CW01661820

Praise for *The H*
Psychology a

This handbook stands out for its relat ... grated approach. It focuses on being directly and practic ... vant to trainees and bridges the gap between complex psychological theory and compassionate clinical practice. Editors Charlotte O'Brien and Divine Charura have assembled a diverse range of voices that match the academic rigour required for professional training with the deeply human element of the therapeutic encounter.

Professor Emmy van Deurzen, Director, Existential Academy

The Handbook of Counselling Psychology and Psychotherapy is a perfect companion for those embarking on their counselling psychology journey, as well as those around them. The format of the book makes sure the core parts of who we are is foregrounded, as well as recommendations for core reading around this. I remember in my own training that some of my peers seemed to have read things that were new to me, and I felt 'out of the club' initially. A resource like this ensures that the foundational aspects to the training are made explicit, and as well as the parts we need to nurture throughout our journey into qualifying.

The content is accessible and would be a worthwhile purchase for trainees, as well as those who supervise them, especially if you are a non-counselling psychologist. There are exercises for reflection which allows for this to be part of a shared journey with fellow trainee (and supervisors). I recommend this fantastic resource to those thinking about counselling psychology, and those who support them. Welcome to the club!

Dr Brian Murray, Chair, BPS Division of Counselling Psychology

In this rich compendium, Charlotte O'Brien and Divine Charura bring together an impressive group of leaders in our field to provide insights into the forms of support needed by those training to be counselling psychologists and psychotherapists. Throughout, the contributors encourage trainees to immerse themselves compassionately and reflexively in their learning, towards the goal of becoming truly reflective practitioners. Trainees are encouraged to focus on the philosophical and theoretical scaffolding that, in tandem with practice, underpins their journey, and to identify their own specific voice and values through wider dialogue, research and writing.

I love the underlying spirit of this book, which is to identify the 'companions' – the supportive relationships – which provide us practitioners with sources of 'wisdom, comfort, knowledge and encouragement'. I also applaud the diverse exercises and inclusive questions offered throughout, all geared to stimulating deeper reflection and enhanced social and cultural sensitivity.

Dr Linda Finlay, Integrative Psychotherapist and Academic Consultant

Training as a therapist is life-changing, and this book provides an essential companion for all those undertaking the journey of becoming through immersion in the complex world of therapy. By recognising that being a therapist is a personal experience, built on our own perspectives and life-worlds, this book encourages and supports the reflexive incorporation of knowledge and understandings which will serve throughout a therapist's career.

Starting from an understanding of where approaches to therapy come from, the work highlights the vital importance of philosophical, theoretical, practice and research groundings in our approach to working, but also shows the reader how these manifest in our ways of knowing, everyday thinking, and application in the room. From these firm foundations the authors show us how this influences our ways of meeting and knowing our clients relationally, how we can navigate our work with them, and how we can recognise and collectively resist epistemic and societal injustice. Alongside covering key considerations of being a practitioner, it introduces thinking points and reflections to translate complexities in to personal perspectives in a way which counters concerns that arise for students and early stage-practitioners in making sense of their learning.

This remarkable book provides a unique growth-oriented perspective on the process of becoming a contemporary therapist. I highly recommend it to all those undertaking training, and also to practitioners who wish to remind themselves of the richness and meaning of our work in the modern world.

Kate Smith, Professor and Head of Department of Mental Health and Well-being, University of Aberdeen

The Handbook of Counselling Psychology and Psychotherapy uses a warm, accessible, and conversational tone, inviting readers to engage closely with the insights of Drs. Charura, O'Brien, and their contributors. They guide readers from foundational philosophical, theoretical, and relational concepts to the attitudes, values, competencies, and skills essential during training and professional practice in counselling psychology and psychotherapy. With contributions from internationally recognized and seasoned practitioners, clinical supervisors, and academics, it provides one of the most comprehensive introductions to psychotherapeutic practice grounded in relational ethics and a deep commitment to social justice. This book champions a global and decolonial perspective on psychological therapies, encouraging readers to embrace anti-oppressive and just practices as central to their professional identity. Students, instructors, and supervisors alike will find value in the research-informed perspectives on timely issues such as telepsychology and AI, practical guidance on developing a professional voice, and thought-provoking questions to foster reflexivity, skill development, and a successful transition into professional roles.

Sophie Yohani, PhD., R Psych. Professor & Counselling Psychology Programs Coordinator, University of Alberta, Canada

The Handbook of Counselling Psychology and Psychotherapy will be an invaluable resource for trainees, supporting them to critically reflect on their own development as practitioners, and how they are metabolising the learning from modules, placements and supervision. With its central commitment to anti-oppressive practice, the handbook encourages trainees to develop both cultural humility and their own identity and voice as practitioners. Through content often not formally included in therapy training – such as tips for how to survive training through self-care and how to navigate accreditation – the handbook offers practical support. With suggested activities, further readings and reflexive questions that prompt active engagement with the material, the handbook offers an engaging and helpful companion on the often long and stressful journey of training to be a therapist.

Naomi Moller, Professor of Psychology and Psychotherapy, The Open University

As a counselling psychologist, academic and practitioner, I am deeply appreciative of how this handbook positions counselling psychology and psychotherapy as relational, ethical and socially situated practices. It offers far more than a technical guide to training: it is a thoughtful companion that recognises becoming a practitioner as an ongoing, reflexive and value-laden process.

With a sustained commitment to anti-oppressive practice and decolonisation, the editors and contributors locate power, difference and social justice as central to therapeutic work, training and research. The chapters invite readers to critically examine the historical, cultural and political foundations of the psychological therapies, while also offering grounded ways of practising with greater humility, accountability and care. This feels both necessary and timely.

As someone teaching on a Doctorate in Counselling Psychology and Psychotherapy, I see this handbook as addressing a significant pedagogical need. It speaks directly to trainees' experiences, normalising uncertainty and encouraging reflexivity, while also providing educators and supervisors with accessible frameworks, exercises and language to support ethically informed learning. The emphasis on relational ethics, positionality and the therapist's use of self, aligns closely with contemporary professional values and regulatory expectations.

In my independent practice, I am reminded daily that therapy unfolds within wider systems of inequality and privilege. This handbook reflects that reality, encouraging practitioners to hold individual distress alongside social context, and to work in ways that resist reductionism and exclusion.

Overall, this is a generous, courageous and ethically grounded contribution to the field, and one that I expect will become a valued resource for trainees, practitioners and educators alike.

Dr Sue Whitcombe BSc MA DCPsych CPsychol, Counselling Psychologist and Senior Lecturer, Metanoia Institute

The Handbook of Counselling Psychology and Psychotherapy

A training companion

Edited by
Charlotte O'Brien and Divine Charura

PCCS BOOKS

First published 2026
Product code – 015002026

PCCS Books Ltd
Wyastone Business Park
Wyastone Leys
Monmouth
NP25 3SR
United Kingdom

contact@pccs-books.co.uk
www.pccs-books.co.uk

This collection © PCCS Books, 2026
The individual chapters © the contributors, 2026

All rights reserved.

No part of this publication may be reproduced, stored in a retrieval system, transmitted or utilised in any form by any means, electronic, mechanical, photocopying or recording or otherwise, without permission in writing from the publishers.

The authors have asserted their right to be identified as the authors of this work in accordance with the Copyright, Designs and Patents Act 1988.

The Handbook of Counselling Psychology and Psychotherapy: A training companion

British Library Cataloguing in Publication data: a catalogue record for this book is available from the British Library.

ISBNs paperback – 978 1 915220 74 5
ePub – 978 1 915220 75 2

Cover design by
Typeset in-house by PCCS Books using Minion Pro and Myriad Pro
Printed in the UK by Bell & Bain Ltd, Glasgow

This product has been assessed as low risk and can be used safely without safety information.

The manufacturer's authorised representative in the EU for product safety is:
Easy Access System Europe – Mustamäe tee 50, 10621 Tallinn, Estonia
gpsr.requests@easproject.com

Contents

SECTION THREE – BECOMING A PRACTITIONER AND BEYOND

Dedication

To everyone who is be-ing-becoming, and to the trainees and learning facilitators who are already shaping the world that is to come.

About the contributors

The editors

Professor Divine Charura MBE (he/him) is Professor of Counselling Psychology at York St John University, UK. He is also a counselling psychologist and a coaching psychologist, registered and licensed as a practitioner psychologist with the Health and Care Professions Council (HCPC) in England (UK). Divine is an honorary fellow of the UK Council for Psychotherapy (UKCP) and an adult psychotherapist. Divine has co-authored and edited numerous books, including *Love and Therapy: In Relationship* (co-edited with Stephen Paul), and with Colin Lago has co-edited *Black Identities + White Therapies: Race Respect and Diversity* (2021). His latest books are *The Handbook of Social Justice in Psychological Therapies: Power, Politics, Change* (co-edited with Laura Winter, 2023) and *Trauma Demystified: A Guide for Students and Practitioners* (2024) co-edited with Mark McFetridge and Emma Bradshaw. For more of Divine's publications, please see https://ray.yorksj.ac.uk/profile/2104

Dr Charlotte O'Brien (she/her) is Editor-in-Chief for Psychology at Wiley. She is an HCPC-registered counselling psychologist, British Association for Counselling and Psychotherapy (BACP)-registered psychotherapist and associate fellow of the British Psychological Society (BPS). She is a passionate and creative clinician, supervisor, author, educator and researcher, having worked as programme director for the Doctorate in Counselling Psychology programme at the University of Manchester, UK and as training and education lead for the BPS Division of Counselling Psychology. Charlotte has a special interest in social justice and the use of anti-discriminatory approaches in psychotherapeutic leadership, training and practice. Charlotte's private and NHS clinical work focuses on working with individuals experiencing complex trauma, and she is an expert reference group member for the BACP's UK Trauma Competency Framework for Adults. Charlotte is currently researching embodied trauma and global mental health priorities for displaced individuals. She is also writing the BPS Core Text *An Introduction to Counselling Psychology* with Laura Winter and Terry Hanley. For more, please see: https://orcid.org/0000-0002-9903-3325

The contributors

Dr Byron Al-Murri is a lecturer in counselling psychology at undergraduate and doctoral level, at York St John University, UK. He is an HCPC-registered and BPS-chartered counselling psychologist, clinical and research supervisor, and his research interests are in difference and diversity in psychotherapy, multicultural competence and social justice. He has contributed to several publications on these topics, including a chapter in *The Handbook of Social Justice in Psychological Therapies: Power, Politics, Change* (co-authored with Jasmine Childs-Fegredo, 2023) and a chapter in *Reimagining Race in Psychology: Challenging Narratives and Widening Perspectives in Training and Practice*, focusing on racial trauma (co-authored with Divine Charura, 2024). Byron has worked as a clinician in the third sector with clients from across the lifespan. He is a pluralistic practitioner, integrating CBT, psychodynamic psychotherapy and humanistic philosophy.

Mary Atito is an accredited integrative psychotherapist, with a special interest in spirituality, identity and transcultural approaches to mental health and the impact of trauma. She is completing her PhD and working in private clinical practice, exploring Black British men's perception of therapy. Mary is passionate about adequate psychological services for the Black community in London and promoting therapy to those who would most benefit from engaging with it. Mary's professional background is within the private, public and voluntary sector, working with individuals presenting with multiple emotional and mental difficulties. Mary specialises in single-session therapy, intrapersonal and interpersonal relational difficulties, particularly divinity and romantic relationships, with an emphasis on perseverance, love and confidence. Mary is a board member of the Society for Psychotherapy Research UK chapter and has a particular aspiration to promote and encourage Black British students to pursue higher education and for therapists/counsellors to become research practitioners, researching phenomena within their communities.

Sofie Bager-Charleson is a senior lecturer and research fellow at the Metanoia Institute, London. She is also a UKCP- and BACP-registered psychotherapist, and an honorary senior research fellow at City University, London, UK. She specialises in research methodology, research training and supervision. She chairs the Metanoia research group, Therapists as Research-informed Practitioners (TRP), which develops training and policy to support psychotherapists and counselling psychologists in research. She is also the co-founder of the annual Metanoia Research Academy for practitioners, and has published widely in the field of research methodology and reflexivity. Her recent textbooks include *Enjoying Research in Counselling and Psychotherapy* and *Supporting Research in Counselling and Psychotherapy* (Bager-Charleson & McBeath (Eds.) 2020; 2022).

Emma Bradshaw is a counselling psychologist registered with the HCPC. She is also a chartered member of the BPS and an EMDR Europe accredited practitioner. She currently works in private practice in York, adopting an integrative relational approach to her therapeutic work with adults, both in person and online. She is also a clinical supervisor and educator. Over the years, Emma has worked with a wide range of people in a variety of settings and was previously a senior lecturer on the Doctorate in Counselling Psychology programme at York St John University. She is particularly interested in helping those who have experienced psychological trauma and is co-author of the book *Trauma Demystified* (2025; with Divine Charura and Mark McFetridge).

Sarah Corrie is Professor of Cognitive Behaviour Therapy and Counselling at the University of Suffolk, UK, where she is also joint head of counselling, psychology and social work. As a consultant clinical psychologist and accredited therapist, supervisor and trainer with the British Association for Behavioural and Cognitive Psychotherapies (BABCP), she has particular expertise in cognitive behaviour therapy. Her work in this field is extensive and has spanned innovations in practice, training and supervision. Formerly chair of the BABCP's course accreditation committee, she was awarded a fellowship of the BABCP in 2017 for her contribution to training and supervision. Sarah has authored approximately 100 articles for academic journals and trade magazines as well as 10 books. She is also a chartered coaching psychologist and registered certified professional executive coach with the Association for Professional Executive Coaching & Supervision. In 2016, she received the BPS Achievement Award for Distinguished Contributions to Coaching Psychology.

Amira-Deka Dirie is a registered psychotherapist (qualifying) with the College of Registered Psychotherapists of Ontario (CRPO), Canada, where she is deeply passionate about the transformative potential of psychotherapy, especially in its ability to facilitate healing and personal growth in her clients. Amira is a graduate with an MEd in Counselling Psychology and Psychotherapy from the University of Toronto's Ontario Institute for Studies in Education (OISE). With a multi-disciplinary background in psychology, biology and women and gender studies, Amira is committed to exploring the human experience through a decolonial and anti-oppressive lens. She is deeply driven by the desire to integrate these diverse perspectives into therapeutic practice, contributing to a richer and more holistic understanding of mental health. As a project coordinator at the I AM Research Lab, she is dedicated to conducting research and writing that amplifies the voices and experiences of marginalised communities, striving to create spaces for their stories to be heard and understood.

Lynne Gabriel OBE is Professor of Counselling and Mental Health at York St John University, UK. She is a BACP-accredited and registered counsellor and psychotherapist, and an honorary fellow of the association. Lynne is the founder director of the York St John Communities Centre and is also a trained supervisor of practitioners working within the counselling, mental health and helping professions. Originally trained as a mental health nurse, Lynne has been a key player in the counselling and mental health fields for many years, contributing at local, regional, national and international levels, and is currently president of the BACP. Lynne's research interests include public mental health, relationship abuse, approaches to ethics for the counselling professions, group interventions for bereavement and loss, and the use of standardised mental health measures in counselling and psychotherapy. Lynne has published books on ethics in practice and research papers on multiple aspects of work in the counselling professions. Lynne co-edits (with Andrew Reeves) the *Ethics in Action* series and they recently published *Relational Ethics in Day-to-Day Practice* (2024).

Dr Keisha Greene is a registered psychotherapist, clinical supervisor and sessional lecturer at the University of Toronto, Canada, where she teaches the Critical Multicultural Practice: Diversity Issues in Counselling and Psychotherapy course. Keisha completed her MA in Counselling & Clinical Psychology at McGill University and completed her EdD in Clinical and Counselling Psychology at the University of Toronto. Keisha has been a practising clinician for over 10 years with BIPOC 2S+ populations and has experience working with clients in community mental health, outpatient mental health and private practice. Her clinical work focuses on mental health within perinatal populations (specifically pregnancy and postpartum), addictions, complex trauma, and racial trauma. Keisha's research interests are in understanding how racialised individuals can be best served in the therapeutic process so that they achieve their desired outcomes.

Terry Hanley is Professor of Counselling Psychology at the University of Manchester, UK, and visiting professor at York St John University, UK. He is a fellow of the BPS and a Health and Care Professions Council-registered counselling psychologist. Terry is co-editor of the fourth and fifth editions of *The Handbook of Counselling and Psychotherapy* (with Laura Winter), co-author of *Introducing Counselling and Psychotherapy Research* (with William West and Clare Lennie), and lead editor of *Adolescent Counselling Psychology*. With Laura Winter, he is currently writing a commissioned text titled *Key Issues in Counselling Psychology*. He has worked as a therapist with young people and young adults, facilitated a football therapy project for survivors of torture and provided clinical supervision for a service user-led mental health group. He is interested in further understanding the way that therapists will be involved in co-creating ecosystems of support for those seeking support.

Gerrie Hughes is a UKCP-registered gestalt psychotherapist and supervisor with more than 30 years' experience, and is based in South Wales. She is the author of *Competence and Self-care for Counsellors and Psychotherapists* (2014). Having revisited the topic for this publication, she realises how much the world has changed over the course of a decade, particularly because of the Covid-19 pandemic. She feels that so-called competence seems more appropriately talked about as self-awareness, and self-care as one facet of an interconnected culture of care, which is influenced by the professional, social and political environment and is concerned with social justice. A second edition of *Competence and Self-care for Counsellors and Psychotherapists*, encompassing these wider themes, is currently in preparation and is expected to be available in 2026.

Ariana Jordan is Senior Lecturer at Metanoia Institute, UK, a chartered counselling psychologist in both the NHS and private practice, and a clinical supervisor. Having studied Psychoanalytic Developmental Psychotherapy at the Anna Freud Centre/UCL and Systemic Practice with Families and Couples at the Institute of Family Therapy/Birkbeck College, Ariana works with adults as well as young people, providing therapy for individuals, couples and families. Ariana's research interests include psychological wellbeing at midlife, and masked autism traits, particularly in women and girls. She recently led a BACP-funded project on the use of avatars in therapy with autistic adults from Black and minoritised ethnic communities, and was co-researcher in a case study project looking at long-term emotion-focused therapy. Ariana runs two monthly groups for adults and young people on the autistic spectrum and founded a Croydon psychologists' film club.

David A. Lane contributed to research and the development of counselling psychology as a profession, provided counselling to children and adults, in education, in the NHS and charities, in the field of trauma and in a wide range of organisations including major consultancies, multinationals, and public sector and government bodies. He was chair of the British Psychological Society Register of Psychologists Specialising in Psychotherapy and convened the European Federation of Psychologists Association's group on psychotherapy. He co-founded The European Association for Counselling and has served on the section and special group in counselling psychology and the working party to establish it as a discipline with the BPS. His published work comprises many chapters, journal papers and books, including *The Modern Scientist Practitioner* (2007), *Making Successful Decisions in Counselling and Psychotherapy* (2012), *CBT Supervision, First Steps in Cognitive Behavioural Therapy* (2015) and *Constructing Stories: Telling Tales, Supervision in the Psychological Professions* (2018).

Colin Lago was director of the counselling service at the University of Sheffield (UK) from 1987 to 2003. He now works as an independent therapist, trainer and supervisor. He is a fellow of the BACP, with which he is an accredited counsellor/psychotherapist. Deeply committed to *transcultural concerns,* he has had articles, videos and books published on the subject. He has been awarded a D.Litt for his contributions to the literature on multicultural therapy. Having experienced academic failure at school, Colin is sensitive to the challenges of learning. Profoundly inspired by the writing of Carl Rogers almost a decade before he trained as a therapist, Colin has had the good fortune to develop his own 'person-centred practice' in individual, small group and large international group work.

Dr Alistair McBeath is Senior Lecturer at the Metanoia Institute, teaching on the Doctorate in Counselling Psychology programme. He is a BPS-chartered psychologist and associate fellow, a UKCP-registered psychotherapist and registered with the General Psychotherapy Council (GPsyC). Trained at Regent College and Guy's Hospital, he is a senior practitioner member of the BPS Register of Psychologists Specialising in Psychotherapy. Alistair considers himself to be a researcher–practitioner and is keen to promote this identity within the psychotherapy profession. He has published widely and is co-editor, with Sofie Bager-Charleson, of the popular books *Enjoying Research in Counselling and Psychotherapy* (2020) and *Supporting Research in Counselling and Psychotherapy* (2022). Alistair works for an Edinburgh-based therapeutic consultancy. His primary research interests are in mixed-methods research, the process of research supervision, the motivations of psychotherapists and the creative use of online surveys.

John McLeod has a degree and PhD in psychology from Edinburgh University, and trained as a person-centred counsellor and psychotherapist. He has held positions as a counsellor, educator and researcher at Wolverhampton, Keele and Abertay universities in the UK, and visiting professor appointments at Massey University Aotearoa New Zealand, University of Padua, University of Oslo, and the Institute for Integrative Counselling and Psychotherapy in Dublin. His work has been characterised by three main themes: the relevance of qualitative and case study research as a source of knowledge to inform and enrich therapy practice; narrative and socio-political perspectives on the aims and process of therapy; and the development of flexible, co-produced pluralistic ways of working with clients. He is the author of *An Introduction to Counselling and Psychotherapy: Theory, Research, Practice, and Social Purpose* (7th ed., 2025), as well as books and articles on a range of therapy topics.

Alan McPherson is the deputy programme leader for the BACP-accredited BSc(Hons) degree in Counselling and Psychotherapy at the Sherwood Psychotherapy Training Institute, Nottingham, UK, and the review manager for the *European Journal for Qualitative Research in Psychotherapy*. Alan is a BACP-accredited and UKCP-registered psychotherapist in private practice in Leicester, UK. Viewing himself as an independent therapist–researcher, he is pursuing a PhD with the Metanoia Institute and Middlesex University, London partnership, exploring the experiences of practising counsellors, psychotherapists, and counselling psychologists who also create and publish their own research independent of academia. Alan's professional background includes multiple careers, including engineering in the private sector and local government adult social care. As a psychotherapist, Alan specialises in working with adult survivors of childhood sexual abuse, the LGBTQ+ community and survivors of spiritual abuse.

Roy Moodley, PhD, is Associate Professor in Clinical and Counselling Psychology, and the director of the Centre for Diversity in Counselling and Psychotherapy (CDCP) at the University of Toronto, Canada. Roy's research and publications include critical multicultural/diversity counselling and psychotherapy, race in psychotherapy, interracial relationships, traditional healing practices, and gender and identity.

Dr Nahid Nasrat is a psychologist and professor in the Clinical Psychology programme at The Chicago School, USA. With over 20 years of experience in teaching and mentoring, she is an expert in refugees' and immigrants' mental health, as well as conflict-related psychosocial issues. Nahid has received numerous prestigious awards, including the Outstanding Dissertation Award for her clinical manual on Afghan refugee women, the 2015 Ignacio Martín-Baró Lifetime Peace Practitioner Award, and the 2016 Anthony J. Marsella Prize for Peace Psychology. She has also been honoured with the NCSPP Diversity Award and the 2020–2021 Distinguished Multicultural Teaching Excellence Award. She previously served as vice president of Afghan Education for a Better Tomorrow and collaborated with the Substance Abuse and Mental Health Services Administration (SAMHSA) to enhance Afghanistan's mental health services. A frequent media contributor, she publishes research on liberation psychology and mental health.

Sarah Niblock is a professor, CEO, consultant and thought leader specialising in psychological wellbeing, ethics and media. With a PhD in psychoanalytic theory, she has held senior leadership roles in academia and the charity sector, shaping policy and practice at national and international levels. Her work bridges psychotherapy, social justice and public engagement, challenging traditional models of mental health to foster more collective, compassionate solutions. As a journalist, she brings a critical lens to dominant narratives, advocating for systemic change in how we understand resilience, trauma and human connection. She has broadcast live on BBC Radio 4, authored numerous books and articles, and advised major institutions in the UK and overseas. She was CEO of the UKCP between 2017 and 2022.

Peter Pearce is Director of Clinical Training at Metanoia Institute, UK. He plays a pivotal role in shaping professional identity, standards and development for therapists, overseeing post-qualification career progression programmes, new pathways into the profession aimed at contributing to the development of a more representative psychological therapies workforce, and leads a range of innovative initiatives. Peter has long experience in both clinical practice (within NHS multi-disciplinary teams, the voluntary sector, EAPs and private practice) and in training and academic curriculum development. He led the Metanoia team that collaborated with the NHS and BACP to develop the National Curriculum for Person-Centred Experiential Counselling for Depression (PCE-CfD), now an approved therapy within NHS Talking Therapies (formerly IAPT). He is a member of the NHS Talking Therapies Expert Advisory Group, and has contributed to a variety of national training standards, remote therapy adaptations and the development of new NHS-funded counselling curricula.

Professor Andrew Reeves is Emeritus Professor in Counselling Professions and Mental Health at the University of Chester, UK, a BACP senior accredited counsellor/psychotherapist, a European Mentoring and Coaching Council senior accredited coach and coach supervisor, and a registered social worker. He has worked in a full range of practice contexts over his 40 years of work, including statutory mental health/crisis intervention services, schools, universities, the third sector and private practice. He has published extensively around ethics, training, working with risk, mental health and other practice areas. He is a past chair of BACP.

Robin Shohet (www.cstdlondon.co.uk) has been supervising since 1976. He has written extensively on the subject, including *In Love with Supervision* (2020) and *Supervision as Spiritual Practice* (2024). He has organised two international conferences on forgiveness inspired by *A Course in Miracles* (1975), of which he is a long-time student.

John Wilson is a co-founder and director at Onlinevents, committed to democratising learning in the helping professions and developing the world's largest video learning library, akin to Netflix for these fields. He is also a director at Temenos Education, where he leads the counselling and psychotherapy programme and supports students in developing their personal and professional potential. With over 20 years of experience, John runs a private practice as a psychotherapist and supervisor, offering services via video, text chat and virtual environments. He facilitates groups and participates in the Going Global and La Jolla programmes, which are rooted in Carl Rogers' Encounter Group movement. Previously, John served as chair and is now an honorary fellow at the Association for Counselling and Therapy Online (ACTO). He also spent six years on the board of the World Association for Person-Centred & Experiential Psychotherapy & Counselling.

Laura Anne Winter (she/her) is Reader in Education and Counselling Psychology at the University of Manchester, UK, where she is also the School of Environment, Education and Development Director of Equality, Diversity and Inclusion, and is the deputy chair of the BPS Training Committee in Counselling Psychology. Laura was the previous programme director for the Doctorate in Counselling Psychology at the University of Manchester, UK (2020–2024). Laura is a fellow of the Higher Education Academy, a BPS chartered psychologist and a HCPC-registered counselling psychologist. Her research focuses on the connections between social justice and politics, and applied psychology and education. She led on editing *The Handbook of Social Justice in Psychological Therapies* (with Divine Charura, 2023). She also edited the fourth and fifth editions of the *Sage Handbook of Counselling and Psychotherapy* (with Terry Hanley) and is currently writing (with Terry Hanley) a commissioned text on *Key Issues in Counselling Psychology*. She is white, not currently disabled, and a mother of three young children.

Acknowledgements

We would like to sincerely thank the wonderful team at PCCS Books, and especially our commissioning editor, Camilla Erskine, for her endless support and encouragement, and for the extraordinary literary talents that she has shared with us in creating this handbook. Your patience, Camilla, has been a steady hand guiding each word home. With thoughtfulness, generosity and unwavering grace, you have helped to shape this book into what it is today – something truer, deeper, more whole than we could have imagined. Thank you!

We are also deeply grateful to all the authors who have contributed to this handbook, generously giving their time and expertise as educators, supervisors, practitioners, trainers, researchers, trainees and academics. Without your wisdom and knowledge, this book would not have been possible. We thank each one of you wholeheartedly and treasure your invaluable contributions.

Charlotte writes:
I would like to thank my family for all their love and support on this journey – to Chloe and Will, my sunshine and joy, and to my mum Yvonne, sister Carrie and nieces Abigail and Grace, for always being my cheerleaders and strong foundations. I am truly blessed to have you all in my life.

To all the clients, students and teachers who have touched my life in relationship, from whom I have had the privilege to grow and change – thank you for all that you have shared with me, and for contributing to my learning and to this book. A special thank you to Dr Emma Bradshaw, my teacher and supervisor, for being such a wonderful role model.

To Divine – for your inspiration, passion, energy and nurture. Thank you for your catalytic collaboration on this wonderful project, which has brought so much joy and fulfilment, and for offering a power-with relationship that has helped me to do what sets my soul on fire.

Finally, to everyone who may read this handbook. I hope it holds a candle to your steps as you embark on your own treasured journey towards becoming the practitioners you wish to be. We are with you all the way.

Divine writes:
I would like to offer a very special thanks to my loving family: my father Alois and mother Letisia, who teach me so much about life and love. Also, to Helen, Elizabeth, Alois, you are the quiet strength beneath my wings, the warmth that guides each thought, and each dream. Thank you for your unending love, support, the laughter and fun we share. To my brothers, sister, nephews and nieces who bring me so much joy. What a loving and amazing collective! I am because we are!

To Charlie – in the quiet rhythm of shared thought and the vibrant pulse of collaboration, this book was born. Each page truly carries the echo of our creative conversations, the harmony of our ideas, and the joy of minds and hearts meeting in purpose. Writing and editing this book together has been a wonderful journey of shared insight, creativity and mutual respect. It is a pleasure and an honour to collaborate with you. You are a soul of grace – thoughtful, generous, and ablaze with inspiration and talent. May this work be a testament to what unfolds when hearts meet in purpose, and words are woven with love for those who walk beside us in our lives and work.

To everyone who contributed to the pages of this book, thank you for your unwavering commitment, your wisdom, and the spirit of collegiality that made this process not only productive but deeply fulfilling. Like threads in a tapestry, your contributions have woven beauty and depth into every chapter. With heartfelt thanksgiving.

Abbreviations

ACA	American Counseling Association
ACT	acceptance and commitment therapy
ACTO	Association for Counselling and Therapy Online
ADHD	attention deficit hyperactivity disorder
AI	artificial intelligence
APA	American Psychological Association
BAATN	Black, African and Asian Therapy Network
BABCP	British Association for Behavioural and Cognitive Psychotherapies
BACP	British Association for Counselling and Psychotherapy
BIPOC 2S+	Black, Indigenous, People of Colour, Two Spirit, plus
BPC	British Psychoanalytic Council
BPS	British Psychological Society
CAMHS	Child and Adolescent Mental Health Service
CBT	cognitive behavioural therapy
CDCP	Centre for Diversity in Counselling and Psychotherapy
CFS	chronic fatigue syndrome
CFT	compassion-focused therapy
CGT	constructivist grounded theory
CMHT	community mental health teams
COSRT	College of Sexual and Relationship Therapists
CPD	continuing/continued professional development
CRPO	College of Registered Psychotherapists of Ontario
CT	cognitive therapy
CYP	children and young people
DBT	dialectical behaviour therapy
DIY	do it yourself
EAP	Employee Assistance Programme
EMDR	eye movement desensitisation and reprocessing
FND	functional neurological disorders
GD	guided discovery
GP	general practitioner
GSERD	gender, sexual, erotic and relationship diversity

HCPC	Health and Care Professions Council
IAPT	Improving Access to Psychological Therapies
IPA	interpretative phenomenological analysis
LGBTQ+	lesbian, gay, bisexual, transgender, and queer/questioning
MBCT	mindfulness-based cognitive therapy
MDT	multi-disciplinary team
ME	myalgic encephalomyelitis
MHWP	mental health wellbeing practitioner
NCS	National Counselling Society (now NCPS, see below)
NCPS	National Counselling and Psychotherapy Society
NCSPP	National Council of Schools and Programs of Professional Psychology
NHS	National Health Service
NICE	National Institute for Health and Care Excellence
OISE	Ontario Institute for Studies in Education
PPD	personal and professional development
PRISMA	Preferred Reporting Items for Systematic Reviews and Meta-Analyses
PSA	Professional Standards Authority for Health and Social Care
PWP	psychological wellbeing practitioner
QAA	Quality Assurance Agency
RCT	randomised controlled trials
RET	rational emotive therapy
SAMHSA	Substance Abuse and Mental Health Services Administration
SCoPEd	Scope of Practice and Education
SET	standards of education and training
TR	therapeutic relationship
UKCP	United Kingdom Council for Psychotherapy
UPR	unconditional positive regard
VT	vicarious traumatisation
WEIRD	Western, Educated, Industrialised, Rich, Democratic

Introduction

Charlotte O'Brien and Divine Charura

A training companion

The vision for this book vividly ignited when we reflected together on our own training journeys into the therapeutic professions and thought about what would have been helpful to know from the very start. As with any great adventure, embarking upon a training journey into a new profession can be daunting. Some of us might begin on this unfamiliar road experiencing a mixture of feelings, such as excitement or trepidation to explore pastures new, or to encounter a new and diverse range of people. We may also be driven to make a change in our career path following our own lived experiences of trauma, relational challenges or childhood difficulties. It could also be that positive life experiences and encounters have inspired us to choose a career in the psychological therapies professions. Whatever the reason that has led us to this place, the pathway of the learning ahead can often feel steep, treacherous and challenging, leading us to wonder if we will ever reach our destination. At times we may find ourselves feeling overwhelmed, or questioning whether we are practically prepared or educationally competent enough to complete the full journey ahead.

'Yet hope remains while the company is true' (Tolkien, 2021, p. 357), and this, dear reader, is where our vision for creating a training *companion* was truly born. Reflexively, we both noticed that our training journeys had been made infinitely lighter by the supportive relationships that surrounded us and provided us with sources of wisdom, comfort, knowledge and encouragement. These have included family, friends and professional relationships such as personal therapists, course tutors and supervisors. Additionally, such relationships have also challenged us and facilitated our growth and personal and professional development (PPD). These relational encounters have instilled in us an appreciation of the centrality of a diversity of relationships in supporting and integrating our learning about ourselves and what it means to become a therapeutic practitioner.

It is with these key relationships in mind that we have gathered together a fellowship of fantastic educators, therapeutic practitioners, researchers, academic writers, trainees and supervisors, whose diverse and yet collective voices have helped us to create this companion for trainees and trainers. Although this book is written as a companion for trainees, it can also be used pedagogically by tutors, educators, trainers and practitioners. The exercises and reflective questions are tailored throughout the book to be used independently by trainees, or collectively in the classroom. They can also be used as teaching aids, or as tools to facilitate dialogue and best practice in the therapeutic professions.

A note on language

Throughout this book you will hear a diverse set of voices who have trodden the trainee path before you, and who will be your companions and guides through each of the chapters to which they have contributed. This is very important to us, as each of your training journeys will be different according to your own background, history, educational and life experiences, and chosen career pathway, to name but a few. We have aimed to create a book that is inclusive of diverse learning styles, embraces different ways of communicating and prizes an array of training experiences and pathways, with professional, ethical, trauma-informed practice and social justice at its core.

With this in mind we have tried, where possible, to simplify our language, be respectful and inclusive of different ways of writing, and overcome any distancing in the text by approaching you, the reader, as a companion, through a conversational style. In this introduction we also emphasise an inclusive approach to a diversity of therapeutic training pathways and use umbrella titles such as 'therapeutic practitioner', rather than counsellor, psychotherapist or counselling psychologist. However, we do also have an appreciation of the nuances of each therapeutic practitioner title and the context and diversity of their ways of working as shared by the authors of each chapter. Whatever our title or modalities of practice that we have trained or are training in, it is important to purposefully acknowledge the shared ground between us, rather than focusing on our differences.

By listening to the different voices of the authors throughout this book, we have noticed a collective longing for a world where we are working together in relationship as a therapeutic field, based on the importance of community, love and human encounters. Therefore, as you read this book, we hope that you will find that it speaks to you and to the unique journey that you are on as a trainee, educator or reflexive practitioner. We hope the simplified approach that we have adopted is sufficient to embrace the considerable spectrum of differing specialist training routes. Fundamentally, however, we want trainees and trainers alike to think about the *relational encounter*, not focusing upon titles but on the work we are doing in relationship with one another, echoing the centrality of the therapeutic relationship (TR) in our work.

Who this book is for

In editing this book together we were inspired by the words from the poem 'The Hill We Climb' by Amanda Gorman (2021), which speaks about the importance of focusing on what unites us rather than divides us. Our aim for this book has always been to focus on what joins us together as practitioners, and while we acknowledge the different therapeutic professions of counselling, psychotherapy and counselling psychology, we are making a call to return to the common factors across each of them. We recognise that all psychotherapeutic practitioners have training approaches that champion inclusivity, anti-oppressive and anti-discriminatory practice, and possess a core of relational ethics, love, humanity and a commitment to therapeutic relationships that aim to facilitate transformation, healing, wellbeing or equilibrium. After all, research on the effectiveness of different types of therapies has identified a so-called Dodo effect that concludes that all psychological therapies are equally effective regardless of the modality (Luborsky et al., 2002). With over 400 varieties of counselling and psychotherapy approaches in use, having a unified stance between practitioners is a complex task. While we acknowledge this breadth of diversity across theoretical models (e.g. psychoanalytic/psychodynamic, behavioural, cognitive, systemic and so forth), formats (e.g. individual, family, group), temporal length and frequency of the sessions, as well as any possible combination of these elements (Garfield & Bergin, 1994), we make a call through this book to return to a more inclusive and equitable approach to our field. This approach means that all practitioners and their plurality of orientations, cultures and training pathways are equally valued. We also appreciate the diversity of approaches used in psychotherapeutic research methods and prize practice-based evidence from all practitioners. This book is therefore written for use by all undergraduate students, postgraduate trainees and for the CPD of qualified therapeutic practitioners and educators. All are welcome!

A commitment to anti-discriminatory, anti-oppressive practice and social justice

As psychotherapeutic professionals, our work is steeped in valuing and upholding anti-discriminatory, anti-oppressive practice, social justice and reflective practice (Lago & Smith, 2010; O'Brien et al., 2025; Winter & Charura, 2023). This book draws from an evidence base that ensures we are engaging with relationally ethical, effective interventions and best practices for our clients. Social justice is a core theme that is interwoven throughout this book as a golden thread tying together everything we do in therapeutic practice and in all our professional relationships. Taking an anti-oppressive stance requires us to critically evaluate the knowledge that we draw from at every stage of our training and professional journeys, including the research, theories, philosophies and approaches that are classically presented to us.

We acknowledge that most psychotherapeutic theories taught on training programmes in the West are often considered to be steeped in Western, Educated, Industrialised, Rich, Democratic (WEIRD) perspectives. In this book we make a firm commitment to using a decolonised approach that acknowledges the diversity of cultures and contexts in which psychotherapeutic practitioners work. We also advocate for engaging with culturally informed practice, seeing the uniqueness of each person and appreciating the intersectionality of selves and our own diverse lived experiences.

Decolonising research and therapeutic approaches also requires us to build an awareness of discriminatory historical research and practice, and to acknowledge its impact on marginalised groups. It therefore requires a radical shift in challenging racial undertones, gender inequality and all forms of so-called 'isms' that breed discrimination (e.g. racism, ableism and sexism) (Charura & Lago, 2021). There is much pre-eminence given to Western models for viewing mental health or ill health using certain nosologic criteria (i.e. specific standards and classification of disease or *dis-ease* such as the *DSM-5* or *ICD-11* diagnostic manuals) even when these do not apply to or fit other groups. Keating (2020) suggested that decolonisation is about breaking down the structures that support power inequalities, discrimination and racism within our profession. This can be done by analysing, challenging and critically examining the beliefs one holds about other groups, including formulations about psychological *dis-ease,* which may not be culturally informed or appropriate. Decolonisation also requires us to be aware of the process of 'othering' and learning to value the views of individuals or groups outside of our own worldview or lens.

Growing and sustaining our identity as reflective and reflexive evidence-based practitioners also comes in different forms. This includes engaging with personal therapy, experiential exercises, supervision, reflective assignments and CPD through learning and research. Given that the therapist's use of self is central to therapeutic processes, we must unpack our worldviews and our identities before meeting those of the clients that we serve. It is therefore imperative that we explore our own perspectives on difference and diversity, power, politics, and other tensions relating to our understanding of the human condition, our relationships and the world. As relationally ethical practitioners, we must also embrace an anti-oppressive stance. In line with this, O'Brien et al. (2025) proposed five core principles (or 5Cs) that facilitate anti-oppressive practice in action. These include the need for continuous self-awareness; collective and relational reflective and reflexive practice; critical conversations;

community involvement; and combating systemic power, politics, policy and privilege. We encourage all practitioners, whatever their training pathway, to adopt with us a firm commitment to social justice, inclusive practice, use of a decolonised curriculum, ethical relationships and anti-oppressive leadership in action. These are common factors across all our training programmes into the psychotherapeutic professions, and run as themes throughout the chapters to set a firm foundation for this book.

How to use this book

Our aim is for this companion to support and guide you as you embark upon your own professional training journey, be that at a foundational or advanced academic level. Our hope is that this book will enable you to dip in, wander around and explore, and travel at your own pace throughout the chapters, in an order that supports your own personal or professional programme or developmental journey. Each chapter follows a common structure that includes an introduction, the scope of the chapter, exercises or case studies, top takeaways, questions for reflection, recommended reading and key resources for your own further exploration. We have laid out the training landscape as a basic map, providing three main sections covering **firm foundations**, **the trainee journey**, and **becoming a practitioner and beyond**, which we will explore with you now.

In Section 1, 'Firm Foundations', you can begin to build your basic knowledge by exploring the historical context and development of the psychological therapies. It is important to understand our radical roots in the psychological professions to appreciate where we have come from and the ways in which we want the field to be decolonised and progress. This includes acknowledging the prevailing white, Westernised, patriarchal theories and philosophical orientations of different modalities. However, we also have a duty to move the field forward and decolonise it by including other cultures, knowledge and contexts that are often excluded, or whose histories have not been encapsulated into the narrative.

It is important that we acknowledge the six major forces of psychology that have influenced our professions, namely: psychoanalysis/psychodynamic; behaviourism/cognitive; existential-humanistic; transpersonal; transcultural; and social justice. However, doing what we have always done is not enough; we also need to build upon and expand our theories, research and practice into contemporary psychotherapeutic applications by committing to societal justice and decolonisation of the curriculum, and understand the ethical importance of adopting therapies that can respond to diverse client needs. This requires evolution towards contemporary, immersive, dynamic and culturally appropriate approaches that are transculturally informed and integrative in practice. This section also introduces the philosophies, paradigms and 'ologies' of psychotherapeutic research and practice, thereby helping you to develop theoretic fluency over time, and acquire skills to integrate into your practice, all built upon a firm ethical foundation.

Section 2, 'The Trainee Journey', will help you to navigate working with difference and diversity, and to develop as an anti-oppressive and anti-discriminatory practitioner (O'Brien et al., 2025). We consider issues and tasks related to human difference within therapeutic training and practice. We also explore why it is vitally important to have more than a weekend's training or the completion of a short module on difference and diversity. Rather, we make the powerful case for threading through iterative and continuous learning and professional development on these themes to work towards becoming anti-oppressive practitioners. We also consider the importance of our positionality of power in the therapy room, and the need to take a stance and for firm commitment to social justice-oriented practice.

This section will also assist you in understanding what psychological assessment and formulation are, why they are useful, and how to develop authentic therapeutic and ethical relationships, rather than seeing people purely through a pathological lens. We consider how to conduct a holistic assessment, and how to integrate different types of assessment information from different contexts. We also consider the formulation process and how it helps us as practitioners to guide our therapeutic interventions, working in collaboration with the client.

We then move on to explore ways of finding your own voice in therapeutic training, enabling you to translate your idiosyncratic learning back into your academic writing, speaking and reading. Developing academic skills in these areas and broadening your repertoire can not only assist you in becoming a better therapist, but can also contribute to building your professional knowledge and continued competence in professional practice.

We then begin to think together about how to navigate your research journey, considering bigger projects such as dissertations or theses. We examine different types of research approach, the importance of performing literature reviews and the need for 'epistemic disruption' to decolonise the field of psychological therapies and move research forward so that it is inclusive of a diversity of worldviews, participant voices and methods. We also think together about what your research means to you, and how to develop your research design to ensure that the research is impactful.

Clinical placements are central to all therapeutic training journeys, and we invite you to consider what is important when starting placements, consider how to use the supervisory relationship, and consider important aspects of safeguarding. Supervision can be a rich experience and we want to support you in making the most out of your placement and supervisory relationships. However, as educators and supervisors ourselves, we also acknowledge that placements and supervision can be challenging, as you may encounter difficult situations and safeguarding matters. Therefore, we hope that the contents in this section of the book will support you in navigating some of the challenges you may face.

Finally, we explore how to become a reflective practitioner and how to look after ourselves with useful self-care practices and personal therapy, and by providing practical survival tips. Undoubtedly, training to be a psychotherapeutic practitioner will have an impact on you as a person and indeed your personal relationships too. Being able to identify your vulnerabilities, responses to stress, biases and prejudices requires a supportive and challenging environment. We delve into what reflective practice is and why we do it, looking at the different styles and contemporary approaches. We also consider the concept of reflexivity and the value of putting our learning back into practice. Our main goal in this section is to help you to find an authentic and sustainable reflective process for you to use throughout your training and CPD.

Section 3, 'Becoming a Practitioner and Beyond', is the final section and will help you to develop your professional practice and identity in your chosen therapeutic field. We explore topics such as ethical issues and contemporary challenges in psychotherapeutic practice, how to develop a congruent professional identity and how to become more aware of our own social privilege, so that we can embody an anti-oppressive practice. This way of being entails developing cultural humility, and sensitivity to and an appreciation of diversity. It also requires the development of professional activism skills, going beyond the therapy room and challenging systemic inequalities. We also introduce career pathways and ways of working in different contexts as a therapeutic practitioner. This includes looking at employment options for newly qualified clinicians and the different contexts and settings within which they may work, such as public and private healthcare sectors, charities, prisons and education environments.

Navigating the current lie of the land in the registration process can be a complex challenge. This section aims to help you to understand the different governing bodies and their roles, exploring which professional registration(s) might suit you and your values, while also considering the challenges that these professional bodies face in the current global climate. Next, we journey alongside two experienced psychotherapeutic practitioners using a duoethnographical approach and reflect with them on their own professional development and learning experiences.

Finally, we move with you beyond your training journey and core curriculum to think more deeply about decolonisation in your future career, research and practice. We then provide a succinct conclusion with key themes and stimuli for continued reflection, where you can access the essence of each chapter in the authors' own words, and collect golden nuggets to take with you as you develop immersive learning across your career.

Finding your voice through this book

In creating this book, we wanted to stay true to the importance of including a diversity of voices, perspectives, modalities, professional identities and career stages. We hope that this integration of different writing styles, approaches, collaborations and knowledge sharing will stimulate and inspire a diverse range of readers. It is our hope that all who read this book will be supported in the immersive process of 'be-ing-becoming' the practitioner that you authentically desire to be. Be-ing-becoming describes a dynamic process of shifts within yourself moment by moment as you develop throughout your life. We encourage you to deeply explore your own lens, positionality, ways of knowing and being known, and the philosophies and theories you are drawn to and why, to inform both your integrative practice and research. We also aim to facilitate you in finding your voice (personally, academically and relationally) throughout your training and professional journeys. As psychotherapeutic practitioners, we work with a diverse range of clients and colleagues, and it is therefore essential for us to be reflective and reflexive practitioners who are open to acknowledging and valuing these differences. In this vein, therefore, we encourage you while reading this book to engage with the diverse writing styles of our international authors, reflect on how they may be different from or the same as yourself, consider what you may learn from them, and use their teaching and ways of being to inform your practice.

A final note

We hope that you enjoy this book and that it acts as a supportive, engaging, enduring and loyal training companion, helping to lighten the load for your journey and reminding you when the training pathway gets steep that you are not walking alone.

References

Charura, D. & Lago, C. (2021). *Black identities + white therapies: Race, respect + diversity*. PCCS Books.

Garfield, S. & Bergin, A. (1994). Introduction and historical overview. In A. Bergin & S. Garfield (Eds.), *Handbook of psychotherapy and behaviour change* (pp. 3–18). Wiley.

Gorman, A. (2021). *The hill we climb: An inaugural poem for the country.* Viking Books.

Keating, F. (2020, November 23). *What does it mean to decolonize knowledge and why is it important in mental health research?* Mental Health Question Time event organised by UCL Psychiatry, The Lancet Psychiatry, Black Thrive and The Mental Elf. [Video] https://www.youtube.com/watch?utm_ign=Black+men+and+mental+health+recovery%3A+An+intersectionalities+approach&utm_source=emailCampaign&utm_content&utm_medium=email&v=jqUlVpvh5A8&feature=youtu.be

Lago, C. & Smith, B. (2010). *Anti-discriminatory practice in counselling and psychotherapy* (2nd ed.). SAGE Publications.

Luborsky, L., Rosenthal, R., Diguer, L., Andrusyna, T.P., Berman, J.S., Levitt, J.T., Seligman, D. & Krause, E.D. (2002). The dodo bird verdict is alive and well – mostly. *Clinical Psychology: Science and Practice, 9*(1), 2–12.

O'Brien, C.V., Chan, K.Y. & Winter, L.A. (2025). How can psychologists lead well? Anti-oppressive leadership principles and practices for practitioner psychologists. In A. Rao (Ed.), *Rethinking leadership for clinical, counselling and health psychologists: Managing complexity and change for thriving workplaces* (pp. 327-349). Routledge.

Tolkien, J.R.R. (2021). *The lord of the rings.* Harper Collins.

Winter, L.A. & Charura, D. (Eds.). (2023). *The handbook of social justice in psychological therapies: Power, politics, change*. Sage.

Section One
Firm Foundations

1.

Historical context and development of psychological therapies

Terry Hanley and Laura Anne Winter

Introduction

This chapter reflects upon the historical context in which the psychological therapies were conceived and outlines six major perspectives, or forces, of development in this area. A brief reflection of the contemporary situation, including the proliferation of therapeutic approaches, is also provided. We discuss the way in which narratives on the development of the psychological therapies, and the lenses through which we view the professions, are often rooted in colonial frameworks that prioritise Western developments and figures. Our intention in this chapter is to sow some seeds that are further developed throughout the rest of the book. While we believe the chapter covers core developments in the growth of the psychological therapies, we acknowledge its inevitable incompleteness and want to be transparent from the outset that any history is subjective and selective in content and substance. We aim to illustrate the way in which we need to think critically about the history and current context of psychological therapies and to acknowledge the social and political factors in which the profession is intertwined. We hope, in doing so, to present something closer to an anti-oppressive history of psychological therapies than has perhaps come before.

Scope of the chapter

We will cover the following key topics:

- the conception of the psychological therapies – the 'talking cure'
- the historical development of the psychological therapies
- where we are now in contemporary practice.

The discussion of these key topics is followed by an exercise and questions for reflection.

The conception of the psychological therapies: The talking cure

To start a chapter about the history of the psychological therapies, it is important to outline what we mean when we use the term 'psychological therapies', as it could be interpreted in numerous ways. Moreover, the individuals who offer these therapies practise under a wide variety of professional titles. Thus, for the purposes here, we view the term as encompassing the work of those in the counselling and psychotherapy professions whose work is explicitly informed by psychological theories. This might therefore be relevant to those who adopt the professional title of counsellor, psychotherapist, practitioner psychologist (clinical, counselling, educational, forensic, health, occupational, and sport and exercise), or more broadly, therapist.

When we ask the question 'where do we begin?' in a chapter focusing upon the historical context of these psychological therapies, it is often noted what a young profession it is. However, importantly, this only holds true when the psychological therapies are considered as 'profession(s)' in a particular socio-cultural and geographical context. If we look for the origin of counselling and psychotherapy, it is often attributed by those in the global north to the work that Bertha Pappenheim entered into with the physician Joseph Breuer in the 1880s. Pappenheim's story of recovery through a 'talking cure' was subsequently outlined in the book *Studies of Hysteria* in which she was referred to as Anna O (Breuer & Freud, 1895). When compared to other professions such as teaching or medicine, the psychological therapies are, without doubt, a new kid on the block. That is not to say that people have not offered psychological support for millennia, because they have. Societies across the globe, and arguably across the whole of human history, have always had individuals who have taken on supportive roles for others. We might characterise societal elders, ancient philosophers, spiritual leaders or those with healing roles as engaging in therapeutic work with those people that they supported. Indeed, it is important to recognise the various ways in which cultures understand mental health and culturally bound (or Indigenous) ways of approaching distress. The psychological therapies might, therefore, be viewed as one contemporary take on the supportive roles that humans offer to one another.

In line with important developments around decolonial theory and practice in psychology, we recognise that colonialism has shaped, and continues to shape, the values and practices in psychological therapies (Oulanova et al., 2023; Wilcox et al., 2024). With this in mind, the history of these therapies might be better understood when situated within broader traditions of healing, rather than as a distinct medicalised 'profession' or as something limited to the global north (Wampold, 2001). If, in this chapter, we only continued to tell the story of the development of psychological therapies that have been prioritised in WEIRD nations for many years (i.e. those psychological therapies developed only in the global north by middle-class white men), then we would be perpetuating a colonialist narrative (Fernando & Moodley, 2018). As you will see, we challenge this view in this chapter, while acknowledging throughout that we are limited by our own positioning. Consistent with a liberation psychology perspective, we encourage readers to critically question and 'de-naturalise' taken-for-granted discourses about the historical context of psychological therapies (Martín-Baró, 1986).

Before delving further into the ways that people have attempted to harness theories for the good of others, it is also helpful to consider what this means more broadly. Probably the most common view is that therapies aim to reduce distress for individuals. This is certainly a dominant view within healthcare settings (e.g. people might end up less anxious or happier as a consequence of attending therapy) but it is by no means the only one (Hanley, 2023). Numerous therapeutic approaches view their role to be more of an existential exploration. For instance, in contrast to working to reduce distress caused by problems (a deficit model), people might want to learn more about themselves and see themselves as growing as a consequence of attending therapy (a potentiality, or growth-focused model).

While it is important to understand how psychotherapy affects an individual, it is also necessary to question whether psychotherapy has a wider societal impact. Certainly, many therapies focus upon the individual needs within the therapy room, but more systemic, socio-political motives also play an important role. For instance, schools might offer psychotherapeutic services because they want pupils to stay in school and achieve good grades. Likewise, health settings might ultimately want to support people in getting well enough to return to work. These two examples relate to getting individuals to contribute to the economy rather than focusing *solely* on their wellbeing. There are also numerous instances where psychological theory, and therapy itself, has been used as a form of explicit control. Frameworks that are dominated by diagnostic categories, and thus clear perceptions of what is viewed as 'normal' or 'abnormal' have been used to prize dominant viewpoints and to be more punitive towards less dominant ones. One only needs to look to the recent publications from the American Psychological Association (APA) on the discipline's history of racism, and their apology to people of colour with a historical addendum outlining psychology's involvement in perpetuating structural racism as an example of this (American Psychological Association, 2021).

The early therapeutic years

The simplistic answer to the conception of the psychological therapies, which is often presented by those in the global north, might be marked by the publications of Sigmund Freud, chronicling the work that he and his colleagues had embarked upon with people seeking support. Forgoing the complexity of the many strands that led to Freud's writing, and the minimisation of the role of the individuals who had accessed this therapy, these certainly marked a seminal period for the growth of therapy as we now know it. From his early writing, Freud described his version of a 'talking cure' at the end of the 1800s and published his *Introduction to Psychoanalysis* (*Vorlesungen zur Einführung in die Psychoanalyse*) in 1916. His thinking was influenced by many European philosophers who were embedded in a time that was both concerned with ongoing conflicts between nations and the growth of the scientific method. Further, acknowledging the problematic patriarchal systems within which Freud's work was embedded is important. Early women's liberation movements in England later rejected psychoanalytic theory (Mahoney, 2023). While Freud undoubtedly made an important contribution to the development of psychological therapies, it is vital not to forget the significant histories of the global south and the 'early years' that preceded the work of Freud and other global north scholars.

Moodley and van der Tempel (2018) describe the history of global south psychologies and reflect upon the significance of religion, magic and supernatural forces, and spirituality in the understanding of psychological healing. They emphasise the various histories and importance of Afrocentric healing traditions, Chinese medicinal approaches and Asian religious healing practices. Far earlier than Sigmund Freud's writing and work in the 1800s, Islamic hospitals formed the basis of perhaps the earliest institutionalised mental health systems, and authors have suggested that the first psychiatric ward globally was established in 705 in Baghdad (Awaad et al., 2019). Later, psychiatric hospitals developed in places such as Damascus, Alexandria and Cairo (e.g. Qalawun Hospital in Cairo, Egypt, which was developed in the 1280s). These early psychiatric hospitals were largely focused on treating mental health as a physical malady, with Islamic psychotherapy approaches that looked at the cognitive rooting of distress developing later. In many cultures and parts of the world there are minimal written records that predate European colonialism, which further compounds the colonialising of the history of psychological therapies (Paul & Charura, 2014).

In the global north, psychoanalysis continued to grow during the early 1900s, with Freud's thinking also spurring on many variants. Influential disciples of Freud's thinking, such as Alfred Adler, Carl Jung, Melanie Klein and Otto Rank, built on his theories and, often without the blessing of Sigmund Freud himself, took it in their own directions. Frantz Fanon, a French-speaking psychiatrist and freedom fighter born in Martinique, also significantly developed psychoanalytic thinking by reflecting upon the ways that racism and racist societies have an impact on individuals' psychological wellbeing (Fanon, 1961). Thus, while Freud's influence was not uncontested, his thinking provided the central reference point from which much of 20th-century psychoanalytic thought emerged.

Freud travelled widely to introduce others to his ideas. When travelling across the Atlantic to the USA, and indicative of his view of the human, he is said to have whispered to Carl Jung, 'They don't realize we're bringing them the plague'

(Rottenberg, 2020, p. 210). This remark captures Freud's anticipation that his theories would be disruptive and unsettling to existing ways of thinking. Much has also been written about how Freud's psychotherapy was subsequently metamorphosed in the process of being translated into different languages from its original. In *Freud and Man's Soul* (1984), Bruno Bettelheim considers the way in which the anglified version of psychoanalysis, which can be literally translated as 'analysis of the soul', became more medicalised in tone for its English-speaking audience.

The start of the 1900s marked the beginning of the second force of therapeutic development in the global north. In 1913 John B. Watson published his classic paper, 'Psychology as the Behaviorist Views it' (Watson, 1913). This paper, which proposed that behaviours are fundamentally the result of experience, was a forerunner to the work of psychologists such as Burrhus Skinner and Ivan Pavlov, whose work is a staple in introductory units to psychology degrees. The behaviourist approach became increasingly popular in psychology, with the historian Edwin Boring noting that, 'For a while in the 1920s it seemed as if all America had gone behaviourist' (Boring, 1950, p. 645). As the approach grew, influential behavioural psychologists such as Hans Eysenck and Joseph Wolpe published new developments in this area. This included their influence in launching the journal *Behaviour Research and Therapy*, the first issue of which was published in 1963.

Behaviour therapy aligned well with the medical model, which was prevalent in hospitals in Western societies. Its influence continued to grow and, while widely critiqued, was seen as a less medically intrusive alternative to the procedures (e.g. lobotomies or electroconvulsive treatments) and medications being used within the world of psychiatry in the 1940s and 1950s. Behaviour therapy fits well within healthcare settings, which commonly work with a deficit model of support (i.e. if you break a leg, they will help mend it). The growth of behavioural psychology was followed by the development of cognitive psychology. Cognitive therapy theorists, for example Aaron Beck (Beck, 1976) and Albert Ellis (Ellis, 1973), believed that problematic feelings and behaviours are formed through our relationships with and perceptions of them. As such, understanding these relationships more fully and, where necessary, challenging them and devising appropriate plans of action can lead to positive changes for those in distress. While the cognitive therapy and behavioural therapy elements were clearly related, they were more formally brought together within theories during the 1980s. This saw the growth of numerous difficulty-specific approaches to what has now become known as cognitive behavioural therapy (Clark, 1986; Salkovskis, 1985). This development has proven incredibly popular and the growth of CBT has been astronomical.

The humanistic psychology movement is often cited as the third force of applied psychology (sometimes referred to as the humanistic-existential movement). This perspective was articulated by individuals who had been trained in psychoanalytic or behavioural models of psychology but did not see either approach as reflecting their core philosophy or view of the way that humans engage within the world. Key individuals in this movement, people such as Charlotte Bühler, Abraham Maslow and Carl Rogers, devised a set of five postulates summarising the core principles of those identifying as humanistic psychologists (Bugental, 1964). These included the view that all individuals are unique, have the potential to constructively grow given the correct environment and have some choice and agency in the decisions that they make. Practically speaking, those working in the humanistic psychology movement varied greatly in their therapeutic approaches. Probably the most well-known approach was that articulated by Carl Rogers, the person-centred approach (sometimes referred to as non-directive or client-centred therapy) (Rogers, 1951). Rogers' perspective purposefully contrasted to the proactive interventionalist approaches adopted by the psychoanalysts and behavioural therapists of the time, with the importance of the therapist's way of being and the therapeutic relationship being prized more than the specific techniques of therapists.

While it might be believed that the humanistic psychology movement grew separately from the CBT movement, it should be noted that this is not the case. In his book outlining rational emotive therapy (RET), a theory that is credited as a forerunner to CBT, Albert Ellis did so under the title *Humanistic Psychotherapy* (Ellis, 1973). In this text he calls RET a 'revolutionary humanistic approach to psychotherapy' (p. 4) and outlines 10 reasons why cognitive therapy (CT) and RET are 'among the most humanistic of psychological treatment procedures' (p. 9). Thus, while there are those that place CBT in opposition to humanistic approaches, the reality is not quite so simple, and caution needs to be taken not to make sweeping misconceptions of different approaches.

To date there have been many claims to the development of a fourth, fifth and even sixth force in the world of therapy. While different accounts sometimes refer to different forces, the fourth is commonly referred to as transpersonal psychology, which extends therapeutic thinking beyond the individual self to include spirituality, altered states of consciousness, and the search for meaning beyond the personal (Sutich, 1969). The fifth force is often described as multicultural or transcultural approaches, and the sixth, social justice. Building momentum in the late 1990s, the fifth force focuses on *culture*, which was at least initially narrowly defined in terms of someone's racial and ethnic backgrounds. But as the transcultural movement developed, a broader understanding of culture that encompasses multiple aspects of someone's social identity became the focus (Pedersen, 1998). Further developments and debates have emerged regarding multicultural and cross-cultural competencies for therapists. These have been followed by an urgent need for work on transcultural humility rather than cross-cultural competencies. The sixth force of social justice broadens and builds on transcultural approaches, although some have considered these 'two sides of the same coin' (Ratts, 2011). The social justice agenda urges therapists to consider the social and political context, and to move beyond individual focused understanding and actions to include advocacy in our understanding of a therapist's role (Winter & Charura, 2023).

Where we are now

The psychological therapies are now relatively mainstream and have become an accepted, if often misunderstood, means of obtaining support. Therapy, of course, continues to evolve, and the forces previously mentioned are not static entities, but developing movements and shifts in understanding and practice. At the current time, numerous news reports highlight concerns for the mental health and wellbeing of various groups and communities, in the UK and beyond.

One of the misunderstandings regarding therapy is that it is a single activity and that every therapist offers the same type of service. As evidenced previously, numerous forces have influenced therapeutic thinking and, as a consequence, hundreds of approaches have been developed (Karasu, 1986). The urge to count the number of approaches has waned somewhat since the 1980s but, while the core approaches remain, new approaches continue to be developed. For some, this is a bit like a quest for a magic bullet, aiming to identify the perfect 'one-size-fits-all' therapeutic approach. For others, one approach will never be sufficient to accommodate the needs of everyone. During the 1960s, Gordon Paul (1967) noted that we need to address the following question: 'What treatment, by whom, is most effective for this individual with that specific problem, and under which set of circumstances?' (p. 111). Arguably, whether we advocate for one or multiple approaches, much research conducted in the psychological therapies only scratches the surface of the different elements of this question and often prioritises those approaches rooted in Western, colonial ways of conceptualising and approaching distress. We have a long way to go in fully understanding the work of therapy and therapists.

CBT has probably become the dominant force within the psychological therapies. Its resonance with the more medicalised view of therapy, alongside a large volume of controlled quantitative research, has aided its growth and made it a very attractive proposition with those commissioning services. However, alternative and more inclusive evaluations of the impact of therapy reflect that each major force of therapy can be effective some of the time, for some people. This perspective is often described as the Dodo bird verdict, a phrase coined by Luborsky et al. (1975) to reflect the chaotic nature of the evaluation of the psychotherapies. This is highlighted not to undermine the ascendence and contribution of CBT, which is clearly a very effective way of supporting large numbers of people, but to place it within an understanding of the broader, more complex, context.

A relatively recent development has been the acceptance of mediated therapeutic work (i.e. the therapist and client are connected at distance by technology such as phone, chat, videoconferencing, apps, social robots and so on). Prior to the Covid-19 pandemic, offering computer or telephone mediated therapy was a relatively niche endeavour. Since then, however, mediated work has become relatively commonplace (Hanley, 2021) and these are new frontiers that therapists need to understand. New technologies continue to be created that will impact upon the practices of therapists across the globe. There remains a need to expand the knowledge base in psychological therapies to amplify different voices, including those who have been marginalised.

Exercise: Reflecting on *our* historical perspective

As two white cisgendered authors trained as counselling psychologists in the UK, we invite the reader to consider how this perspective might have shaped what we have written. As noted in the introduction, all writing is selective and at least in part reflects the identities of those who have written it. Now that you have finished reading this chapter, we invite you to consider its contents in relation to us, the authors, and you, the reader. In turn, close your eyes and spend a few minutes considering your responses to the following set of questions:

- What do you think it tells you about us and who we are?
- What messages are we trying to convey about the political landscape of the development of therapy?
- What are the ways in which therapy services are positioned in society?
- What are the best therapeutic approaches?
- What is your view of the nature of the human?
- In what ways might you have written the chapter differently? Are there things that you consider important that we have not covered?

Top takeaways

- The psychological therapies reflect the work of a relatively new professional group, when considered from a Western perspective. While new, however, the type of work that they do resonates throughout human history, and adopting a global, decolonial understanding of mental health and healing opens up an understanding of psychological therapies as older and more varied than is often presented in texts written by anglophone authors.

- The growth of the psychological therapies is multifaceted and can be categorised as having six major forces: (i) psychoanalysis/psychodynamic; (ii) behaviourism/cognitive; (iii) existential-humanistic; (iv) transpersonal; (v) transcultural; and (vi) social justice.
- There is no one-size-fits-all therapeutic approach. Certain approaches appear to be more effective ways of helping with different challenges in life than others, but all dominant approaches to therapy appear to be effective, with some people, some of the time.
- Therapeutic theory and practice continue to change to fit their circumstance. New challenges for humans, technological developments and increasing awareness of societal injustices and inequalities will shape the future of those working in the psychological professions (counsellors, psychotherapists, practitioner psychologists, mental health key workers and so forth) and how they go about their clinical practice.

Questions for reflection

1. The most well-known historical figures in the development of the psychological therapies are white men. Why do you think this is the case?
2. The perspectives of the clients or patients that have sought support have often been ignored in therapeutic theory. Going forward:
   a) Why might including the views of these individuals be important in developing therapeutic theory?
   b) What ethical considerations need to be made when including these hidden figures in the development of therapeutic theory?

Recommended reading and key resources

- Fernando, S. & Moodley, R. (Eds.). (2018). *Global psychologies: Mental health and the global south*. Palgrave Macmillan.

An excellent edited text providing an internationally relevant overview of the psychological professions.

- Hanley, T. & Winter, L. (Eds.). (2023). *The Sage handbook of counselling and psychotherapy* (5th ed.). Sage.

This includes numerous chapters that reflect upon the history of the psychological therapies as a whole. It also includes introductions to specific therapeutic approaches.

References

American Psychological Association. (2021). *Apology to people of color for APA's role in promoting, perpetuating, and failing to challenge racism, racial discrimination, and human hierarchy in U.S.* https://www.apa.org/about/policy/racism-apology

Awaad, R., Mohammad, A., Elzamzamy, K., Fereydooni, S. & Gamar, M. (2019). Mental health in the Islamic golden era: The historical roots of modern psychiatry. In H.S. Moffic, J. Peteet, A.Z. Hankir & R. Awaad (Eds.), *Islamophobia and psychiatry: Recognition, prevention, and treatment* (pp. 3–17). Springer International Publishing. https://doi.org/10.1007/978-3-030-00512-2_1

Beck, A.T. (1976). *Cognitive therapy and the emotional disorders*. International Universities Press.

Bettelheim, B. (1984). *Freud and man's soul: An important re-interpretation of Freudian theory.* Knopf Doubleday Publishing Group.

Boring, E. (1950). *A history of experimental psychology*. Appleton-Century-Crofts.

Breuer, J. & Freud, S. (1895). *Studien über Hysterie* [Studies on hysteria]. F. Deuticke.

Bugental, J.F.T. (1964). The third force in psychology. *Journal of Humanistic Psychology, 4*(1), 19–26. https://doi.org/10.1177/002216786400400102

Clark, D.M. (1986). A cognitive approach to panic. *Behaviour Research and Therapy, 24*(4), 461–470. https://doi.org/10.1016/0005-7967(86)90011-2

Ellis, A. (1973). *Humanistic psychotherapy: The rational emotive approach*. McGraw Hill.

Fanon, F. (1961). *The wretched of the earth* (C. Farrington, Trans.). Penguin Classics.

Fernando, S. & Moodley, R. (2018). Introduction to global psychologies: Mental health and the global south. In S. Fernando & R. Moodley (Eds.), *Global psychologies: Mental health and the global south* (pp. 1–17). Palgrave Macmillan.

Freud, S. (1916). *Vorlesungen zur Einführung in die Psychoanalyse.* Hugo Heller & Cie.

Hanley, T. (2021). Researching online counselling and psychotherapy: The past, the present and the future. *Counselling and Psychotherapy Research, 21*(3), 493–497. https://doi.org/10/gk87gz

Hanley, T. (2023). What do people come to counselling and psychotherapy for? In T. Hanley & L.A. Winter (Eds.), *The Sage handbook of counselling and psychotherapy* (5th ed.) (pp. 14–18). Sage.

Karasu, T.B. (1986). The specificity versus nonspecificity dilemma: Toward identifying therapeutic change agents. *American Journal of Psychiatry, 143*(6), 687–695. https://doi.org/10.1176/ajp.143.6.687

Luborsky, L., Singer, B. & Luborsky, L. (1975). Comparative studies of psychotherapies: Is it true that 'everyone has won and all must have prizes'? *Archives of General Psychiatry, 32*(8), 995–1008. https://doi.org/10.1001/archpsyc.1975.01760260059004

Mahoney, K. (2023). *Feminist mental health activism in England, c. 1968–95.* Manchester University Press.

Martín-Baró, I. (1986). Hacia una psicología de la liberación [Toward a psychology of liberation]. *Boletin de Psicologia (El Salvador), 5*(22), 219–231.

Moodley, R. & van der Tempel, J. (2018). Contexts, epistemologies and practices of global south psychologies. In S. Fernando & R. Moodley (Eds.), *Global psychologies: Mental health and the global south* (pp. 59–74). Palgrave Macmillan.

Oulanova, O., Olga, J. & Moodley, R. (2023). Engaging with minoritised and racialised communities. In L.A. Winter & D. Charura (Eds.), *The handbook of social justice in psychological therapies: Power, politics, change* (pp. 10–21). Sage.

Paul, G.L. (1967). Strategy of outcome research in psychotherapy. *Journal of Consulting Psychology, 31*(2), 109–118. https://doi.org/10.1037/h0024436

Paul, S. & Charura, D. (2014). *An introduction to the therapeutic relationship in counselling and psychotherapy*. Sage.

Pedersen, P. (1998). *Multiculturalism as a fourth force*. Routledge.

Ratts, M.J. (2011). Multiculturalism and social justice: Two sides of the same coin. *Journal of Multicultural Counseling and Development, 39*(1), 24–37. https://doi.org/10.1002/j.2161-1912.2011.tb00137.x

Rogers, C.R. (1951). *Client-centered therapy*. Constable.

Rottenberg, E. (2020). At witz end: Theory in a time of plague. *Derrida Today, 13*(2), 210–216. https://doi.org/10.3366/drt.2020.0240

Salkovskis, P.M. (1985). Obsessional-compulsive problems: A cognitive-behavioural analysis. *Behaviour Research and Therapy, 23*(5), 571–583. https://doi.org/10.1016/0005-7967(85)90105-6

Sutich, A.J. (1969). Some considerations regarding transpersonal psychology. *Journal of Transpersonal Psychology, 1*(1), 11–20.

Wampold, B.E. (2001). Contextualizing psychotherapy as a healing practice: Culture, history, and methods. *Applied and Preventive Psychology, 10*(2), 69–86. https://www.sciencedirect.com/science/article/abs/pii/S096218490180007X

Watson, J.B. (1913). Psychology as the behaviorist views it. *Psychological Review, 20*(2), 158–177. https://doi.org/10.1037/h0074428

Wilcox, M.M., Pérez-Rojas, A.E., Marks, L.R., Reynolds, A.L., Suh, H.N., Flores, L.Y., McCubbin, L.D., Wilkins-Yel, K.G. & Miller, M.J. (2024). Structural competencies: Re-grounding counseling psychology in antiracist and decolonial praxis. *The Counseling Psychologist, 52*(4), 650–691. https://doi.org/10.1177/00110000241231029

Winter, L.A. & Charura, D. (2023). An introduction to the handbook of social justice in psychological therapies. In L.A. Winter & D. Charura (Eds.), *The handbook of social justice in psychological therapies: Power, politics, change* (pp. 3–9). Sage.

2.

The relevance of philosophy to therapy practice and research

Byron Al-Murri, Divine Charura, Charlotte O'Brien and John McLeod

Introduction

For many students entering into a psychological or therapeutic training pathway, the idea of engaging with philosophical perspectives can feel like a strange or unexpected detour within their learning journey. Certainly, in our own experience as students, it was not until later on in our careers that we recognised the vital importance of gaining a firm foundation in philosophy for both our therapeutic practice and our research. In this chapter we aim to explore with you why understanding your own philosophical outlook is an important aspect of training to become a therapist. Additional discussion of this topic can be found in Chapter 4 on integration and Chapter 9 on undertaking impactful psychotherapeutic research.

Du Plock (2017) reminds us that psychotherapy is fundamentally informed by questions about what it means to be *human*. Our sense of being human can be understood, from a philosophical standpoint, as comprising our sense of what exists (ontology), and how we learn about the objects or phenomena in the world around us (epistemology) and how our actions are an expression of moral values (axiology). How we position ourselves in relation to truth, existence, value and learning has profound implications for the way that we engage in psychotherapy as clients, or show up in the therapeutic relationship and integrate theory as practitioners.

Scope of the chapter

There are many ways that philosophical insights have the potential to inform therapy research and practice. The following sections offer an overview of:

- the relationship between philosophy and psychotherapy

- how philosophical ideas are embedded in therapy practice
- how philosophical perspectives can enhance therapeutic practice and understanding.

The relationship between philosophy and therapy

Philosophy is an academic discipline, and more generally a dimension of collective intellectual practice and meaning-making that has been in existence, in some form or another, throughout all human civilisation. Philosophy seeks to develop an understanding of fundamental questions relating to the nature of reality, knowledge and values. As a result, philosophical concepts underpin all research, inquiry and decision-making, and are relevant to all aspects of human life. In earlier historical periods, philosophical thinking took place through myth, religion, spiritual practice, law and oratory, and was part of everyday discourse. With the development of printing and universities as centres of learning, philosophy gradually became a specialist field of knowledge. Philosophy can be seen as the academic root discipline. Academic disciplines such as physics and psychology originally existed as branches of philosophy, and their work continues to refer to, and draw on, philosophical insights.

In terms of its relationship to psychology and psychotherapy, the main functions of philosophy are to question taken-for-granted assumptions, maintain clarity in the use of language and concepts, identify emergent topics, establish principles for rational analysis, and offer transdisciplinary points of connection between different areas of inquiry. In a similar fashion to psychotherapy, the philosophy literature has until recently been largely grounded in the ideas of a set of key figures, such as Descartes, Kant, Hume and Locke – all white European men (Beaney, 2023). The more recent development of philosophy has been driven by an appreciation of its cultural narrowness, matched by an intention to take account of African, Asian and Indigenous philosophical traditions, and the writing of women. Unlike psychotherapy, which has been largely organised around mostly self-contained schools or approaches (psychoanalysis, humanistic, cognitive behavioural), philosophical writing has largely avoided the creation of monolithic systems of thought, and instead has tended to be grounded in dialogue between contrasting perspectives on a topic.

Because the philosophy literature is wide-ranging and multi-layered, it can be hard for those who have not received philosophical training to engage with it. Accessible introductory sources for those new to philosophy include Bakewell (2017), Blackburn (2017), Craig (2020) and Magee (2026). Philosophical ideas tend to receive limited attention in professional programmes in counselling, psychotherapy and psychology. Philosophical discussion of issues in counselling and psychotherapy have tended to originate in the writing of individual therapists with prior training in philosophy, rather than being spread through all sectors of the profession: there are no journals or special interest groups devoted to philosophical aspects of therapy. An important bridge between philosophy and therapy has been the application of existentialist and phenomenological philosophical concepts within existential therapy. There is a thriving tradition of philosophical counselling or practice that invites clients to look at how the issues they bring to therapy are shaped by their personal philosophical worldview and assumptions (Louw, 2013). Sources that explore how philosophy can be used to critique and support therapy practice can be found in Downing (2000), Gipps and Lacewing (2019), King-Spooner (2001), Lowenthal and Snell (2003), Mace (1999), Miller (2004), and Smoliak et al. (2026).

Personal reflection exercise: Taking stock of your relationship with philosophy

What is your own personal engagement with philosophy? Which philosophers or philosophical concepts have been meaningful for you in your life up to this point? In what ways – if any – have you found philosophical insights valuable for your therapy practice, research and personal/professional development? What is your philosophy learning agenda – which thinkers or ideas are you curious to know more about?

How philosophical ideas are embedded in therapy practice

Working with clients rarely draws on philosophical ideas in any kind of direct manner. As a therapist, one's attention in a session is focused on listening to the client and using counselling skills to facilitate their exploration of personal issues and concerns, guided by a theoretical framework. However, these processes are underpinned by the position one takes in relation to one's core philosophical standpoint. One of the major dividing lines in mental (ill) health, treatment and therapy is the contrast between psychiatric and medical approaches. Both approaches reflect what philosophers might describe as a positivist, realist or objectivist stance that assumes that the ultimate nature of reality (ontology) consists of atoms, molecules, neuro-biochemistry, genetics and physiology. Such a stance is also associated with an epistemology or way of knowing that emphasises scientific measurement and experimentation. By contrast, counselling, psychotherapy and counselling psychology practice can be viewed as grounded in a relational (Slife & Wiggins, 2009) and humanist (Wampold, 2007) ontology that is based in a sense of people acting together to co-construct the world they experience. Much therapy practice draws on phenomenological epistemology. Phenomenology is a way of knowing linked to existentialism, based on an understanding that the essential nature of any aspect of everyday human experience can be brought into awareness by bracketing off taken-for-granted assumptions and gradually revealing the multifaceted, dynamic qualities. Finlay (2021) offers a detailed account of how these phenomenological concepts and procedures inform therapeutic work. Psychotherapy practice is also informed by hermeneutics – an epistemological perspective that was originally developed by philosophers and theologians to guide the interpretation of sacred texts. Counselling and psychotherapy also operate in accordance with professional ethical codes that make use of ideas from moral philosophy, such as virtue ethics.

In addition to these broad sources of philosophical influence, specific therapy approaches are identified with particular philosophical concepts and perspectives. The first waves of therapy approaches – psychoanalysis, humanistic and cognitive behavioural – positioned themselves within contrasting philosophical traditions. Psychoanalysis was influenced by philosophical insights with respect to interpretation, the nature of mind and consciousness, and biological determinism (libido). The humanistic therapies such as the person-centred approach and gestalt therapy drew heavily from ideas in phenomenology and existentialism, as well as from ideas about the existence of a future-oriented life force or actualising tendency that was highly influential in early 20th-century European and North American philosophy, and which was most clearly articulated in the work of Henri Bergson. By contrast, behavioural and cognitive behavioural therapy adopted a pragmatic and flexible philosophical stance, incorporating elements from both a behaviourist realist-objectivist ontology alongside a constructivist position on epistemology in which the individual was seen as creating reality through their own cognitions and appraisals (lenses of interpretation and meaning). The strands of thinking come together in a pragmatic realism within CBT, through recognising the existence of an objective external world in which a client's subjective (individually constructed) cognitions can be tested (Kaushik & Walsh, 2019). CBT epistemology uses empirically quantifiable, psychometric, thought and behavioural records to measure change, intensity, frequency and the observable 'data' of actions and thoughts (intensity, frequency, duration), which also places importance on subjective experiences, such as physical sensations, emotions, thoughts and actions. CBT reached back into the history of philosophy to retrieve and repurpose the practice of Socratic questioning as a method of collaborative inquiry based on a guided discovery (GD) process.

Subsequent waves of therapy theories have tended to use philosophical ideas to mark out their distinctive identity as approaches offering something new and different that has emerged from critiques of the underlying conceptual assumptions used in earlier models of therapy. Statements of philosophical positioning can often be found in the early books and articles that announce the arrival of a new approach. Narrative therapy used poststructuralist philosophical perspectives, as exemplified in the work of Michel Foucault, to provide a rationale for its critique of how power and control are maintained through narrative and storytelling. Acceptance and commitment therapy defined itself as being based in functional contextualism, with an emphasis on values. Pluralistic therapy is oriented around a philosophical stance that argues that there are no single or monolithic truths, and that human society and progress is associated with a commitment to dialogue. Open dialogue therapy is an expression of the work of the Russian philosopher Mikhail Bakhtin on the philosophy of language and communication. Feminist, social justice-oriented and decolonising approaches to therapy are influenced by critical theory and philosophical analyses of the concept of justice.

Overall, it is possible to see that counselling and psychotherapy theories and approaches take philosophical ideas as points of reference that contribute to depth of understanding, while engaging in practice that is predominantly guided by psychological concepts. However, this way of relating to philosophy – as a kind of intellectual super-power and unique selling point – is far from straightforward. Clients generally live their lives without devoting much time or thought to ontology, epistemology or moral reasoning. Instead, they operate on the basis of an eclectic mix of common-sense ideas that are highly responsive to the specific contexts within which they find themselves. The implication of such everyday ontological, epistemological and values fluidity is that it is essential for therapists to be able to be responsive to, and respectful of, the philosophical stances adopted by clients, regardless of their own philosophical position or that of the therapy approach they espouse. The challenge during therapy training, and also throughout one's subsequent career, is to continue to explore philosophical concepts that are personally relevant, as a means of becoming able to articulate one's authentic position. At the same time, being open and curious about all philosophical perspectives allows one to be open to the authentic positions of clients and colleagues.

Being open to new philosophical perspectives

The capacity to use philosophical ideas to deepen one's practice is a skill that needs to be cultivated and practised. Hopefully, the period of time during which a counsellor, psychotherapist or professional psychologist undergoes primary training, would provide opportunities to develop such skills. As well as the time-consuming and intellectually challenging task of reading philosophical books and articles, it can be valuable to find other ways to keep one's philosophical understanding alive. The BBC Radio 4 programme and podcasts *In Our Time* offers many opportunities for low-intensity, enjoyable philosophical learning. Each episode comprises three experts engaging in respectful, informed dialogue around a topic, with many focusing on philosophical concepts or the lives of particular philosophers. These podcasts offer insights into the social and cultural context in which philosophical ideas emerged, the person behind the concept, and the enduring significance of ideas. It can be useful to listen to episodes, not just in terms of the information that is being shared, but also in terms of what it means to you personally, and to your work as a therapist. Previous episodes can be downloaded for free, and the programme website includes suggestions for further reading.

Using art and music to experience unfamiliar ontological realities

For many counselling psychologists, counsellors and psychotherapists, philosophical writing can be difficult to follow. To explain their ideas, a philosopher may need to refer to the work of other philosophers with whom the reader may not be familiar. In addition, much philosophy seeks to explore phenomena and experiences that are not readily captured in existing language – the author may need to use analogies and metaphors, or even invent new words. These challenges are particularly evident in philosophy that touches on ontological, existential and metaphysical issues. An alternative way to engage with ontological perspectives is through music and art. In relation to art as a means of depicting different realities, the book *Ways of Seeing* by John Berger (1972) – and his many subsequent essays and books on this theme – provides a good starting point around being able to use paintings as entry points into different worlds. Music can serve a similar function. Contemporary popular and rock music largely depicts an individualised and lonely reality mitigated by occasional romantic attachments, received by a passive audience. By contrast, other musical traditions evoke collective realities – for example, work songs and gospel, where everyone takes part. Some music, such as the Aborigine and Torres Straits Islanders' Indigenous music, refers to the existence of a more-than-human world. The most downloaded Beatles song is 'Here Comes the Sun'. Both music and art also provide many opportunities to engage with the kind of fragmented reality implied in postmodern philosophy. A useful exercise, in relation to constructively engaging with philosophical texts, can be to identify creative visual and musical sources that are evoked by what you are reading, and open yourself to the feelings and insights that they produce in you.

How philosophical perspectives can enhance therapeutic practice and understanding

In addition to providing conceptual grounding for therapy theories and approaches, philosophical perspectives have the potential to contribute to the capacity of counsellors and psychotherapists to respond effectively to challenges arising from the relationship between therapy practice and the socio-political environment within which it exists. The following sections highlight current examples of how philosophical insights can function in this manner.

Social and epistemic justice

A growing proportion of counsellors and psychotherapists are finding it meaningful to adopt a social justice-oriented approach in their work. Social justice-oriented therapy refers to a wide-ranging set of ideas and practice, including access to therapy for members of marginalised communities, inclusion of more individuals with disabilities and people of colour as therapists and trainers, and re-focusing therapy theory and practice to take account of structural inequality and adversity (Winter & Charura, 2023). While the development of social justice-oriented therapy represents a response to social activism, cultural change and political context, it has also been shaped by ideas from philosophy. One set of ideas is connected to philosophical work on ethics, which has argued that while professional contractual codes of ethics are necessary in therapy, it is also essential to take account of wider moral issues associated with human rights and a relational ethics of care.

A further philosophical perspective that underpins a social justice approach originates in the concept of epistemic justice (Fricker, 2017). The notion of epistemic justice refers to the relative status and credibility of different epistemologies or ways of knowing. In the fields of counselling, psychotherapy and healthcare, much greater weight tends to be given to the ways of knowing exhibited by trained professionals (i.e. therapists) rather than the knowledge-from-experience possessed by clients and service users. A notable recent site of epistemic justice has been the insistence by health professions that chronic fatigue syndrome (CFS)/myalgic encephalomyelitis (ME) is a psychological condition that should be treated by exercise regimes and CBT, rather than – as believed by most people suffering from this condition, and their carers – that it is fundamentally a physical and biological process that has psychological effects (Byrne, 2020). A further area of therapy practice associated with epistemic injustice has been the extent to which therapy theory, practice and training have downplayed the significance of transcendent epistemology for many clients – the belief that prayer, meditation, pilgrimage, and manifestations of the sacred in everyday life can be meaningful sources of knowing that can be highly relevant for their therapeutic healing (Captari et al., 2022). The concept of epistemic justice provides a framework for understanding how a therapist's lack of humility around a client's knowledge and beliefs is not only due to lack of skills, but is also a wider phenomenon rooted in their fundamental epistemological stance.

Using research to inform practice

There is a general appreciation, both within the therapy and mental health professions and more widely across society as a whole, that therapy practice should be research-informed, evidence-based and accountable. As a consequence, learning about research methodologies, critical reading of research articles, and designing and conducting research studies, are significant elements within any training curriculum. A capacity to use research to inform practice requires an understanding of the philosophical assumptions that underpin different research paradigms. A research paradigm comprises a matrix of ideas and procedures that have been developed by a scientific community as a basis for carrying out research within a particular area of knowledge. The field of psychotherapy research is organised around two contrasting paradigms. On one side sits quantitative research, which reflects realist, objectivist and scientific ontological and epistemological assumptions. On the other side is qualitative research, which is broadly constructivist, interpretivist, relational and phenomenological in how it sees the world (Ponterotto, 2005). Although these paradigms can combine, overlap and merge in many ways – for example, in mixed-methods research designs or a critical realist philosophical perspective (Bhaskar, 2015) – they influence and inform therapy practice in distinct ways. On the whole, quantitative research, which seeks to measure abstract factors within large data sets, provides useful evidence for policy decision-making around such questions as the effectiveness and cost-effectiveness of different types of therapy that might be provided within a national health service. By contrast, qualitative research, which describes and analyses lived experience using such methods as interviews and ethnographic participant observation, offers an understanding of how social reality is constructed through purposeful action in a context of meaningfulness. Both paradigms are necessary, but contribute to practice in different ways. The accumulated findings of measurement-based research, and their application to the client–therapist working alliance, summarised by Wampold and Flückiger (2023), clearly demonstrate that the relationship exerts a significant impact on client outcomes, and as a consequence needs to be taken seriously in training, supervision and practice. By contrast, qualitative studies such as Grindheim et al. (2025) and Oddli and Rønnestad (2012) provide examples and insights around what therapists actually do to facilitate a productive alliance.

A growing appreciation of the potential value of qualitative research as a source of evidence for practice has led to a wide-ranging programme of epistemological inquiry into the question of how to maximise the relevance and credibility of qualitative studies (Tracy, 2010). An important answer to this question emphasises the philosophical coherence of a study – the extent to which its ontological, epistemological and values stances are consistent with how data were collected, analysed and written up (Levitt et al., 2021). What this means is that being philosophically informed and literate is an important aspect of competence as a qualitative researcher (Brinkmann, 2017; Cushman, 2022; Finlay, 2011; McLeod, 2011; Nordstrom & Ulmer, 2017; Smith et al., 2021).

The nature of causality

Some clients may be interested in making sense of causes of the difficulties and concerns that have brought them to therapy (Larkings et al., 2019). An understanding of causes may also be relevant to preventing problems from re-occurring, by building awareness of precipitating situations. However, therapists may be cautious about talking about such processes because their thinking is dominated by the kinds of highly demanding rules for establishing causality associated with randomised clinical trials. In many situations within the field of healthcare – for instance, in respect of medically unexplained symptoms – clinicians may feel that they are ethically barred from engaging in conversations about causality at all. In response to these dilemmas, there has emerged an extensive philosophical literature that has started to build frameworks that practitioners can use with clients, which facilitate exploration of everyday causality in terms of such concepts as dispositions (Anjum et al., 2020), vectors (Low, 2017) and affordances (Bohart, 2007).

The use of technology in therapy

A significant area of innovation and development in contemporary psychotherapy concerns the impact of technology – for instance, through the use of online therapy, apps, feedback and monitoring systems, and AI. Debates within the therapy and mental health professions have tended to focus on such issues as cost, cultural inclusiveness, therapeutic effectiveness, consequences for the client–therapist relationship, and data security. By contrast, the majority of philosophers would take the view that there is no such thing as value-free technology, and that all of these technological adjuncts to therapy contribute to a subtle reshaping of what it means to be human. An example of such a perspective can be found in the work of the philosopher Shannon Vallor (2024a, 2024b) on the implications of AI. The use of technology represents an area in which philosophers are able to articulate and explore concerns that therapists may feel at an experiential level but struggle to put into words.

The tension between worldviews of the global north and those of the global south

The current book has a firm commitment to the promotion of social justice as a key goal of therapy training. In relation to using training to develop a deeper appreciation of what is involved in social justice-oriented practice, it is essential to engage with the diverse range of philosophies and worldviews that exist outside the European or Ameri-centric philosophical traditions of the global north. Such engagement involves knowledge of philosophies from Islam (Akhavi, 2003), Hinduism (Bernard, 1999), Buddhism, Taoism and Confucianism (Reader, 2015), and Indigenous (Chilisa, 2012; Topa & Narvaez, 2022; Yunkaporta, 2019) and

African philosophical perspectives (Masolo, 1994; Sefotho & Letseka, 2024). As discussed in Chapter 1, these perspectives have often been marginalised in our therapeutic histories. Although each offers its own unique approach to making sense of reality, ways of knowing and values, they tend to share certain features that are largely absent in philosophies of the global north: acknowledgement of spirituality and the sacred; place-based or land-based knowing; and an assumption of the inter-relatedness of all things. Critical engagement with these diverse philosophies, theories, belief systems and worldviews, from a position of openness, curiosity and cultural humility about the diversity of our clients' backgrounds and cultural identities, contributes to deepening and enriching our therapeutic encounter and relational depth.

Personal reflection exercise: Seeing yourself as others see you

Choose one philosophical tradition that is different from your own personal primary belief and value system. Allow yourself some time to read and learn about that way of seeing the world – if possible, augmented by dialogue with individuals who identify with that worldview. What are the implications of what you have learned for your therapeutic work with clients who identify, partly or entirely, with that way of seeing the world? Finally, how might such a client view you, and the philosophical stance and values that you represent? What have you learned about yourself, as a person and as a therapist, from seeing yourself through their eyes?

Top takeaways

This chapter has demonstrated the value of philosophical understanding for therapy practice and research, and offered some starting points for exploring this topic during training and throughout your professional career. Philosophy is a wide-ranging discipline that has the potential to connect with therapy in many different ways. To be able to use philosophical insights to deepen your practice, it is important to identify specific philosophical concepts and writing that are most meaningful and relevant for you, in respect of particular challenges that arise in your work with clients.

Questions for reflection

1. What is reality and truth for you (your ontological position)?
2. What is your epistemological position? What are the ways of knowing that are most meaningful and credible for you in your work as a therapist?
3. What are the values and moral principles that are most significant for you, in your professional role?
4. What are the philosophical concepts or ideas that are available to you, to support and inform your reflection on your ontological, epistemological and axiological positions?
5. To what extent, and in what ways, do you engage with the ontological, epistemological and axiological positions of your clients?
6. What are the opportunities that are available to you in your training, for developing your philosophical understanding? What can you do to maximise your use of these opportunities?

Recommended reading and key resources

- Hastings, J. (2020). *Mental health ontologies: How we talk about mental health, and why it matters in the digital age.* University of Exeter Press.

An accessible and rich exploration of how philosophical perspectives can contribute to more integrated, consistent and holistic ways of understanding mental health and treatment.

- Laing, R.D. (1965). *The divided self: An existential study in sanity and madness.* Penguin Books.

A compelling account of how ideas from existential philosophy can be used to generate new ways of thinking about the aims and process of therapy. In particular, the section on ontological insecurity highlights the value of being able to engage with client suffering at its most fundamental ontological level.

- Ponterotto, J.G. (2005). Qualitative research in counseling psychology: A primer on research paradigms and philosophy of science. *Journal of Counseling Psychology*, *52*(2), 126–138.

A hugely influential analysis of how research paradigms in the field of psychotherapy and counselling psychology are grounded in different philosophical assumptions.

- Willig, C. (2019). Ontological and epistemological reflexivity: A core skill for therapists. *Counselling and Psychotherapy Research, 19*(3), 186–194.

A clear explanation, with examples from practice, of how and why an understanding of one's own philosophical position is an essential dimension of being an effective therapist.

The work of Brent D. Slife, whose long career was devoted to critiquing the underlying philosophical assumptions of therapy practice and research, represents an invaluable learning resource for anyone interested in learning about these topics: https://www.brentslife.com/about

References

Akhavi, S. (2003). Islam and the west in world history. *Third World Quarterly*, *24*(3), 545–562. https://doi.org/10.1080/0143659032000084465

Anjum, R.L., Copeland, S. & Rocca, E. (Eds.). (2020). *Rethinking causality, complexity and evidence for the unique patient. A causehealth resource for healthcare professionals and the clinical encounter*. Springer.

Bakewell, S. (2017). *At the existentialist café: Freedom, being, and apricot cocktails.* Vintage.

Beaney, M. (2023). Open-mindedness and ajar-mindedness in history of philosophy. *Metaphilosophy*, *54* (2–3), 208–222.

Berger, J. (1972). *Ways of seeing*. Penguin.

Bernard, T. (1999). *Hindu philosophy*. Motilal Banarsidass Publications.

Bhaskar, R. (2015). *The possibility of naturalism: A philosophical critique of the contemporary human sciences* (4th ed.). Routledge.

Blackburn, S. (2017). *Truth*. Profile Books.

Bohart, A.C. (2007). An alternative view of concrete operating procedures from the perspective of the client as active self-healer. *Journal of Psychotherapy Integration*, *17*(1), 125–137.

Brinkmann, S. (2017). *Philosophies of qualitative research*. Oxford University Press.

Byrne, E.A. (2020). Striking the balance with epistemic injustice in healthcare: The case of chronic fatigue syndrome/myalgic encephalomyelitis. *Medicine, Health Care and Philosophy*, *23*(3), 371–379.

Captari, L.E., Sandage, S.J. & Vandiver, R.A. (2022). Spiritually integrated psychotherapies in real-world clinical practice: Synthesizing the literature to identify best practices and future research directions. *Psychotherapy*, *59*(3), 307–320.

Chilisa B. (2012). *Indigenous research methodologies*. Sage.

Craig, E. (2020). *Philosophy: A very short introduction*. Oxford University Press.

Cushman, P. (Ed.). (2022). *Hermeneutic approaches to interpretive research*. Routledge.

Downing, J.N. (2000). *Between conviction and uncertainty: Philosophical guidelines for the practicing psychotherapist*. New York Press.

Du Plock, S. (2017). Philosophical issues in counselling psychology. In D. Murphy (Ed.), *Counselling psychology: A textbook for study and practice*, (pp. 36–51). Wiley.

Finlay, L. (2011). *Phenomenology for therapists: Researching the lived world*. Wiley-Blackwell.

Finlay, L. (2021). The phenomenological use of self in integrative psychotherapy: Applying philosophy to practice. *International Journal of Integrative Psychotherapy*, *12*, 114–141.

Fricker, M. (2017). Evolving concepts of epistemic injustice. In I.J. Kidd, J. Medina & G. Pohlhaus, Jr (Eds.), *Routledge handbook of epistemic injustice*. (pp. 53-60) Routledge.

Gipps, R. & Lacewing, M. (Eds.). (2019). *The Oxford handbook of philosophy and psychoanalysis*. Oxford University Press.

Grindheim, Ø., Moltu, C., Iversen, V., McAleavey, A., Tømmervik, K., Govasmark, H. & Brattland, H. (2025). Points of departure: A qualitative study exploring relational facilitators and barriers in the first treatment session. *Psychotherapy Research*, *35*(1), 155–169.

Kaushik, V. & Walsh, C.A. (2019). Pragmatism as a research paradigm and its implications for social work research. *Social Sciences*, *8*(9), 1–17. https://doi.org/10.3390/socsci8090255

King-Spooner, S. (2001). *Spirituality and psychotherapy*. PCCS Books.

Larkings, J.S., Brown, P.M. & Scholz, B. (2019). 'It's often liberating': Consumers discuss causal beliefs in the treatment process. *Journal of Mental Health*, *28*(4), 397–403.

Levitt, H.M., Morrill, Z., Collins, K.M. & Rizo, J.L. (2021). The methodological integrity of critical qualitative research: Principles to support design and research review. *Journal of Counseling Psychology* *68*(3), 357–370. https://doi.org/10.1037/cou0000523

Louw, D. (2013). Defining philosophical counselling: An overview. *South African Journal of Philosophy*, *32*(1), 60–70.

Low, M. (2017). A novel clinical framework: The use of dispositions in clinical practice. *Journal of Evaluation in Clinical Practice, 23*(5), 1062–1070.

Lowenthal, D. & Snell, R. (Eds.). (2003). *Post-modernism for psychotherapists: A critical reader.* Routledge.

Mace, C. (1999). *Heart and soul: The therapeutic face of philosophy*. Routledge.

Magee, B. (2026). *A history of philosophy.* Dorling Kindersley.

Masolo, D.A. (1994). *African philosophy in search of identity*. Indiana University Press.

McLeod, J. (2011). *Qualitative research in counselling and psychotherapy* (2nd ed.). Sage.

Miller, R.B. (2004). The moral content of theories of clinical practice. In R.B. Miller, *Facing human suffering: Psychology and psychotherapy as moral engagement* (pp. 71–114). American Psychological Association.

Nordstrom, S. & Ulmer, J. (2017). Postqualitative curations and creations. *Reconceptualizing Educational Research Methodology, 8*(3). http://journals.hioa.no/index.php/rerm

Oddli, H.W. & Rønnestad, M.H. (2012). How experienced therapists introduce the technical aspects in the initial alliance formation: Powerful decision makers supporting clients' agency. *Psychotherapy Research, 22*(2), 176–193.

Ponterotto, J.G. (2005). Qualitative research in counseling psychology: A primer on research paradigms and philosophy of science. *Journal of Counseling Psychology, 52*(2), 126–136.

Reader, I. (2015). Religions of East Asia. In J.D. Wright (Ed.), *International Encyclopedia of the Social & Behavioral Sciences*, (pp. 366–372). Elsevier.

Sefotho, M.M. & Letseka, M. (2024). Botho/Ubuntu paradigm as cognitive justice in psychology. *School Psychology International, 45*(3), 233–253.

Slife, B.D. & Wiggins, B.J. (2009). Taking relationship seriously in psychotherapy: Radical relationality. *Journal of Contemporary Psychotherapy, 39*(1), 17–24.

Smith, J.A., Larkin, M. & Flowers, P. (2021). *Interpretative phenomenological analysis: Theory, method and research* (2nd ed.). Sage.

Smoliak, O., Tseliou, E., Strong, T., Bava, S. & Muntigl, P. (Eds.). (2026). *The Routledge International handbook of postmodern therapies*. Routledge.

Topa, W. & Narvaez, D. (2022). *Restoring the kinship worldview: Indigenous voices introduce 28 precepts for rebalancing life on planet Earth*. North Atlantic Books.

Tracy, S.J. (2010). Qualitative quality: Eight 'big-tent' criteria for excellent qualitative research. *Qualitative Inquiry, 16*(10), 837–851.

Vallor, S. (2024a, May 23). The danger of superhuman AI is not what you think. *Noema*. https://www.noemamag.com/the-danger-of-superhuman-ai-is-not-what-you-think/

Vallor, S. (2024b). *The AI mirror: How to reclaim our humanity in an age of machine thinking.* Oxford University Press.

Wampold, B.E. (2007). Psychotherapy: *The* humanistic (and effective) treatment. *American Psychologist, 62*(8), 857–873.

Wampold, B.E. & Flückiger, C. (2023). The alliance in mental health care: Conceptualization, evidence and clinical applications. *World Psychiatry, 22*(1), 25–41.

Winter, L.A., & Charura, D. (2023). An introduction to the handbook of social justice in psychological therapies. In L.A. Winter & D. Charura (Eds.), *The handbook of social justice in psychological therapies: Power, politics, change* (pp. 3–9). Sage.

Yunkaporta, T. (2019). *Sand talk: How indigenous thinking can save the world.* Text Publishing.

3.

Developing theoretical fluency

John McLeod, Divine Charura and Charlotte O'Brien

Introduction

The experience of training involves not only learning *about* theory, but also participating in a process of critically reflecting on what *theory means to you* at both personal and professional levels, and developing a capacity to *use* theory to inform your work with clients and facilitate dialogue with colleagues. This chapter does not try to describe and explain specific theoretical perspectives – your training course is already doing that, and there are many excellent books that provide access to that knowledge. However, the following discussion refers to the analysis of existing and emergent theory clusters, developed by Fleuridas & Krafcik (2019), as a means of characterising the landscape of counselling and psychotherapy theory as a whole. Theoretical fluency or competence is multifaceted, and that effectiveness as a practitioner requires attention to a range of ways that theoretical knowledge and skills can both help and hinder your development and work with clients. This chapter invites you to stand back and reflect on the function and role of theory in therapy practice and research, and identify your personal strategies for making the most of the theoretical learning opportunities offered by your training programme.

Scope of the chapter

In this chapter we will cover the following key topics:

- being on a theoretical journey
- the foundational and emerging psychological forces (building on Chapter 1)
- what a theory is
- the importance of belonging to a community of practice

- the use of theory within the therapy process
- theorising and learning theory
- the limitations of theory
- ethical and metaphysical uses of theory.

We will also explore some exercises and reflective questions throughout the chapter.

Being on a theoretical journey

Your theoretical journey to becoming a therapist and beyond will inevitably be influenced by a set of theoretical perspectives or 'forces' that underpin research and practice in psychology (Fleuridas & Krafcik, 2019; Paul & Charura, 2015). There are six main forces: psychoanalytic/psychodynamic; behaviourism/cognitive; existential-humanistic; transpersonal; transcultural; and social justice, plus integrative, inclusive and holistic (see Table 3.1).

Personal reflection exercise 1

Reflection on your engagement with these theoretical clusters offers a valuable means of taking stock of where you are in your own theoretical learning journey. At the earliest stage of that journey, before you had any thought of training to be a therapist, you will still have needed to guide your life according to implicit, common-sense assumptions about what makes people the way they are, and what you (and others) want and need from life. You would also have your own understanding of how to handle difficulties in your life – painful emotions, conflict with others, dilemmas about choices that you might need to make. Your mode of understanding would also have included ideas related to morals, values and spiritual guidelines. Allow yourself some time to reflect on that journey, and perhaps write down key personal discoveries and turning points in notes or a list.

At some point in your life you would have come across psychological and psychotherapeutic concepts and theories for the first time. Can you recall when this was? Who was the first therapist you heard about? What was the first therapy book or article you read? What impact did these encounters have on you? To what extent, and in what ways, have these first contacts with therapy theories set the direction of your development as a therapist? If you have changed direction at some stage, what were the reasons behind that shift?

More recently, your studies and training would have required engaging with therapy theory in a more formal way. It is likely that this engagement would have included acquiring in-depth understanding of perhaps one or two core theoretical models, alongside a broad appreciation of the wide range of therapy theories that currently exist. Where do you see yourself in relation to the field of therapy theory as a whole? If you think about the general counselling or psychotherapy textbooks that you have used in your studies, which are the theory chapters that have been most, or least, meaningful for you? Which ones have challenged you?

As discussed in Chapter 1, it can be helpful to think about the historical development of therapy in terms of a series of theoretical themes and forces, starting with psychoanalysis, then moving through humanistic-existential, CBT and multicultural theories, leading to the more social justice-oriented and holistic models that have emerged in recent years (Fleuridas & Krafcik, 2019; O'Brien & Charura, 2023). When you consider the theoretical landscape of therapy as a whole, what are the territories that you might wish to explore in future? An article by Hansen (2024) offers an insightful discussion of the value of maintaining theoretical fluency rather than basing one's practice in a single theoretical perspective.

An important aspect of any therapist's theoretical journey concerns their roads not travelled – the theoretical ideas and traditions that do *not* have meaning for them, or that may even be perceived as unhelpful or misguided. It is likely that there are ideas and traditions that are significant, meaningful and helpful for many colleagues and their clients, but not for you. What can you learn about yourself as a person and a therapist by asking yourself why you *reject* certain concepts and theories?

In a study by Råbu and McLeod (2018), senior therapists at the end of their careers described how their theoretical understanding had evolved and changed over the course of their working lives (see also Chapter 4). In some cases, this involved arriving at a deeper appreciation of the meaning of key concepts. In other cases, it involved learning new ideas. For those who are at earlier stages of training, these findings raise the question: what might you be doing now that could create a platform that would support your ongoing theoretical learning?

What is a theory?

A theory is a set of interconnected concepts that can be used to make sense of a specific aspect of the world. A theory is a statement about what the world is like. Such statements can be used to *explain* what happens in the world in terms of causal sequences, or to *interpret* what happens in terms of its meaning. Taken together, these functions of theory have the potential to feed into action: they sensitise us to future possibilities and allow us to anticipate, predict and possibly control future events.

Table 3.1 Foundational and emerging forces of psychology: key dimensions

Forces	Methods	Position of therapist	Place of the relationship in therapy	Aim of therapy
Psychoanalysis (and later, also psychodynamic)	Interpretation, working with transference, countertransference and resistance. Identification of relational patterns, unconscious processes and maladaptive behaviours that may be the root of distress.	Blank screen and works with dynamics of transference and countertransference between patient and therapist. Offering of interpretations and resisting unconscious or conscious invitations to destructive relational patterns.	Working with the here and now to resolve past difficulties. Providing boundaries and a therapeutic frame that hold and contain the dynamics and enactments between therapist and patient.	To adjust and to live more fully in the present reality based on the past (relationships, attachments, trauma and other difficulties).
Behaviourism (and later, cognitive)	Deciding goals, action plans, new ways of behaving and thinking. Identifying core beliefs, rules of living, strengths, critical incidents, systems and areas required for change.	Psycho-educator and trainer.	Focus on practical goal-based approach within a collaborative working alliance.	To change maladapted thoughts, feelings, actions or behaviours, and how one responds to body sensations.
Humanistic–existential	Human encounter. In some cases, particular techniques may be used – for example, wholebody focusing, expressive movement, object elicitation, empty chair.	Facilitator or catalyst.	Central, focused on working in the here and now through authentic relational encounter.	To live an authentic and full life, and to continually work towards one's potential.

Transpersonal	Dialogue, creative visualisation and imagery.	Guide, facilitator, educator.	To facilitate holistic change.	To achieve spiritual growth and to become integrated in mind, body and spirit.
Transcultural	Human encounters where the emphasis is on cultural humility, curiosity, awareness and conveying/working through the acceptance of difference and diversity.	Facilitator and learner.	To model acceptance of cultural difference and demonstrate anti-discriminatory practice, challenging oppression and power imbalances.	To live a full life and achieve authentic acceptance of the cultural self. Facilitated through the valuing of different psychological constructs and their ways of being presented by people of different cultures.
Social justice	Participatory. Affirming of human agency and capacity for working collaboratively with others to create change. This is done through sharing power ('power-with'), facilitating consciousness raising, building on strengths, leaving clients with the tools for social change, and giving voice.	Activist, advocate, facilitator, catalyst, educator, learner, disruptor of oppressive and colonial systems.	Respect ing of human diversity and group differences, and modelling appreciation of valuing social justice and decolonised practice. This is relayed through challenging inequality, oppression, marginalisation and discrimination.	Emancipation, transformation and change in personal contexts and wider society, with the ultimate goal of social justice.
Integrative, inclusive and holistic	Acknowledges diverse perspectives on conceptualising the forces of psychology. The development of theoretical fluency involves a shift from a modality-specific orientation towards seeing the person as a whole, engaging with a bio-psycho-social-sexual spiritual-existential and cultural framework for practice and adopting a decolonising stance in our engagement with theory, methods, positionality and relationships.			

As counselling and psychotherapy are ultimately applied disciplines and forms of practice, therapy theories never stand on their own, but are always part of a more all-encompassing set of skills, interventions, ways of doing research, and institutions (e.g. conferences, journals, professional associations, training centres). Such wider assemblages of psychotherapeutic theory and practice tend to be described as approaches, paradigms or traditions.

In a classic paper from the 1950s, two leading psychoanalysts, David Rapaport and Merton Gill (1959), argued that it is useful to see any theoretical model used in counselling and therapy as comprising three levels of abstraction:

1. statements about *observational* data
2. theoretical *propositions*, which make connections between different observations
3. Underlying *philosophical assumptions*.

This framework allows us to be more aware of how we are using theory in relation to our work as therapists. For example, a person-centred therapist might use the concept of *congruence/incongruence* as a shorthand way of describing a pattern or way of responding that they observe in themselves, or in a client. However, this observational concept forms part of the more elaborate theoretical proposition articulated in the propositions around *necessary and sufficient conditions* for change, as developed by Carl Rogers (1957). It also refers to, and gains an added depth of meaning from, an underlying concept: the *actualising tendency*. The observational element of this theoretical framework (congruence) is relatively easy to verify and learn and is largely interchangeable with other concepts such as transparency and authenticity. The existence of degrees of congruence can be measured by questionnaires that ask a person to respond to a series of simple statements that capture various aspects of this phenomenon. By contrast, the propositional dimension (how congruence leads to positive change) can only be inferred from observations: it is a process that unfolds over time. The ways in which congruence leads to positive change has also been the subject of many research studies. Finally, the construct that underpins all person-centred theory – actualisation – is not observable at all, but rather reflects a fundamental sense of what it means to be human. Rapaport and Gill (1959) trace these three aspects of theory in relation to psychoanalytic theory. In principle, any theory of therapy can be deconstructed along the lines described above.

The practical value of Rapaport and Gill's (1959) framework lies in its capacity to highlight points of contact between theory and practice. Being able to draw on a rich array of observational concepts enhances awareness of multiple processes that may be occurring in a therapy session. If–then causal propositions refer to change mechanisms that might be facilitated through particular therapy skills and interventions. A philosophical meta-perspective, such as the actualising tendency, the unconscious, or (in CBT) contextualism, may allow a therapist to offer their clients a powerful and coherent vision.

An important implication of Rapaport and Gill's (1959) model is that observations and propositions are fairly readily translatable across theoretical approaches, while underlying philosophical stances are not. There are many books and articles that have sought to compare alternative theoretical interpretations of the same case. On the whole, although different readers of case material may use quite different terminology, their analysis of the case generally ends up highlighting the same themes and similar proposals for what might help the client to change – see, for example, an interesting and accessible paper by Persons et al. (1991) that compared psychodynamic and cognitive behavioural formulations of a single case.

Personal reflection exercise 2

Take a few minutes to generate a list of theoretical concepts that you have drawn on in your practice. Go through the list, and label each item as an observational concept, theoretical proposition or underlying philosophical assumption. What have you learned about your theoretical resourcefulness from this exercise?

Belonging to a community of practice

A key development within contemporary thinking around the nature of therapy training has been a realisation of the value of seeing a training programme as an opportunity to be part of a learning community whose members accept an ethical commitment to engage in mutual support and constructive challenge (Johnson et al., 2014; Mendoza-Newman & Erickson Cornish, 2023). A crucial aspect of a communitarian approach to training is that it prepares students to be actively involved in practice networks throughout their career. Reducing professional isolation in this way can help to minimise burnout and moral injury, and maintain standards of competence and ethical practice. A crucial aspect of a training course community is developing this ability to use a common shared theoretical language. At later stages of a career, it is more likely that colleagues working in a particular service, or across a specific area of interest (e.g. eating disorders), will possess slightly different theoretical languages. The capacity for being able to translate across theoretical terminologies, without losing meaning, is therefore a crucial skill in maintaining the cohesiveness of communities of practice within organisations and professional interest groups. An important implication of an appreciation of how theory operates to support one's identity as a member of communities of practice is that the development of theoretical competence involves not just cognitive learning, but also being able to use theoretical ideas in conversations with colleagues in a way that has the potential to support interpersonal and emotional learning.

Using theory within the therapy process

Ultimately, the most important function of theory is using it for the benefit of the client. A key way of accomplishing this is being able to refer to relevant concepts and models within supervision, in ways that facilitate the emergence of a better understanding of the options that are available in one's work with a client. Such conversations comprise reflection *on* practice – looking back at what happened in a therapy session with a client. However, it is also possible to use theory as a means of reflection *in* practice, by drawing on concepts and models as resources for handling critical points in the therapy process and relationship.

Something to hang on to: Structure in the face of chaos

Through their presence, emotional availability and willingness to listen, there are times when a therapist may be drawn into the confusing and frightening reality being lived and experienced by a client. On other occasions, a therapist may have strong feelings and reactions in response to a client, which are similar to conflictual relationships between that client and other members of their family with whom they are having difficulty. The quality of theoretical understanding of the therapist is a crucial aspect of the capacity to constructively manage potentially destabilising countertransference reactions (Fang, 2017). Therapists (i.e. counsellors, psychotherapists and counselling psychologists) who trust their theoretical understanding as a reliable guide to action are better able to enter the chaos in the knowledge that they will be able to navigate a way out (Pérez-Rojas et al., 2017).

Offering the client a way of making sense

A therapy theory can be viewed as a story about what it means to be a person, and in particular, a way of accounting for how personal troubles develop and are maintained, and how they may be resolved or healed (Hansen, 2006). For example, the underlying structure of CBT theory is a story about learning, while a psychodynamic narrative centres on becoming able to gain a rational understanding of internal and relational processes that had previously operated out of conscious awareness.

By offering life-enhancing stories to live by, therapy theories can be significant for clients who have acquired highly destructive self-stories that they are worthless, a failure, or should never have been born. There exists a vast array of popular books and websites that invite readers to think about their lives in terms of various therapy theories such as CBT, psychodynamics and transactional analysis. Some therapists explicitly teach their theory to their clients (psycho-education). Theoretical narratives may also be conveyed through case formulation (see Chapter

7). The process of informed consent at the start of a therapeutic relationship can be another occasion where a practitioner offers the client a theoretically informed account of what might happen in their work together.

Many clients are desperate to make sense of the awful things that are happening in their lives, and may find that therapy theories or narratives offer them hope for the future, and a sense of purpose and control. As a result, competence in the use of therapy theory is not merely a matter of being able to use concepts and models behind the scenes, in conversations with colleagues and supervisors. It is also essential to be able to engage in theory talk with clients. To do this effectively requires an ability to explain therapy ideas in everyday vivid language, using metaphors, images, stories, examples or diagrams.

Personal reflection exercise 3

How do you explain your theoretical ideas to your clients? How might you respond when a client says, 'I don't understand how what you are suggesting (or the way we are working) will help me'? What might you do to learn more about how you can engage in client-friendly ways of explaining and communicating therapy concepts?

Theorising

Clients have their own theories, arising from a combination of cultural knowledge and their own capacity to find meaning. The client's own theory of healing and change is an explicit aspect of both strengths-oriented approaches to therapy (Duncan & Miller, 2000) and therapy approaches that take account of the client's cultural identity, or reflect a decolonising stance.

Unlike therapists, clients do not generally have much prior experience in articulating their implicit theories. For a therapist to invite the client's understanding or explanatory assumptions into the therapy process requires humility, curiosity and a capacity to bracket off their own theoretical assumptions. An important skill in respect of this work is to be open to moments when, either verbally or nonverbally, the client says 'no', signifying that they are aware of an alternative perspective.

In relation to working collaboratively with a client, it can be useful to think in terms of a process of co-productive *theorising*, rather than a process of implementing a pre-existing formal theory (Swedberg, 2016). The concept of theorising introduces a playful and improvisational dimension to the activity of using concepts and propositions in therapy. It also implies that the validity of the theory that is co-produced is evaluated not against external scientific criteria, but in terms of its unique pragmatic utility for a specific client.

Learning theory

On most counselling and psychotherapy training programmes, therapy theories are taught through lectures, seminar discussion, writing essays, and demonstrating practical application through case study reports. Although these activities are valuable, they are not sufficient in themselves. As outlined previously, therapy concepts and models serve multiple functions, both inside the therapy room and in the wider professional community. In particular, using theory within the therapy process calls for a fluid and flexible theoretical understanding that is highly responsive to the client and the clinical context. At least some of the time a practitioner needs to be able to think theoretically when under considerable emotional and time pressure. In addition, an authentic relationship with theory means that their clients experience them as genuinely believing what they are talking about.

Betan and Binder (2010) argued that to be able to use concepts and models effectively in their work with clients, therapists need to have *metabolised* theory. In other words, key ideas need to have been understood at a deep personal level, integrated into the practitioner's way of seeing the world, and be entirely accessible in the moment. The process of learning theory therefore needs to involve self-practice in which the trainee applies concepts and techniques from a particular theory to their own life (Bennett-Levy & Finlay-Jones, 2018).

Personal reflection exercise 4

Choose one therapy theory, or an element of that theory, and devote at least one month to attending to, and experimenting with, its practical utility in relation to issues or challenges in your own life, along the lines suggested by Bennett-Levy and Finlay-Jones (2018).

Accepting the limitations of theory

Theory represents one way of knowing. The practice of therapy calls for an ability to bring together insights not only from theory, but also from several other ways of knowing: ethical, cultural, scientific, embodied. This requires appreciation of the limits of theory in terms of situations in which being guided by theory could be unhelpful or disrespectful. Charura (2024) interviewed therapists about their experiences of working with refugees and asylum seekers who had been tortured. A recurring theme in these interviews was a sense that being open to the stories and needs of these clients was personally highly challenging in ways that took the therapists beyond the type of understanding available to them through the theory of therapy within which they had been trained. These findings illustrate the principle that human experience is broader and more complex than can be accommodated within any theory of therapy. Erikson and Erlandson (2015) invite their students to see a theory as a *map* that may function as a useful guide to getting from one place to another, emphasising that the map is not the territory – the reality of any journey always involves obstacles and features not captured in the map.

Ethical issues in the use of theory

Training as a counsellor, psychotherapist or practitioner psychologist involves considerable grounding in professional ethics. Competence around such areas as maintaining confidentiality, negotiating informed consent, maintaining the security of personal information, and other aspects of ethical practice, are necessary in order to respect the client's rights and autonomy and minimise the risk of harm. In general, the use of theory has not been regarded as an ethical issue. However, the philosopher Miranda Fricker (1999) developed the concept of *epistemic privilege* as a means of making sense of encounters between practitioners and patients/service users where the therapist imposes their own ideas, theory or knowledge – typically presented as objective scientific evidence – in ways that disregard the insights and perspective of the client.

An example of how this process can be harmful has been the treatment of CFS/ME, where until recently most health professionals have insisted on operating from a theoretical stance that assumes that this condition has no physical basis but is an expression of a psychological disorder (Blease et al., 2017). A further example of epistemic injustice can be found in the writing of prominent influential psychologists and researchers who have played a role in advancing a biological theoretical perspective that seeks to explain human behaviour in terms of race (Charura & Clyburn, 2023).

The existence of epistemic privilege suggests that it is not appropriate to assume that the use of theory in counselling and psychotherapy is ethically neutral. Rather, it may operate as a site for the enactment of power, control, privilege and microaggression in ways that both undermine the confidence of a client in their own status as a knower and perceiver of reality, and impede recovery by not allowing the client's personal knowledge and learning to inform therapeutic work.

Meta-theoretical perspectives

There are many theories of theory: on what basis, then, does a trainee or experienced practitioner choose which theory to learn and apply? To some extent, the answers to that question are shaped by practical considerations such as where one can get a job or the affordability of alternative training options. However, at a deeper level, both individual practitioners and the field of counselling and psychotherapy as a whole, tend to be profoundly influenced by *meta-theoretical perspectives* that operate at a more general societal level. The whole historical course taken by the counselling and psychotherapy profession has been heavily influenced by meta-perspectives offered by science, medicine, feminism, multiculturalism, pluralism and theology. Most recently, there are approaches to therapy that are positioned in relation to the socio-political agendas outlined by social justice (Winter & Charura, 2023), decolonisation (McLeod, 2025; Turner, 2025) and ecology (Ingle, 2021).

Personal reflection exercise 5

What are the meta-perspectives that are closest to your own values and worldview? In what ways, and to what extent, do these meta-perspectives afford you a critical perspective from which you evaluate the mainstream therapies in which you are being (or have been) trained? What are the implications of your reflection around these questions for your future development as a therapist?

Top takeaways

- The issues discussed in this chapter can all be regarded as associated with the idea of theoretical *fluency*.
- As a metaphor, fluency draws attention to the similarities between learning and applying theory, and learning and using a new language.
- There is much value in engaging as a member of a community of practice because it is a way of developing theoretical competence.
- The value of theory and theorising is not only for development and learning, but also to help clients to make sense of their own experiences and ways of healing using their own positionality, perspectives and strengths.
- It is essential that we continue to critique and decolonise theory and our own theorising in order to move the field of counselling and psychotherapy forward.

Question for reflection

Please see and engage with the personal reflection exercises throughout this chapter.

Recommended reading and key resources

Sources that offer further exploration of themes introduced in the present chapter include:

- Evans, M.R. & Dealey, R.P. (2021). Theory in practice. In R. P. Dealey & M.R. Evans (Eds.), *Discovering theory in clinical practice* (pp. 1–11). Springer.

This chapter offers a wealth of examples of how counsellors and psychotherapists can use theory to enhance practice.

- Gedo, P.M. (2011). An island in a sea of madness: The uses of theory for in-patient adolescent treatment. *Clinical Social Work Journal, 39*(2), 132–138.

This article explores the importance of theoretical grounding when working with clients who have complex and challenging difficulties.

- Hansen, J.T. (2014). Connecting theories to practice: A model for categorizing theories according to use. *International Journal for the Advancement of Counselling, 36*, 384–394.

This article uses a critical philosophical perspective to suggest new ways of thinking about the role of theory in therapy practice – an entry point into the enormously valuable body of work produced by James T. Hansen.

References

Bennett-Levy, J. & Finlay-Jones, A. (2018). The role of personal practice in therapist skill development: A model to guide therapists, educators, supervisors and researchers. *Cognitive Behaviour Therapy, 47*, 185–205.

Betan, E.J. & Binder, J.L. (2010). Clinical expertise in psychotherapy: How expert therapists use theory in generating case conceptualizations and interventions. *Journal of Contemporary Psychotherapy, 40*, 141–152.

Blease, C., Carel, H. & Geraghty, K. (2017). Epistemic injustice in healthcare encounters: Evidence from chronic fatigue syndrome. *Journal of Medical Ethics, 43*(8), 549–557.

Charura, D. (2024). Therapists' experience of working with refugees and asylum seekers who have been tortured: An interpretative phenomenological analysis. *Psychological Trauma: Theory, Research, Practice, and Policy, 16*(Suppl 3), S521–S531. https://doi.org/10.1037/tra0001709

Charura, D. & Clyburn, S. (2023). Critical race theory: A methodology for research in psychotherapy. In K. Tudor & J. Wyatt (Eds.), *Qualitative research approaches for psychotherapy* (pp. 72–86). Routledge.

Duncan, B.L. & Miller, S.D. (2000). The client's theory of change: Consulting the client in the integrative process. *Journal of Psychotherapy Integration, 10*, 169–187.

Erikson, M.G. & Erlandson, P. (2015). Theories as maps: Teaching psychology beyond mind and behavior. *Scholarship of Teaching and Learning in Psychology, 1*(1), 92.

Fang, N. (2017). On (not) listening for theory: The trainee's use of theory as defence against the stress of beginning psychodynamic practice. *Psychodynamic Practice, 23*(3), 269–281.

Fleuridas, C. & Krafcik, D. (2019). Beyond four forces: The evolution of psychotherapy. *Sage Open, 9*(1). https://doi.org/10.1177/2158244018824492

Fricker, M. (1999). Epistemic oppression and epistemic privilege. *Canadian Journal of Philosophy, 29*(1), 191–210. http://dx.doi.org/10.1080/00455091.1999.10716836

Hansen, J.T. (2006). Counseling theories within a postmodernist epistemology: New roles for theories in counseling practice. *Journal of Counseling and Development, 84*, 291–297.

Hansen, J.T. (2024). Lessons contemporary counselors can learn from exploratory therapies. *Journal of Counseling & Development, 102*(4), 385–393.

Ingle, M. (2021). Western individualism and psychotherapy: Exploring the edges of ecological being. *Journal of Humanistic Psychology, 61*(6), 925–938.

Johnson W.B., Barnett J.E., Elman N.S., Forrest L., Schwartz-Mette R. & Kaslow N.J. (2014). Preparing trainees for lifelong competence: Creating a communitarian training culture. *Training and Education in Professional Psychology, 8*(4), 211–220.

McLeod, J. (2025). *An introduction to counselling and psychotherapy: Theory, research, practice, and social purpose* (7th ed.). Open University Press.

Mendoza-Newman, M. & Erickson Cornish, J.A. (2023). Creating a communitarian, multiculturally sensitive, and socially just training culture. In R.A. Schwartz-Mette, E.A. Hunter & N.J. Kaslow (Eds.), *Supporting trainees with competence problems: A practical guide for psychology trainers* (pp. 9–24). American Psychological Association.

O'Brien, C.V. & Charura, D. (2023). Refugees, asylum seekers, and practitioners' perspectives of embodied trauma: A comprehensive scoping review. *Psychological Trauma: Theory, Research, Practice, and Policy, 15*(7), 1115–1127. http://doi.org/10.1037/tra0001342

Paul, S. & Charura, D. (2015). *An introduction to the therapeutic relationship in counselling and psychotherapy*. Sage.

Pérez-Rojas, A.E., Palma, B., Bhatia, A., Jackson, J., Norwood, E., Hayes, J.A. & Gelso, C.J. (2017). The development and initial validation of the Countertransference Management Scale. *Psychotherapy, 54*(3), 307–319.

Persons, J.B., Curtis, J.T. & Silberschatz, G. (1991). Psychodynamic and cognitive-behavioral formulations of a single case. *Psychotherapy: Theory, Research, Practice, Training, 28*(4), 608–617.

Råbu, M. & McLeod, J. (2018). Wisdom in professional knowledge: Why it can be valuable to listen to the voices of senior psychotherapists. *Psychotherapy Research, 28*(5), 776–792.

Rapaport, D. & Gill, M. (1959). The points of view and assumptions of metapsychology. *International Journal of Psycho-Analysis, 40*, 153–162.

Rogers, C.R. (1957). The necessary and sufficient conditions of therapeutic personality change. *Journal of Consulting Psychology, 21*(2), 95–103. https://doi.org/10.1037/0033-3204.44.3.240

Swedberg, R. (2016). Before theory comes theorizing or how to make social science more interesting. *British Journal of Sociology, 67*(1), 5–22.

Turner, D. (2025). *Decolonising counselling and psychotherapy*. Routledge.

Winter, L.A. & Charura, D. (Eds). (2023). *The handbook of social justice in psychological therapies: Power, politics, change*. Sage.

4.

Developing an integrative therapeutic practice

Charlotte O'Brien and Divine Charura

Introduction

This chapter outlines the many varied perspectives and themes of traditional and contemporary integrative therapeutic practice. At heart, we argue that the process of integration is lifelong, iterative, reflexive, dynamic and, perhaps most importantly, *authentic* to our own personal development and professional practice. As trainees and practitioners, our integrative therapeutic practice is informed by our *ontology* or way of being in the world and by our *epistemology* or views on how we know what we know (see Chapter 2 for a more detailed explanation of these terms). We also present our own conceptualisation of integration using what we have termed an 'integration by immersion' model (O'Brien & Charura, 2024). To bring this model to life, we present a brief duoethnographic case study and invite the reader to engage with it, applying their own unique lens to create their own dynamic and idiosyncratic integrational approach.

Scope of the chapter

- an outline, exploration and critique of commonly used models of integration
- presentation of our case study of the process of integration by immersion
- engagement with a duoethnographic process of integration.

At the end of this chapter we offer reflective questions that the reader can use to explore their own unique approach to integration.

Outline, exploration and critique of commonly used models of integration

We begin by offering a summary of integration that we have conceptualised and applied to therapeutic practice.

> Integration is the way in which we combine psychotherapeutic theories and their associated tools or skills into a coherent therapeutic practice approach, which is authentic to ourselves as practitioners and appropriate for the client(s) we serve.

In this section we present five different forms of integration, namely assimilative, eclecticism, common factors, theoretical and pluralism.

1. **Assimilative:** This is a mode of conducting therapy in which a technique, concept or perspective is incorporated into one's preferred core therapeutic approach (Messer, 2015). For example, one might have a person-centred foundational approach, and incorporate psychodynamic concepts. In this form of integration, the therapist practises mainly within one modality, and as experience is gained, includes features from another. A common critique is that when components are combined using assimilative integration, they are theoretically changed when synthesised, thereby affecting their original potency.

2. **Eclecticism: This** is the use of therapeutic techniques from a variety of sources without any regard for theory. Eclecticism instead aims to improve therapeutic outcomes without the need to create a new model or theory. For example, eclectic practice could be seen as the use of interventions such as mindfulness, without understanding the full richness and depth of its different spiritual and cultural world origins, contemporary theoretical underpinnings, and neuroscientific developments. A key critique of eclecticism is that it lacks systematic criteria to guide the decisions concerning the interventions used by the therapist. Arguably, this results in challenges in articulating the process of change due to a lack of holistic synthesis that is grounded in firm theoretical foundations.

3. **Common factors:** This approach to integration identifies the common factors that exist among practitioners regardless of their theoretical

orientation. These include, for example, the understanding that we are relational beings and therefore require a relationship, or explicitly a *therapeutic relationship*, to work through difficulties. In the common factors approach, an appreciation of the facilitative conditions that are beneficial to the therapeutic process is required. These facilitative conditions include empathy, congruence and unconditional positive regard (UPR), which, depending on the modality practised, can be provided or experienced in different ways. For example, a psychoanalyst may convey empathy towards a patient in a different way to a person-centred therapist towards a client. Another example is the acknowledgement of the importance of a psychological formulation of the client, which enables a conceptualisation of their challenges. A fundamental critique of this approach is that there is not a consistent or definitive list of what the common factors are; neither is there an evidence base of their combined efficacy. Where such research evidence is provided within the psychotherapeutic literature, it is argued that there are many methodological challenges to its further development.

4. **Theoretical:** This approach strives to achieve a unified model through the combination of theoretical concepts from disparate models that may arise from fundamentally diverse worldviews. It involves integrating in depth at theory level rather than intervention level (Cutts, 2011). This is achieved through the formulation of specific problems, using a theoretical exposition of the therapeutic change process combined with a decision-making model regarding the sequence of interventions employed (Charura, 2016; Wolfe, 2001). A key challenge in this integrative approach is how we reconcile both a theory of the stability of behaviour, with a theory concerning the nature of change of that behaviour, which remains enigmatically elusive. An additional critique is that no single theoretical model is comprehensive enough to conceptualise and fully articulate the complexity of the human experience across the lifespan.

5. **Pluralism:** Another contemporary approach to integration is pluralism (Cooper & McLeod, 2011), which acknowledges that 'any substantial question admits of a variety of plausible but mutually conflicting responses' (Rescher, 1993, p. 79). Pluralism adopts a stance that values the social, cultural and political contexts in which the therapeutic professions have developed and in which therapeutic work is undertaken. The pluralistic integrational approach offers a framework to make sense of some of the tensions present within and

> across the core therapeutic models. As with the other approaches, pluralism has also been critiqued. It has been argued that pluralism is an aspect of resolution for dealing with, for example, potential tensions that arise from the application of multiple perspectives in psychotherapeutic practice, rather than being a model of integration itself (Athanasiadou, 2012).

In the next section we present a case study of the process of integration by immersion (O'Brien & Charura, 2024) to exemplify how we as practitioners have continued to develop in our unique integrational journeys. Our personal critique of the approaches outlined previously is that there is limited research on them, or on their correlation to therapeutic outcomes. Secondly, we argue that a paradigm shift is urgently required to decolonise integrational approaches and challenge the status quo in counselling and psychotherapy, enabling us to conceptualise the human condition across the lifespan as applied to diverse client groups and communities.

Case study of integration by immersion

Integration by immersion aims to provide a new decolonised, anti-oppressive lens and positionality within which to explore the creation, development and evolution of a model of integrative psychotherapeutic practice. This dynamic integrational approach focuses on the development of a practitioner's theoretical and philosophical understanding across the human lifespan (Erikson, 1963; Lewis, 2008), and their own personal development through reflective and reflexive activities (see Chapter 11).

What is integration by immersion?

In conceptualising our model of integration by immersion, we draw upon the definition of *immersion* as the state of being immersed to the point of absorbing involvement or extensive exposure to the object of study. It can also be understood from its origins in the early Judaic and Christian scriptures relating to the act of baptism through full immersion in water (O'Brien & Charura, 2024). We argue that the process of training to become a psychotherapeutic practitioner is an immersive experience, which includes learning new theories, philosophies, ways of being in relationship with others, and engaging with reflection and reflexivity. Therefore, we assert that integration by immersion in psychotherapeutic practice is only possible by holistically drawing upon our own idiosyncratic bio-psycho-social-sexual-spiritual-existential and cultural experiences (O'Brien & Charura, 2023). Through immersive engagement with these holistic aspects of self in relationship with others, integration by immersion provides us with a unified pathway across a diversity of approaches, modalities, research findings, processes and techniques of psychotherapy. The resulting model delivers a holistic and comprehensive framework for integration, which can then be idiosyncratically applied by each practitioner.

Integration by immersion is a cyclical process repeated across the lifespan as we develop as human beings and practitioners, learning from being in relationship with ourselves, others and our clients. Pedagogically, this contemporary model of integration also enables educators to move beyond the constraints of traditional models, including their theoretical frictions or clash of approaches. It embraces a wider school of thought that engages with each individual and their client work across all realms of human development (O'Brien & Charura, 2023).

The following diagram (Figure 4.1) helped us to conceptualise integration by immersion using a swimming pool analogy (O'Brien & Charura, 2024). Using a duoethnographical approach, we will now explain and apply each of the aspects of immersion, namely the immersion in self, theory, practice, philosophy, the use of a framework of love and relationship, and the importance of the processes of reflection and reflexivity.

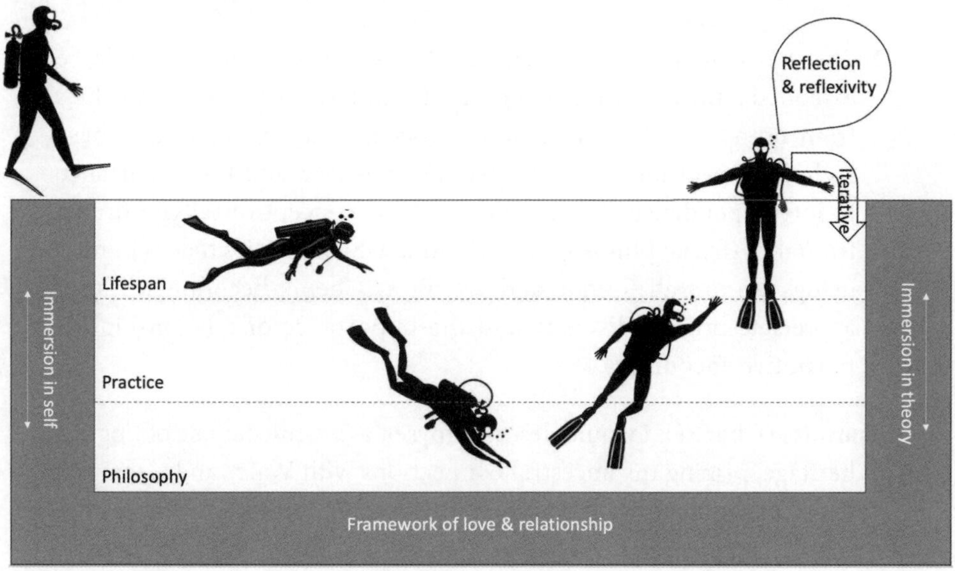

Figure 4.1 Diagram of integration by immersion (O'Brien & Charura, 2024)

Engaging with duoethnography in our process

In this section we present excerpts of our dialogue over the last couple of years regarding our unique approaches to integration. Our process aligns with Norris et al.'s (2012) assertion that through a duoethnographic process, personal beliefs, meta-narratives and diverse experiences are juxtaposed with those of the other's and 'neither position can claim dominance or universal truth' (2012, p. 15). We also encourage the reader, through reflective questioning, to immerse themselves alongside us in the process, establishing their own unified integration by immersion for psychotherapeutic practice.

Immersion in the self: Understanding the self concept

The *self* in its most basic form can be conceptualised as human existence in opposition to death (Scalabrini et al., 2021). However, our definition of self can be more fully explained as that which encompasses our holistic, biological-psycho-social-sexual-spiritual-existential elements (O'Brien & Charura, 2023), inherently including our idiosyncratic intersectional parts of difference and diversity that make us unique (Burnham, 2013; Crenshaw, 1989; Moodley, 2005). The self can be seen to develop and change intra- and inter-subjectively across the lifespan, in parallel with the developments and changes across all the streams as part of the iterative process of integration by immersion.

Q1: What aspects of self are important to you in your integration by immersion for psychotherapy?

Divine: I would describe myself as a Black British man from a large extended family of African heritage. I synthesise aspects of my values from both my Afrocentric and Eurocentric upbringing, and these include respect for others, respect for diversity, and the importance of interdependence. These values and my concept of self are drawn from the African philosophy of Ubuntu, which implies that as human beings we are all unique and are always 'being-becoming'. Thus I appreciate human diversity and the importance of relationship for reparative encounters.

Charlotte (Charlie): I would describe myself as a white female of English heritage, prizing my ancestral connections with Wales and Germany. I was brought up with traditional Christian values, including love, respect and service for others. Based on this I value a holistic conceptualisation of self and its intersectional parts in psychotherapy (O'Brien & Charura, 2023). I use a humanistic lens, which sees us all as parts of an interconnected human family and as metaphysical particles of matter in the universe. I embrace my female gender, and also my experiences of intersectional discrimination surrounding power and the patriarchy.

A framework of love and relationships

As human beings, from the moment we are born we are in relationship with our primary caregivers, with the love that we receive in our formative attachments establishing patterns that affect our relationships throughout our lives (Charura & Paul, 2015). We also note the importance of relationship, love and attachment to all our human relationships across the lifespan, including those relationships that are central to our roles as authors, ethical researchers and practitioners, and also held within the supervisory relationship (Hiebler-Ragger et al., 2021). Therefore, the framework of love and relationships, both in the therapeutic relationship and beyond, can be seen as one of holding, containing and creating an underlying foundation to unifying integrative practice.

Q2: How are your conceptualisations of love and relationships important in your integration by immersion?

Divine: I believe that we are relational beings. Contemporary research on the neuroscience of interpersonal biology highlights that we are wired for relationship, and without love and relationship, ultimately, we die. In terms of integration, I have consequently immersed myself in contemporary neuroscience and psychotherapy research, continually learning different theories on lifespan development and the importance of love and attachments as cornerstones for healing and transformation within relationship (Charura & Paul, 2015).

Charlie: Through my own life experiences and psychotherapeutic practice, I have found that love, relationship and attachment are fundamental human needs, as vital as the basic physiological needs on Maslow's hierarchy (2013). If thwarted at any stage of development the result can be trauma (Rogers, 1959). I also believe in the healing potential of the therapeutic relationship, which offers the necessary and sufficient conditions with love (Rogers, 1959).

Immersion in human development across the life span

Life is a process of human development, learning, change and actualisation across time, which can be conceptualised across theories, and observed across modalities in whichever guise it may manifest itself (e.g. Erikson, 1963; Freud, 1991; Piaget, 1952; Rogers, 1959; Vygotsky, 1978). When considering integration throughout the human development phase, we must also include any psychopathological impacts, trauma, or psychological maladjustment that we may encounter along our way, in the self or in relationship to others, to which even the practitioner is not immune (Victor et al., 2022).

Q3: How has your own development across the lifespan impacted your integration by immersion?

Divine: Through my own development, I have been privileged to engage in personal therapy and work through my own relational traumas, impact of discrimination and experiences of racism, and to explore my intersectionality and privilege. This has informed my valuing of psychodynamics and clients' lived experiences, and thus I hold an appreciation of their 'be-ing-becoming' (Medlock & Charura, 2024) and the place for a therapeutic relationship that facilitates hope, working through trauma, recovery and post-traumatic growth. As such, regarding integration, I have come to accept that no single orientation is solemnly comprehensive enough to conceptualise the complexity of the human experience across the lifespan.

Charlie: Reflecting on my own developmental experiences across the lifespan, I draw attention to the periods of difficulty and trauma in my life. I notice how, by engaging with my own therapy, those road blocks along my path have shifted or been repaired, which has given me hope in the recovery process for others as they develop across their lifespan. This reflection has helped me better understand my firm foundational framework of love in my relationships, including the centrality of the therapeutic relationship. It also makes me reflect on the maturity of practice, which comes with personal and professional development and lived experiences across the lifespan. This has given me an appreciation for what it means to practise from the stance of the wounded healer (Jung, 1951).

Immersion in theory: Understanding your theoretical approach

One of the key pillars to providing a unified pathway to integration in psychotherapy alongside development of the self is immersion in theory. Immersion into psychological theory can be seen as a life's work, from the formative training years where we begin at the surface, exploring the shallows of one or two core theoretical approaches according to the dominant approach of the course or educational institution (Lewis, 2008). This iterative process takes place across our development as human beings and as therapists or practitioner psychologists, as we grow in our practice and maturity, learning from our clients and our own lived experience, integrating, and unifying our knowledge further.

Q4: How has integration by immersion been helpful for your theoretical development?

Divine: Through immersion I have noted how different theories and cultures all relay the experience of relational trauma as having an impact on the individual. However, trauma manifests differently across cultures. Our research on embodied trauma exemplified this, where we noted culturally diverse embodied expressions of trauma (O'Brien & Charura, 2023). Here we found the body sharing the speechless horrors of trauma where there are no universal words to describe it (Van der Kolk, 2014). However, it has also remained the case that I hold irreverently what I have learned, and appreciate that I continue to develop and learn from each client or family I work with, as well as from research.

Charlie: Integration by immersion has been vital to my theoretical development. As a trainee I swam at the surface of my theoretical knowledge and understanding, and assimilated it with a core of person-centred theory (Rogers, 1959), integrating other theoretical principles and techniques according to the needs of the client, but also that were congruent with my foundational model. However, by gaining a deeper understanding of my philosophical underpinning through my research, I was able to swim to the bottom of the pool, coming up reflexively and reflectively for air, to begin to unify my pathway of diverse theoretical and philosophical concepts and learning through practice. This iterative process has shown me that integrational practice in psychotherapy is dynamic, being shaped by evidence-based discoveries and practice-based learning, which continue across my lifespan.

Immersion in practice

Rogers (1961) noted that in order to truly understand another person, we ourselves must also be changed. This is true of the journey throughout our therapeutic practice, whereby (whatever our modalities of practice) our encounter with the client changes us as practitioners. It also arguably requires an individualised assessment, formulation and treatment plan according to each person's needs, which may unify and develop within us as practitioners a different integration of skills or a deeper understanding of advanced psychological process.

Q5: How have your experiences with clients affected your integration by immersion for psychotherapy practice?

Divine: I value a relational, trauma-informed, non-pathologising, compassionate stance in my practice. Based on this and my experience of working with a diverse range of clients presenting with relational trauma, my positionality is what happened to you, rather than what is wrong with you (Charura & Smith, 2024). Hence, my stance is of turning towards the client with authenticity to contain and hold what they bring with curiosity, compassion, openness to listen, and encounter their narrative and everything that emerges in the relationship moment-by-moment.

Charlie: My psychotherapeutic practice with clients has deeply affected my integration by immersion. In fact, I would say, in agreement with Rogers (1961), that through the immersive work I have done in understanding and accepting my *self* just as I am, I am changed, but I am also changed by being in the therapeutic relationship with another.

Immersion in philosophy: Establishing ontology and epistemology

Perhaps the bedrock of integration by immersion is the philosophical underpinning that encapsulates our ontology and epistemology for practice. In our experience as trainees and subsequently as practitioners, this is arguably the last part to be explored and understood after the inevitable and organic immersion in human development across the lifespan – our examination of the self in training and personal therapy, and the exploration of theory and experiential practice within the relational framework.

Q6: How has your philosophical development changed over time and affected your integration by immersion?

Divine: Alongside valuing the Ubuntu African philosophical concepts that inform my integrated components of humanity and unified appreciation of the biological, psychosocial, spiritual, sexual, environmental and existential aspects of life (Chigangaidze et al., 2022), I also integrate the postmodernist philosophical tenet of dialectics in being able to hold and reconcile two positions, accepting the 'both/and' rather than 'either/or' positions. This allows me to gather additional positionality and perspective to better synthesise and analyse various viewpoints (Charura & Lago, 2021). It also enables me to unify theories, approaches or philosophies that may seem opposing – for example, Eurocentric and Afrocentric perspectives of trauma, and conceptualisations of mental health and healing.

Charlie: I don't believe that I fully understood my ontological and epistemological stance until I explored it fully in my research. Using reflexive thematic analysis (Braun & Clarke, 2022) gave me the opportunity to explore my own philosophical positionality and lens. This brought with it an awareness of self and what I was bringing as a person to my research. It was only after deep diving into the depths of these philosophical concepts that I was then able to reflect on whether my theoretical stance and approach to client work aligned with my grounding philosophy, which enabled me to make adjustments where necessary – for example, in becoming more transculturally attuned.

Immersion in reflection and reflexivity: Taking breath and considering the lens

Willig (2019) asserted that reflexivity is the key to developing an awareness of one's own ontology and epistemology, therapeutic model and understanding of ourselves and our clients, which is vital in order to ethically bracket our own assumptions and not impose them on the other. As we, as the learners, engage in tangible experiences that we observe and reflect on, they develop into conceptualisations that are then tested with further experience (Stella & Taggart, 2020). This is a central process to our theory of integration by immersion (please also see Chapter 11 for more on becoming a reflective practitioner).

Q7: How have reflection and reflexivity affected your integration by immersion?

Divine: I have different pathways to engage with reflection and reflexivity – for example, through supervision, therapy, reflective practice groups and self-care. By immersing myself in reflexivity and reflection, I can constantly review my practice and development, what have I done well, what do I need to change, what have I learned. The blessing of therapy, supervision and other professional relationships offers me space as well as opportunities for exploring domains that may be areas of weakness, or prejudices I need to work on. Reflecting on therapy dynamics (i.e. transference and countertransference dynamics), or feedback from clients, also offer me opportunities to explore what I may need to change, or to celebrate what I may be doing well. Thus, I see reflection and reflexivity as the lynchpins to ethical practice and integration by immersion.

Charlie: For me, reflective spaces have helped me immerse not only into my client work, but also into my *self*, enabling me to reflect on my phrase-by-phrase interventions, and also on my motives for doing so. Immersion in reflection and reflexivity via supervision and reflective groups has been vital, as the process has given me a more rounded and externalised view of what I do and who I am. It has also given me the opportunity to observe my areas of challenge and enabled me to reflexively circle back to my immersion in self, rethinking my philosophy or re-integrating theory, and sifting out those parts of my practice that have the capacity to negatively affect myself or the client.

Thank you for journeying alongside us in our duoethnographical exploration of our own integration by immersion. We hope that you will find it helpful in informing your own continuing journey. We will now provide you with some top takeaways from this chapter, and further questions for your own reflective development.

Top takeaways

- Integrative practice is dynamic and changes across the developmental lifespan and professional practice.
- Integrative practice is a personal approach, which should not be held as the 'truth applying to all cases' (Nuttall, 2006).
- Whichever integrational approach you use, it should be open to critique, and should be dynamic, anti-oppressive, decolonised and transculturally oriented.
- Reflective and reflexive processes and practices are key to formulating and evaluating the efficacy of integrated components.
- A key point of reflection is the iterative process required to integrate authenticity of self, while valuing the client's experiencing moment-by-moment, and paying attention to theoretical and philosophical synthesis.

Questions for reflection

1. How are your own conceptualisations of love and relationships important in your integrational approach?
2. How has your own development across the lifespan affected your practice and integrational approach to date?
3. How have your experiences with clients affected your integrational approach and practice?

Recommended reading and key resources

- O'Brien, C. & Charura, D. (2024). 'Integration by immersion': A contemporary model of integration for psychotherapeutic and pedagogical practice. *Counselling and Psychotherapy Research, 25*(2). e12833. *https://doi.org/10.1002/capr.12833*

This is the original research article that introduces the contemporary model of integration by immersion.

References

Athanasiadou, C. (2012). Pluralism as the forerunner of integration? A reflective account. *Counselling Psychology Review*, *27*(4), 18–26.

Braun, V. & Clarke, V. (2022). *Thematic analysis: A practical guide*. Sage.

Burnham, J. (2013). Developments in social GGRRAAACCEEESSS: Visible-invisible, voiced-unvoiced. In I. Krause (Ed.), *Cultural reflexivity* (pp. 23–35). Karnac.

Charura, D. (2016). A 5,000 word personal philosophy statement in which the trainee articulates their personal creative synthesis/theoretical standpoint. [Unpublished manuscript.]

Charura, D. & Lago, C. (Eds.). (2021). *Black identities + white therapies: Race, respect & diversity*. PCCS Books.

Charura, D. & Paul, S. (Eds.). (2015). *Love and therapy in relationship*. Karnac.

Charura, D. & Smith, P. (2024). A duoethnographic exploration of relational psychotraumatology: Research, training, and practice considerations. *Counselling and Psychotherapy Research*, *24*(3), 972–981. https://onlinelibrary.wiley.com/doi/10.1002/capr.12749

Chigangaidze, R.K., Matanga, A.A. & Katsuro, T.R. (2022). Ubuntu philosophy as a humanistic–existential framework for the fight against the COVID-19 pandemic. *Journal of Humanistic Psychology*, *62*(3), 319–333. https://doi.org/10.1177/00221678211044554

Cooper, M. & McLeod, J. (2011). *Pluralistic counselling and psychotherapy*. Sage.

Crenshaw, K. (1989). Demarginalizing the intersection of race and sex: A black feminist critique of antidiscrimination doctrine, feminist theory, and antiracist politics. In K.T. Barlett & R. Kennedy (Eds.), *Feminist legal theory: Readings in law and gender* (pp. 57–80). Routledge.

Cutts, L. (2011). Integration in counselling psychology: To what purpose? *Counselling Psychology Review*, *26*(2), 38–48.

Erikson, E.H. (1963). *Childhood and society* (2nd ed.). W.W. Norton & Co.

Freud, S. (1991). *The Penguin Freud library: Volume 1. Introductory lectures on psychoanalysis*. Penguin.

Hiebler-Ragger, M., Nausner, L., Blaha, A., Grimmer, K., Kolarth, S., Mernyi, M. & Unterrainer, H.F. (2021). The supervisory relationship from an attachment perspective: Connections to burnout and sense of coherence in health professionals. *Clinical Psychology & Psychotherapy*, *28*(1), 124–136. https://doi.org/10.1002/cpp.2494

Jung, C.G. (1951). *Aion: Researches into the phenomenology of the self*. Routledge.

Lewis, Y. (2008). Counselling psychology training: Implications for 'self'. *Counselling Psychology Review*, *23*(4), 63–69. https://doi.org/10.53841/bpscpr.2008.23.4.63

Maslow, A.H. (2013). *A theory of human motivation*. Martino Publishing.

Medlock, G.E & Charura, D. (2024). On becoming a coaching practitioner-researcher: A duoethnographic study. *The Coaching Psychologist, 20*(1), 16–27. https://doi.org/10.53841/bpstcp.2024.20.1.16

Messer, S.B. (2015). Assimilative psychotherapy integration. In E.S. Neukrug (Ed.), *The Sage encyclopedia of theory in counseling and psychotherapy* (Vol. 2, pp. 64–66). SAGE Publications Inc.

Moodley, R. (2005). Diversity matrix revisited: Criss-crossing multiple identities in clinical practice. Keynote paper at Multicultural and Counseling Symposium. Cornell University.

Norris, J., Sawyer, R. & Lund, D.E. (2012). *Duoethnography: Dialogic methods for social, health, and educational research*. Left Coast Press.

Nuttall, J. (2006). Researching psychotherapy integration: A heuristic approach. *Counselling Psychology Quarterly, 19*(4), 429–444. https://doi.org/10.1080/09515070601090121

O'Brien, C.V. & Charura, D. (2023). Refugees, asylum seekers, and practitioners' perspectives of embodied trauma: A comprehensive scoping review. *Psychological trauma: Theory, Research, Practice and Policy, 15*(7), 1115–1127. https://doi.org/10.1037/tra0001342

O'Brien, C. & Charura, D. (2024). 'Integration by immersion': A contemporary model of integration for psychotherapeutic and pedagogical practice. *Counselling and Psychotherapy Research, 25*(2). e12833. *https://doi.org/10.1002/capr.12833*

Piaget, J. (1952). *The origins of intelligence in children*. International Universities Association.

Rescher, N. (1993). *Pluralism: Against the demand for consensus*. Oxford University Press.

Rogers, C.R. (1959). A theory of therapy, personality, and interpersonal relationships as developed in the client-centred framework. In S. Koch (Ed.), *Psychology: A study of a science, formulations of the person and social context* (Vol. 3, pp. 184–256). McGraw Hill.

Rogers, C.R. (1961). *On becoming a person*. Constable.

Scalabrini, A., Xu, J. & Northoff, G. (2021). What COVID-19 tells us about the self: The deep intersubjective and cultural layers of our brain. *Psychiatry and Clinical Neurosciences, 75*(2), 37–45. https://doi.org/10.1111/pcn.13185

Stella, M. & Taggart, J. (2020). Attachment, learning and embodied reflective practices in clinical supervision. *Body, Movement and Dance in Psychotherapy, 15*(4), 295–308. https://doi.org/10.1080/17432979.2020.1783572

Van Der Kolk, B.A. (2014). *The body keeps the score: Brain, mind, and body in the healing of trauma*. Viking.

Victor, S.E., Schleider, J.L., Ammerman, B.A., Bradford, D.E., Devendorf, A.R., Gruber, J., Guanaydin, L.A., Hallion, L.S., Kaufman, E.A., Lewis, S.P. & Stage, D.L. (2022). Leveraging the strengths of psychologists with lived experience of psychopathology. *Perspectives on Psychological Science, 17*(6) 1624–1632. https://doi.org/10.1177/17456916211072826

Vygotsky, L.S. (1978). *Mind and society: The development of higher mental processes*. Harvard University Press.

Willig, C. (2019). What can qualitative psychology contribute to psychological knowledge? *Psychological Methods, 24*(6), 796–804. https://doi.org/10.1037/met0000218

Wolfe, B.E. (2001). A message to assimilative integrationists: It's time to become accommodative integrationists: A commentary. *Journal of Psychotherapy Integration, 11*(1), 123–131. https://doi.org/10.1023/A:1026637226683

5.

Developing relational ethics competencies for counselling psychologist and psychotherapist training

Lynne Gabriel and Andrew Reeves

Introduction

Therapy does not exist in a vacuum, since everyone in therapy is also a citizen who works, relates and lives within diverse and contested economic, geopolitical, social, cultural and ecological systems. Additionally, we live in a competitive neoliberal 21st century, in which many individuals and communities face oppressive, limiting and negatively affecting experiences. These influences play out alongside other intersecting disadvantages for increasing numbers of people. These intersecting factors include, for example, social and cultural heritage, poverty, ethnicity and disability. Such a complicated context means that the fields of counselling psychology and psychotherapy must reflexively respond to ensure trainees gain an understanding of contemporary human challenges in different contexts and circumstances across the lifespan.

In this chapter, we aim to show how a relational ethics approach to day-to-day therapeutic practice can be developed by counselling psychologists and psychotherapists in training. This will assist them in adapting to working within a complex and diverse profession and wider mental health arena. In the context of the chapter, we adopt a relational ontology (Gravett et al., 2021) and refer readers to Chapter 2 in this handbook for further explanation of *ontology*.

In preparing this chapter, we want to acknowledge research conversation contributors whose narratives inform it. The contributors supported development of the central research chapter in our textbook *Navigating Relational Ethics in Day-to-Day Practice* (Gabriel & Reeves, 2025). The research conversationalists who gave generously of their time were Myira Khan, Haydn Williams, John Wilson, Rich Knight, Peter Blundell, Linda Finlay, Gillian Proctor, Dwight Turner and Alistair Ross.

Scope of the chapter

This chapter will cover the following:

- engaging with ethics in theory and practice
- competencies for relational ethics education and development
- demonstrating relational ethics knowledge, understanding and abilities
- building relational, dialectical and dialogical skills
- evidencing a pragmatic pluralistic mindset
- educating the educators
- the development of reflexive ethical literacy.

Engaging with ethics in theory and practice

How ethics education is delivered and researched requires an engaging stance: one that is relational and based on an ethics of engagement and interaction. It also requires an approach that considers the influence of multiple factors (including the rise of AI, global terror and war events, and the climate crisis) to enable full reflection upon *who matters and what counts* in engaging with ethics in theory and practice (Gravett et al., 2021, original emphasis included). From a feminist, posthuman perspective, Barraclough et al. (2024) consider ontological-ethical-relational research and teaching practices and identify the significance of learning and being that 'expands knowing engagement with/in differentiated, in/determinate mo(ve)ments as professional practice educators and researchers' (Barraclough et al., 2024, p. 1). Essentially, they are calling for learning that enables ethically flexible, responsive and relevant ways of being across diverse contexts and practices (Orlinsky et al., 2023). Such skills and ways of working need to be acquired. We believe that relational ethics training should be a core part of counselling psychologists' and psychotherapists' training, and to that end, in this chapter we propose competencies and guidance for the development of relational ethics.

> We define relational ethics as a way of being, working and relating that… acknowledges complex relational and liminal processes through which decisions, nuanced interactions, and meaning-making associated with helping relationships and work are mindfully and reflexively engaged with. A pluralistic approach to relational ethics affords authentic compassionate attention to social, cultural, racial, and political dimensions, as well as to inclusivity, anti-oppression, collaboration, and recognition of the positive impact, contributions, and implications of diverse relational concepts and contexts. (Gabriel & Reeves, 2025, pp. 4–5)

It is a way of working that acknowledges the complex, diverse and challenging contemporary society in which we live and work.

Competencies for relational ethics education and development

Role-related competencies underpin training curricula to form the bedrock of psychotherapeutic practitioner education and development. Within the USA, for instance, practitioner psychologist training tends to be configured around either a *scientist-practitioner* or *scholar-practitioner* model (Hanley & Amos, 2017). UK counselling psychology training leans towards the *scientist-practitioner* and *reflective-practitioner* models and identities. Within psychotherapy and integrative humanistic psychology and counselling, the emphasis is more on educating and developing *reflexive integrative practitioners* (Gabriel & Reeves, 2025) or *reflective practitioners* (Hanley & Amos, 2017).

Given the value placed upon beneficent (for the good of) ethics in helping work and relationships, key competencies to support trainers to develop meaningful and engaging learning and teaching curricula through relational ethics are essential. The competencies here are derived and adapted from research with key ethicists (Gabriel & Reeves, 2025). Additionally, they are informed by decades of experience possessed by both authors in the development and practice of 'ethics in action'.

Meta-competencies, as referred to in Table 5.1, are overarching or 'umbrella' themes that represent a concept and inform learning and associated practice. *Competencies*, however, denote specific and focused knowledge, aptitudes, skills or abilities that fall within the umbrella theme. Competencies provide a map or framework through which trainers and trainees can develop skills and knowledge to navigate the complex and evolving terrain of education, development and practice as a therapist. Although displayed in Table 5.1 in a linear fashion, the competencies intersect and connect across contexts, processes, relationships and dialogues.

Table 5.1 Practitioner competencies for relational ethics

Relational ethics meta-competencies	Associated practitioner competencies
Relational ethics knowledge, understanding and abilities	• understand the core principles and premises of relational ethics, such as inclusivity, anti-discriminatory and anti-oppressive practices • knowledge of a range of philosophical and ethical theories and concepts to inform the translation of therapy theory and approaches into lived ethical and relational practice • acknowledge and understand that seemingly intractable and contradictory factors, forces or variables co-exist in relational situations • understand that differences and dissensus can be collaboratively navigated and relationally managed by the client and therapist working in partnership

	• aptitude and capacity to sustain self and support facilitation of others through this process of collaborative work • use intentional and deliberate practice to actively build ethical literacy and competency • understand and recognise internalised or external oppression, discrimination or injustice encountered by the client • recognise that people may be defensive in therapy and feel unable to share because of their past experiences or trauma • awareness of, and capacity for, trauma-informed ways of working • understanding and experience of being and relating in complex micro and macro relational, social, cultural and professional contexts • knowledge and understanding of the phenomena of oppression, epistemic injustice and discrimination.
Relational, dialectical and dialogical skills	• demonstrate reflexive ethical literacy – able to develop and practise relational reflexivity with self and others in dyadic, group and other relevant contexts • adopts trauma-informed ways of being, relating and working • a compassionate presence • authenticity, congruence and being non-judgemental • relationship formation and moderation • competent communication and dialogical skills • open to learning from clients with lived experience of their presenting difficulties • able to facilitate co-creation and co-production in a helping context that is conducive to collaborative conversations, decision-making and actions • can develop dialectical discussions and navigate these in day-to-day work and practice, as well as in more challenging relational and ethical situations • capacity to identify opposing forces, conflicting or troubled content, people and events, and to generate mediating and enabling dialogues in collaboration with clients and relevant others • able to facilitate collaborative and co-produced meaning-making and decision-making • can challenge their own, clients' and others' internal and external injustices through compassionate conversations and dialogue • able to use meta-communication and deliberate practice throughout individual, group work and relevant other areas of work (including training, supervision and consultation processes).

A pragmatic pluralistic mindset	• co-creation of contracting and decision-making throughout therapy interactions and work, using intentionality and deliberate practice, to evidence reasoned thoughtful meaning-making and decision-making • fostering of client participation, ownership and agency in the helping process • developing therapeutic insights, decisions and practices in collaborative dialogue with the client • collaborating with clients to identify preferences and directions for the therapy work • using evidence-informed deliberate practice in dialogue and in collaboration with clients • generating peer support/peer review/development group contexts to support self-care and the care and support of others.

(Source: adapted from Gabriel and Reeves, 2025)

Demonstrating relational ethics knowledge, understanding and abilities

This meta-competency offers a conceptual 'label' to capture key knowledge, understanding and abilities to support living, being and practising relational ethics. The associated competencies in column two of Table 5.1 provide indicators for trainers, practitioners and supervisors for knowledge exchange, training and trainee mentoring purposes. We leave it to trainers and others to interpret and incorporate the competencies within the context of their training programme, as each training team and programme will bring unique and nuanced interpretations to the competencies. Anti-oppressive knowledge, understanding and practice permeates our ways of being and relating, and for this reason we have made it a central feature of the framework.

Building relational, dialectical and dialogical skills

By using the term 'dialectical' we mean ways of working and meaning-making that, through collaborative conversations between the client and therapist, can be identified and synthesised. The term 'dialogical' is used to convey the process of reaching mutual understanding without necessarily removing or changing points of difference. This particular meta-competency forms the basis of most practitioner training, with variations and nuances according to the core modality and professional role. Here, we focus on ways of being, behaving and interacting in helping relationships – ways that foster and facilitate collaborative intersubjective therapeutic alliances. Texts on integrative, intersubjective or pluralistic approaches to therapy work often provide useful macro level indicators for the type of practice that works within a collaborative relational ethics approach (Gabriel & Casemore,

2009; Gabriel & Reeves, 2025). These indicators for practice include concepts such as authenticity, congruence, compassion, inclusivity, intersubjectivity, and epistemic justice.

A pragmatic pluralistic mindset

This meta-competency is at the core of the pragmatic pluralistic approach that we advocate. By *pragmatic*, we mean resources and interventions that are relevant to therapeutic processes and are agreed to and valued by the client. By *pluralistic*, we are referring to ways of working that encompass therapy theories and practices that are appropriate and contracted as part of the therapy contract. Central to this meta-competency is a collaborative practitioner-client decision-making process about the content and direction of therapy. It also includes the fostering of authentic client participation and agency in the helping process and relationship. Through this groundwork, as well as through collaborative and shared therapeutic insights, the therapy decisions and practices can be co-developed by the practitioner and client.

Educating the educators

A rich heritage for practitioner training and education is evident in the *scientist-practitioner* Boulder model and the more recent Vail *scholar-practitioner* model (Drugas, 2023; Shapiro, 2002), both of which have influenced clinical and counselling psychology in the UK and USA. The scientist-practitioner gives primacy to evidence derived from large-scale quantitative research data to identify best clinical interventions, while the scholar-practitioner education and approach prioritises a research-informed yet relational way of working. Notably, neither approach embeds a critical stance on the dominant Westernised therapy theories and literature – an important ethical dimension for practitioner training and any research on practitioner training.

Fortunately, a growing body of literature, and in particular, textbooks written by Dwight Turner (2021, 2023), question the dominance of Westernised and colonial influences and hold value for those involved in delivering practitioner training. Questioning individualised and autonomous interpretations of human identity, with reference to counsellors-in-training, Barraclough (2023, p. 14) helpfully sets out an alternative notion of practitioner identity, that of 'becoming counsellor'. In the process, they posit a posthuman interpretation of being and relating across diverse peoples:

> As counsellors, through such a posthuman attention, we can pursue a shared aim of participating in, ethically and responsibly, the reconfiguring of the… unsettling and remaking of boundaries and of opening up possibilities for multiple different ways of knowing, being and becoming counsellor.

According to Barraclough (2023), it is our *response-ability* to respond to injustices (our own and others') and it is a relational commitment that is ever-present and never ending. This turn to a posthuman perspective, in which multiple factors and forces are considered as contributors to events and experiences (including non-human ones connected, for example, to the built environment or place) is increasingly evident in recent perspectives papers and in the growth of social change groups within the fields of counselling, psychotherapy and psychology. It is time to consider these philosophical shifts, and associated relational and behavioural changes, in the context of practitioner education (Ferrando, 2019). See also Chapter 2 in this handbook for further explanation of ontology and philosophical concepts of relevance for counselling psychologists and psychotherapists.

From research conversations with people working in the counselling professions (Gabriel & Reeves, 2025), we know that teaching and learning about relational ethics, and the accrual of trainees' understanding about navigating day-to-day ethics, including relational power and oppression, is lacking in training programmes. At best, it may be a 'tick box' exercise either as a stand-alone session or short module. At worst, it can be briefly referenced in relation to professional bodies' ethics codes. Central to all approaches, however, including counselling psychology and psychotherapy, is the ethical principle of 'do no harm'.

Contributors to the ethics research project that forms the core of our textbook on navigating relational ethics in day-to-day practice (Gabriel & Reeves, 2025; Chapter 2) emphasised the importance of facilitating meaningful learning and engaging trainee practitioners with key constructs of importance to developing their approach to relational ethics. This research strongly suggests, therefore, that training programmes should be less about the delivery of multiple theories and concepts and more about developing the self of the practitioner, and learning and exploration of self in relationship with others. Theories and concepts could be engaged with through targeted student reading, and then within the training context, tutors could facilitate discussions to enhance and deepen learning. Shifting the focus within training contexts to facilitating learning and understanding of the inter- and intrapersonal dimensions of therapeutic work brings potential for dynamic and dialectical ways of thinking, relating and being – all supporting the evolution of reflexive practitioners and practices. A relational ethics approach will focus on the unique subjectivities and intersubjectivities of each client and therapist (Finlay, 2019; Khan, 2023; Proctor et al., 2023). Training content, processes and pedagogical tactics can then focus on generating opportunities for trainees to consider and experiment with their ways of being in their work and relationships. Significantly, training curricula that include consideration of the cultural, geopolitical, environmental and economic factors that affect citizens can help prepare trainees to work with people who have been affected by such influences.

Creative use of videos, case studies and role enactments, alongside preparatory off-site reading, can support trainees to develop their understanding of key concepts and therapeutic processes. This also includes developing understanding of compassion, congruence, authentic relating, decolonisation, relational power, oppression, social and epistemic injustices, and anti-oppressive practices – a tall order for trainers and trainees alike: and yet, an essential way forward.

Teaching reflexive ethical literacy

Achieving realistic and relatable ethics is challenging yet crucial. As Linda, another contributor to Gabriel & Reeves' (2025, p. 20) research, comments:

> I think there's a real challenge for the individual practitioner to find their way and know what they're doing in a way that's consistent with their professional frameworks but also that's responsive to the particular client they have… if I had to say one word which I think is the key, I think we need to be reflexive.

By far the largest theme in Gabriel & Reeves' (2025) relational ethics research project was associated with what we refer to as *reflexive ethical literacy*. Teaching and learning about ethics must be engaging, plus based on nuanced real-life complexity. Importantly, trainees must learn about the appropriate use of ethics codes, resources and responses within the context of each unique client(s)/therapist(s) relational dynamics and settings.

Training placements that enable trainees to put into practice their learning and understanding is a crucial part of core training, including anti-oppressive practice, the importance of understanding social justice, epistemic justice and injustices, and the gradual building of understanding and 'fluency' in relation to meaning-making and decision-making in any given therapeutic context. All of these go towards the development of competent and *deliberate practice* (McLeod, 2020) and support deeper understanding and lived experience of ethics in action. Hence, placement settings can provide powerful contexts for trainees to reflexively translate their course-based education and learning about relational ethics into authentic and congruent lived experiences.

During placement, trainees engage with the real-world complexity of client work, where personal, social and cultural factors intersect within each therapeutic relationship. These hands-on encounters provide opportunities to practise relational ethics in action, with trainees noticing how ethical dilemmas and relational challenges emerge in the immediacy of practice. Working alongside others, trainees are supported to reflect critically and reflexively on their responses, helping them to recognise areas of strength and those requiring further development (see Chapter 11). Through this reflective process, they begin to build both confidence and competence in navigating relational ethics, learning to trust the client, themselves and the therapeutic process. In this way, placements become a vital space for developing the reflexivity, courage and ethical awareness that form the foundation of professional practice.

> Supporting practitioners to have a more internal locus of evaluation when thinking about their own practice, or how can we support a therapist to reflect and assess their competence, their prejudices themselves, and not necessarily rely on external people like supervisors, or your professional body, or additional training courses… there's a real risk that people are gathering all these tools, but they're not embedding how they… are… going to use them, how is that going to work in practice? (Peter, in Gabriel & Reeves, 2025, p. 20)

> [T]hat whole idea of, actually, things don't stay static… how do they see their position with regards to keeping the relational flow of ethics within the therapeutic space?… it's that relational understanding of the relational dynamics that then creates a constantly evolving ethical framework for ourselves, for our clients, for our profession, and having that regular dialogue, seeing it as a fluid construct and not just something defined by the organizations [professional bodies]. (Dwight, in Gabriel & Reeves, 2025, p. 24)

The development of reflexive ethical literacy

Developing ethical literacy requires trainees to become reflexively aware of how oppression and inequality shape therapeutic relationships, and to engage with anti-oppressive ways of being and relating with clients (Khan, 2023; Proctor, 2014, 2017). Relational ethics training emphasises that every client–therapist encounter is unique, shaped by the interplay of personal, social and cultural factors. Central to this is the collaborative formulation of therapeutic work, where process and progress are negotiated together. Within this multiverse of relational ethics, dynamics at both micro and macro levels, the 'in here/out there' influences, and the unfolding of therapy processes, are continually brought into reflexive awareness. Training and development activities, therefore, need to create opportunities for trainees to practise recognising, reflecting on and responding to these complexities so they can build the confidence and competence required to work ethically within relational contexts. Training cannot possibly cover all ethical considerations of a given modality; however, as Alistair, emphasised:

> I know this came up in our conversation at the BACP research conference you know; we do have to train the trainers… it's the people

> who are doing the, you know, training in relationship to this and yet we also have to be utterly pragmatic[,] which is that on any training course that you're only going to get you know, one or two or three options to talk about ethics' (Alistair, in Gabriel & Reeves, 2025, p. 20)

Pressures of a full curriculum and workload were conveyed by Gillian:

> A lot of the things that need to be covered could be just uploaded and students can read... do[ing] more of this experiential stuff in groups with people would take much more time and awareness and emotional energy from the tutors. And I don't know, I think most environments are such that there are too few people doing too much work with too many... [we need to] increase people's awareness of their own places of fear, really, to hopefully get to know, recognise, go to those places to be able to come away and then try and go somewhere else... educate people as to what happens when you go to that place and how to mindfully be able to come out of it. (Gillian, in Gabriel & Reeves, 2025, pp. 20–21)

Alternative pedagogies could make positive differences to how trainees engage in learning. As identified by Avci (2023), the 'flipped counselling classroom' is conducive to students exploring learning and building their knowledge through experiential and interactive learning. Students engage in debates, dialogues and experiential activities to more authentically and congruently create opportunities for reflexive meaning-making and development of relational and decision-making skills. This *flipped* educational context provides supported meaning-making in a compassionate training environment. This is especially important, as experiences of training, particularly in the earlier stages, can be discombobulating, as Dwight conveys:

> [T]he ground shifts underneath them, all of a sudden, the idea of this 'what do you do, and how do you do it, what do you get, and what happens when you do A, B and C'? (Dwight, in Gabriel & Reeves, 2025, p. 21)

All research contributors conveyed the importance of understanding 'self as practitioner', as well as the importance of working reflexively and non-defensively, with inclusive, non-oppressive and compassionate care central to the work. Importantly, we need to recognise the personal challenges involved in developing the capacity, reflexivity and responsiveness for relational ethics in practice. As Rich notes:

> I think it's really important that… that hasn't come about easily. It's come from a journey of getting it wrong and learning and realising from getting it wrong and that it's okay to get things wrong. But I'm not sure how often in the profession we say that. (Rich, in Gabriel & Reeves, 2025, p. 22)

Exercise: Introduction to metaphorical ethics allies – Boundary rider, sentinel and ethics warrior

The following exercise invites you to flex your reflexive skills through considering a 'cast of characters' or 'relational ethics allies' that can provide you with rich metaphors to help you navigate ethics in action. First presented by Gabriel (2005), these metaphors provide students and practitioners with tangible, pragmatic and creative tools to bring alive your ways of thinking about ethics in action. The metaphors are offered here as resources for training, CPD and supervision contexts.

Boundary rider: The boundary rider monitors and maintains the limit, scope and extent of a given relationship.

Sentinel: The sentinel can work with complex ethical issues, can embody and epitomise authentic and spontaneous relating, can maintain a capacity for reasoned and ethical responding in chaotic and conflicted relational situations, and has a capacity for an 'eagle eye' perspective on relational processes.

Ethics warrior: The ethics warrior signifies the process of taking up our 'sword' to courageously quest and clear a way through the unexplored or tangled thicket of the relational features confronting us – to the point of either finding a clear enough existing pathway or forging another. Like all warriors, we tire; we cannot go on without sustenance and we need to replenish ourselves intellectually, spiritually and emotionally to undertake our quest. Importantly, in the spirit of all questing, we face towards the unknown. We might draw strength and wisdom from a previous warrior explorer, but we cannot avoid facing unknown territory and thus must become a 'bricoleur' warrior, forging a relational ethic as we ride the boundaries of being with one another.

Activity

Using the metaphors of the boundary rider, sentinel and ethics warrior, as outlined above, consider how you might use these metaphorical aides or allies to support you in navigating relational ethics in your day-to-day practice and work. Reflect on a specific challenge or incident and identify how the boundary rider, sentinel or ethics warrior could have helped you to navigate the situation. When processing options for meaning-making and decision-making, consider how you will make use of opportunities for further feedback and reflection, such as peer review, supervision and training groups for discussion of ideas and potential actions. Feedback from others through these mechanisms can support further thinking and create an opportunity to revisit assumptions and different ways of navigating relational ethics.

In this chapter we have outlined the reasons why navigating ethics in complex day-to-day practice needs to form a core part of practitioner training, both in the classroom and in placements. Importantly, practitioners need opportunities during core training and ongoing development to engage in building their approach to relational ethics and ethics in action. This includes creating space for reflection, dialogue and supervision that acknowledges the inevitable tensions and dilemmas of practice. By developing the capacity to sit with complexity rather than seek quick resolutions, practitioners strengthen their ability to act with integrity and responsiveness in diverse contexts. Ultimately, embedding relational ethics at the heart of training fosters a professional culture that values authenticity, compassion and accountability as ongoing commitments, rather than fixed competencies.

Top takeaways

- The key role of relational ethics is presented as the foundation of being, relating and working in counselling psychology and psychotherapy.
- An evidence-informed approach, grounded in the ethics research project by Gabriel and Reeves (2025), underpins the relational ethics competencies outlined in this chapter and offers practitioners a practical framework for navigating everyday ethical challenges.
- Developing a body of research evidence is essential to inform core training curricula for counselling psychologists, psychotherapists, and all counselling professionals.

Questions for reflection

1. How might you embed a relational ethics approach in your own therapy work?
2. What future research do you think we need to enhance relational ethics for contemporary counselling psychology and psychotherapy, and why?
3. If you are considering becoming a counselling psychologist or psychotherapy trainer, how might you include ethics in action in your training curriculum?

Recommended reading and key resources

The following recommended reading has been selected to extend your knowledge and competence in relational and dialogical skills, and, importantly, in ways that complement the relational ethics approach and competencies set out in this chapter.

- Cooper, M. & McLeod, J. (2010). *Pluralistic counselling and psychotherapy*. Sage.

This seminal text set the foundations for the development of pluralistic therapeutic practice and remains a key 'go-to' book in this area.

- Finlay, L. (2019). *Practical ethics in counselling and psychotherapy: A relational approach*. Sage.

Finlay's work is critically important in helping us to navigate ethics through a relational lens and continues to be a key text when thinking of relational ethics in counselling, psychotherapy and counselling psychology.

- Gabriel, L. & Casemore, R. (2009). *Relational ethics in counselling and psychotherapy*. Routledge.

This book explores the vital role of relational ethics in therapy, emphasising integrity, empathy and mutual respect, all of which are essential for building authentic, effective and ethically sound therapeutic relationships.

- Gabriel, L. & Reeves, A. (2025) *Navigating relational ethics in day-to-day practice*. Routledge.

This text helps practitioners to apply relational ethics every day, fostering genuine connections, cultural sensitivity and accountability. It offers therapists practical tools and enhances self-awareness to help develop and support ethically grounded client relationships.

- Smith, K. & De La Prida, A. (2021). *The pluralistic therapy primer*. PCCS Books.

This text offers an accessible and relevant introduction for therapists who wish to understand more about the development and application of pluralistic principles in practice.

References

Avci, M. (2023). Analyzing the effects of the flipped classroom method on counselling students' competencies and effective counselling characteristics in ethics class. *British Journal of Guidance & Counselling, 52*(1), 81–93. https://doi.org/10.1080/03069885.2023.2170980

Barraclough, S. (2023). On becoming a counsellor: A posthuman reconfiguring of identity formation for counsellors-in-training. *British Journal of Guidance & Counselling*, https://doi.org/10.1080/03069885.2023.2172550

Barraclough, S., Tudor, R. & Warren, A. (2024). Reconfiguring community of practice as socio-material practices for making differences with/in the world: A creative-relational inquiry. *International Review of Qualitative Research. 18*(2), 218–236.

Drugas, M. (2023). The scientist-practitioner and the scholar-practitioner models in psychology. *Psychological Thought, 16*(2), 203–212. https://doi.org/10.37708/psyct.v16i2.904

Ferrando, F. (2019). *Philosophical posthumanism.* Bloomsbury.

Finlay, L. (2019). *Practical ethics in counselling and psychotherapy: A relational approach.* Sage.

Gabriel, L. (2005). *Speaking the unspeakable: Dual relationships in counselling and psychotherapy.* Routledge.

Gabriel, L. & Casemore, R. (2009). *Relational ethics in practice.* Routledge.

Gabriel, L. & Reeves, A. (2025). *Navigating relational ethics in day-to-day practice.* Routledge.

Gravett, K., Taylor, C.A. & Fairchild, N. (2021). Pedagogies of mattering: Re-conceptualising relational pedagogies in higher education. *Teaching in Higher Education, 29*(2), 388–403. https://doi.org/10.1080/13562517.2021.1989580

Hanley, T. & Amos, I. (2017). The scientist-practitioner and the reflective practitioner. In V. Galbraith, *Counselling psychology* (pp. 167–182). Routledge.

Khan, M. (2023). *Working within diversity: A reflective guide to anti-oppressive practice in counselling and therapy.* Jessica Kingsley Publishers.

McLeod, J. (2020). How students use deliberate practice during the first stage of counsellor training. *Counselling & Psychotherapy Research, 22*(1), 207–218. https://doi.org/10.1002/capr.12397

Orlinsky, D.E., Messina, I., Hartmann, A., Willutzki, U., Heinonen, E., Rønnestad, M.H., Loffler-Staska, H. & Schroder, T. (2023). Ninety psychotherapy training programmes across the globe: Variations and commonalities in an international context. *Counselling & Psychotherapy Research, 24*(2), 558–571. https://doi.org/10.1002/capr.12690

Proctor, G. (2014). *Values and ethics in counselling and psychotherapy.* Sage.

Proctor, G. (2017). *The dynamics of power in counselling and psychotherapy: Ethics, politics and practice.* PCCS Books.

Proctor, G., Cahill, J., Gore, S., Lees, J. & Shloim, N. (2023). A not-knowing, values-based and relational approach to counselling education, *British Journal of Guidance & Counselling, 51*(2), 310–321. https://doi.org/10.1080/03069885.2021.1912289

Shapiro, D. (2002). Renewing the scientist practitioner model. *The Psychologist, 15*(5), 232–234.

Turner, D. (2021). *Intersections of privilege and otherness in counselling and psychotherapy: Mockingbird.* Routledge.

Turner, D. (2023). *The psychology of supremacy: Imperium.* Routledge.

Section Two
The Trainee Journey

6.

Navigating difference, diversity and anti-oppressive practice

Nahid Nasrat and Colin Lago

Introduction

The subject of navigating difference, diversity and anti-oppressive practice has the capacity to touch the 'outsider' aspect of ourselves and consequently heighten our awareness of our social and professional vulnerabilities and responsibilities. In recognition of the significance of how cultural contexts shape people's attitudes, behaviours and relational patterns, it is important for us to introduce you, the reader, to our own differing origins and identities as co-authors of this chapter.

Nahid is a psychologist and full professor at the Chicago School of Professional Psychology in Washington, D.C. As a refugee from Afghanistan, her experiences shape her focus on diversity, oppression and racial attitudes. She is dedicated to serving refugees in the USA and worldwide, with expertise in the mental health of refugees and psycho-social issues in conflict settings. Her clinical manual for Afghan refugee women earned her the Outstanding Dissertation Award. Nahid has received multiple accolades, including the 2015 Ignacio Martín-Baró Lifetime Peace Practitioner Award, the 2016 Anthony J. Marsella Prize for her contributions to peace psychology and the 2016 NCSPP Diversity Award for her work with marginalised populations. She also received the 2020–2021 Distinguished Multicultural Teaching Excellence Award from the Chicago School of Professional Psychology.

Colin is a white British male who identifies as heterosexual. He qualified as a counsellor/psychotherapist after already having trained and worked as an engineer, a full-time youth worker in London and a teacher in Jamaica. Recognising the plight of *outsiders* through having weathered many school moves in his upbringing, Colin has always been interested in and motivated to welcome, include and seek to understand those whom society deems as *outsiders* and to oppose discriminatory processes in society. Colin has also written many books and articles exploring the implications of diversity upon the therapeutic relationship. He is a fellow of the British Association for Counselling and Psychotherapy and was awarded an honorary D. Litt in 2009 for his contributions to transcultural psychotherapy.

Scope of the chapter

The key topics that we will focus on in this chapter are:

- the issues and tasks related to human difference for psychology practitioners in training
- difference, diversity and anti-oppressive practice: meanings, implications and power imbalances
- the acquisition of new concepts and terminology
- on experiencing your training journey into diversity
- where do I position myself and what do I believe about human difference?
- how you might prepare yourself for the training.

The issues and tasks related to human difference for psychology practitioners in training

In this chapter we try to make best sense of the long but differing histories of the therapeutic professions' changing relationship to matters of 'difference and diversity', and consequently to acknowledge and embrace the extraordinary range of approaches there are in how difference and diversity is embedded within various course curricula. Some courses might only dedicate a day to this subject, while others might dedicate a semester or even completely underpin the whole duration of the course with an ongoing consideration of the implications of difference upon later professional practice.

When embarking generally upon psychological therapy training, students will be faced with complex and searching internal questions as to their beliefs, attitudes and relational patterns. As you, the student, then move on to specifically addressing the subject of difference and diversity, it is likely that complex questions concerning your own identity, biographical history, attitudes and behaviours – particularly towards those who are deemed different – are raised and highlighted in your ethical pursuit of self-awareness. The study of difference raises the fundamental existential, cultural, spiritual, political and attitudinal questions of 'who am I?' and 'who are you?'. You may thus be faced with a core dilemma of how to honour your own position while simultaneously seeking to accept and understand others' perspectives. This journey of exploration is one of social justice, anti-oppressive practice and openness to work with diversity in all its forms.

We recognise that as students, you, the reader, have been acculturated into society where the sheer complexity and number of identity descriptions has exploded in recent decades. This dramatically expanded vocabulary of identity descriptive terms has paralleled the levels of social attention given to increased accuracy of naming and claiming identity positions. Steinmetz (2014) noted that Facebook, for example, listed 56 gender identity characteristics. In this development Facebook moved away from society's previous usage of simplified descriptions of male/female/intersex. Identity has not only substantially expanded in concept to include those who identify in many other ways – but also, such expansion, by implication, may encourage people to create self-definitions that are not already included. Various 'identity' groups have also reclaimed language and adopted new verbal descriptors – for example, the LGBTQ+ community has reclaimed the word queer as an empowering identity label, while the disability community increasingly prefers terms like disabled person or person with disabilities over handicapped. Similarly, there has been a strong move towards the adoption of pronouns in the professional world, such as including she/her, he/him, or they/them in email signatures, business cards and introductions to promote inclusivity and respect for gender identity.

While in many ways such categorisation has proved helpful, particularly to those directly affected by such identity issues, the subject of difference and diversity, at its very core, raises searching and potentially uncomfortable questions about life itself, about history, about cultural, ethnic and national origins, about long-held attitudes towards other groups, about phenomena such as trans-generational trauma, about hate and conflict, and so much more. The nature of power and powerlessness as wielded by groups and within interpersonal circumstances becomes a fundamental issue for therapeutic consideration between those occupying different identity positions.

As a student approaching and participating in a programme on diversity awareness training, we recognise that you will have little influence, particularly at the beginning of your studies, over the content, the teaching methodology and the staff who deliver this training. Our experience has been that this training area is, in the main, taught by lecturers who are deeply committed to creating a macro-societal and micro-therapeutic climate where discriminatory processes are minimised at worst and banished at best. In addition, given the complexities of this subject, setting a discursive climate of psychological safety for all participants is of paramount importance.

Difference, diversity and anti-oppressive practice: meanings, implications and power imbalances

Difference, diversity and anti-oppressive practice are foundational principles in the fields of counselling, psychotherapy and counselling psychology, and they inform how therapists engage with clients and work towards positive outcomes. Embracing the diversity and intersectionality of human experience, challenging systemic oppression and promoting social justice are essential for creating inclusive and empowering therapeutic environments. By recognising and valuing clients' unique identities and experiences, therapeutic practitioners can foster trust, validation and empowerment, ultimately supporting clients in their journey towards healing and growth.

Difference, diversity and anti-oppressive practice shape how therapists engage with clients and promote positive outcomes. Embracing the diversity of human experience acknowledges that individuals have various backgrounds, identities and lived experiences. Difference refers to the unique characteristics that shape individuals' identities, including but not limited to, race, ethnicity, gender, sexual orientation, socioeconomic status and ability (Burnham, 2013; Pope-Davis & Coleman, 2014). Recognising and valuing these differences is essential for fostering culturally responsive and affirming therapy practices.

Diversity encompasses the range of identities and experiences present within society and within the therapy room. It acknowledges the complexity of human identity and the ways in which multiple intersecting factors shape individuals' lives (Arthur & Collins, 2010; Crenshaw, 1989). In therapeutic practice, embracing diversity involves creating an inclusive and welcoming environment where clients feel respected, understood and empowered to explore their concerns and goals. Therapists strive to be attuned to the unique cultural, social and historical contexts that influence their clients' experiences and worldview, monitoring their approach accordingly to meet clients' needs effectively.

Anti-oppressive and anti-discriminatory practice in psychological helping involves actively challenging systemic oppression and promoting social justice within therapeutic relationships and broader societal contexts (Lago & Smith, 2010). It recognises that individuals may face discrimination, marginalisation and other forms of oppression based on their identities, and seeks to address these power imbalances through advocacy, empowerment and allyship. Anti-oppressive therapists strive to create equitable and accessible services, advocate for systemic change and support clients in navigating oppressive systems while simultaneously respecting their autonomy and agency.

Central to anti-oppressive practice is the recognition of power dynamics and privilege within the therapeutic relationship (Proctor, 2002/2017). Courses on difference and diversity encourage therapists to critically examine their own biases, assumptions and privileges, acknowledging the ways in which their social location may influence their interactions with clients (Sue & Sue, 2022). This self-awareness is essential for counsellors, psychotherapists and counselling psychologists in building trust and rapport with clients, and for avoiding inadvertently perpetuating oppressive dynamics within the therapeutic process. Moreover, anti-oppressive therapists use culturally responsive and strengths-based approaches that honour clients' resilience, cultural assets and coping strategies (Lago & Smith, 2010).

They actively seek to understand clients' unique perspectives and experiences, validating their lived realities and affirming their identities. By centring clients' voices and experiences, they empower clients to reclaim agency and autonomy over their lives and to work towards positive change within themselves and their communities.

The acquisition of new concepts and terminology

Inevitably, the process of embarking on any new subject will entail the introduction of new concepts and their associated terms, many of which are frequently abbreviated, as understanding these abbreviations is essential for engaging effectively with the literature and professional discourse. As these concepts change over time through developing literature, research outcomes, cultural influences and so on, critical judgements are frequently evoked when older descriptions are used. An example of this phenomenon is the changing lexicon attributed to the description of those from minority communities. For example, going back a decade or so within the UK, the use of the term 'coloured' was regularly employed. Later, more explicit terms such as 'Black' and 'white' were introduced into the literature derived from sociological literature as indicating minority (Black) and majority (white) groupings. Following this, the term 'Black, Asian and minority ethnic' (BAME) found contemporary acceptance, and more recently, 'minoritised communities'. Additionally, in recent times, the term 'people of colour' (which is used within the USA) has been used in the British context, somewhat influenced by the Black Lives Matter movement. As trainers, we have witnessed complex, and sometimes tense, confrontations between course participants, with one person using specific terminology that was socially acceptable previously (and which has now been superseded), and another person who objects vehemently to this older usage, finding it so unacceptable that they are driven into critical judgement both of the phrase and of the person. We have even heard course participants requesting lists of currently acceptable conventions, pleading, 'If I knew what to say, I wouldn't get into so much trouble…'. It is sometimes easier to judge a phrase rather than explore the person's meaning of its usage. Within general and therapeutic dialogue, it is important to remember the old adage that meanings are in people, not in words! While words generally convey meaning, the adage invites us to recognise, respect and indeed explore a person's specific use of phrases, to understand their own meanings behind the use.

In addition, we have already noted the recent extraordinary attention to and expansion of gender identity terms that individuals might use as more accurate self-descriptors than hitherto were either available or acceptable. In short, sensitivity to the usage of language and its meanings are critical, and this is very much exemplified within the subject of difference and diversity.

On experiencing your training journey into diversity

We are acutely aware of how complex, frequently uncomfortable and challenging the subject of diversity can be. We also recognise the enormity and breadth of this subject. Over recent decades, societal shifts in attitude, protest and debate have influenced waves of new legislation, led to many publications and attracted academic attention. Inevitably these macro trends have had an impact on interpersonal and professional behaviour, which has led to yet further refinements in thought, professional consideration and therapeutic practice. This meta-view of attitudinal and behavioural change in society in relation to difference and diversity, while generally descriptive, does little to address the potentially enormous impact of actively exploring these dimensions of life within training.

There have been significant shifts in cultural attitudes and language concerning identity, discrimination and oppression. Several critical events have driven these changes, including the repeated police killings of Black people in the United States – most notably the murder of George Floyd – the widespread protests in the UK challenging public statues that honour former slave owners, the global spread of the #MeToo movement and the growing influence of anti-discrimination and anti-hate initiatives in sports. Additionally, the role of social media during the Covid-19 pandemic amplified awareness and created new spaces for reflection on social injustices. While there is a noticeable societal trend towards promoting equality and equity across all identity categories, this broader international and intergenerational shift, as Piketty (2022) argues, remains vulnerable to challenges from political movements and perspectives emerging around the world. Patterson (1977) noted that humans have a natural propensity for learning. He argues that humans are, by nature, curious, exploratory, and desirous of discovery, knowing and experiencing. Yet we also carry an ambivalence towards the act of learning, as significant learning inevitably involves some pain, either connected to the learning itself or with having to re-evaluate earlier learnings. Even learning to walk involves falling over! Significant learning places demands upon our sense of self and our ways of being.

Learning about difference can be immensely impactful and challenging. It can lead to a disruption in how one communicates. Defensive processes such as denial and repression can be unconsciously evoked to protect oneself from the challenge of engaging with the subject. Fellow students, who previously have been friendly and supportive on the course, may express attitudes and sentiments quite different in tone and emphasis to yourself. Such moments can sometimes feel very dramatic, affecting your own sense of thinking you knew this person, to suddenly thinking you don't. Or, after you have expressed a particular opinion, the room has gone silent, or others have been triggered into strong responses. Robin DiAngelo (2018) has explored these difficult, socially charged moments within her anti-racist trainings. Chloe Cooper Jones painfully reminisces about experiences where she, as a disabled woman, not only has to cope with her own physical pain, but the emotional discomfort of others. In her book, *Easy Beauty* (2022), she refers to a conversation with colleagues where she is profoundly confronted by the fact of not even being seen as present or existing, let alone worthy of meeting with other people and social contact. Her experience as a disabled person renders her 'outside the sentence', a conceptualisation employed by Roy Moodley (2014).

Engaging with the broad and complex theme of human difference inevitably exposes us to difficult and painful stories, as well as confronting statistics. At times, this learning process can feel unsettling, even turning our understanding of the world upside down. Diversity courses, in particular, can challenge previously held assumptions and disrupt long-standing perspectives. Our intention is not to alarm you, but to prepare you for the possibility that developing greater awareness and sensitivity to others' lived realities may involve questioning and reshaping your own attitudes and opinions. In this sense, studying diversity is not just an academic exercise – it is an exploration of the lived, experienced world.

Where do I position myself and what do I believe about human difference?

We have already noted that in undergoing a training course that explores issues of diversity, it is likely you will end up asking yourself some very deep questions. One level of self-questioning refers directly to the person you are and see yourself as being. Who are you, in terms of cultural background, lived experience, intersectional identities, attitudes, behaviours and so on? This is in line with Hill Collins and Bilge's assertion that, 'Intersectionality is a way of understanding and explaining complexity in the world, in people and in human experience' (2020, p. 2). Intersectionality recognises how the categories of race, class, gender, sexuality, nation, ability, age and so on are inter-related and affect each other, frequently in complex ways.

Next, you may ask yourself further questions, such as: Does my perception of myself accord with how others perceive me? How might I deal with those who have opposing beliefs and views or those who may have discriminated against me in the past? These questions and many more are likely to emerge strongly, if they haven't already for you, within the learning experience of studying diversity and difference.

Each person has a unique life experience shaped by emotions, relationships and attitudes, all of which are deeply influenced by visible and invisible social, ethnic and gendered locations in society. These factors significantly affect one's opportunities and sense of self. Research shows, for instance, that counselling students from 'minoritised' backgrounds are far more likely to explore their identities within training therapy than those from 'majority' groups, who often avoid addressing these aspects (Dhillon-Stevens, 2004). However, training courses can unintentionally perpetuate oppressive dynamics of 'othering', despite intending to foster inclusion. For minoritised students – who are often numerically few within their cohorts – the study of 'difference' can paradoxically deepen feelings of marginalisation rather than alleviate them (Khan, 2023).

Since psychological therapy first emerged, the field of psychotherapy training has promoted the value of therapists developing self-awareness and self-knowledge. Any exploration of perspectives on identity and intersectionality within a group setting is an intensely delicate personal journey. As we have noted, in our experience, including the nature of identity and intersectionality within dedicated diversity modules can evoke great personal discomfort in the individual and also powerfully affect the relationship dynamics of the study group. This can be particularly so for those who have a minoritised identity. Dual process theories (Strack & Deutsch, 2024) suggest that implicit and explicit processes are supported psychologically within us by fundamentally different psychological systems. Implicit processes are highly contextual and only change in an enduring way after considerable time, effort and intensity of exposure. Whitney et al. (2024) argue strongly, for example, that a single session of anti-racism training is highly unlikely to bring about personal change. The value of this research, among other aspects, lies in its detailed articulation of psychological and emotional processes that are differently experienced by students from majority and minoritised identities.

How you might prepare yourself for the training

In the rest of this chapter, we include several self- and small-group exercises and discussions and a list of recommended reading materials that you could engage with before you start training. We have already noted how unsettling discussion groups on this theme can be and the subsequent impact on the relational dynamics of the group. While such phenomena may prove upsetting and challenging, we believe that the unique learning content and process that might emerge through discursive engagement may prove of immense assistance in your future professional career. Group discussion of challenging material or instances of interpersonal friction offer you opportunities for exercising the relational and therapeutic skills you may already have been learning on the course. These are likely to include: giving attention to another, deep listening, striving to understand the other's experiencing, and offering empathic responses from a position of authenticity. These humanistic therapeutic conditions originally proposed by Carl Rogers have great value in such circumstances – see, for example, Lago (2016) and Jackson (2024).

While these qualities are important, we also acknowledge that the very nature of the subject under discussion evokes strong attitudinal responses within yourself. In such situations, one is faced with the dilemma of how to seek to deeply understand the other person's position while simultaneously feeling disturbed that you do not share their position. You could ask yourself, how might I stay attentive and curious about their stance and find a way of expressing my own truth?

A difference of opinion does not mean the other person is an enemy or being deliberately provocative; rather, their life experiences may simply differ from yours. Both of you may be triggered by the discussion, as memories, past hurts and traumas resurface. Yet, these moments hold extraordinary potential for growth and learning in your developing career – if you can remain engaged in the learning process. As Khan (2023) reminds us, there are always two identities present in the therapeutic relationship, and the therapist's own identity directly affects the process. Diversity-sensitive work requires acknowledging and integrating the 'out there' contexts of clients' lives into the 'in here' therapeutic space, recognising diversity as an inherent and vital part of the shared therapeutic environment.

Exercises

The following questions are aimed at individuals; however, they can also be explored within small and large group discussion as well as with supervisors and mentors. Given the complex attitudinal perspectives that can emerge in training discussions, participants are strongly advised to ensure that the necessary conditions to ensure a climate of physical, psychological and professional safety are established prior to any consideration of the issues.

On identity

How do you self-identify? What, for you, is your predominant aspect of identity? Explore the question of why and what underpins this particular choice.

Exploring your intersectionality

How do you see the interconnecting aspects of your intersectional identity combining, competing and relating in your experiencing? Elements of your intersectional identity will include age, ethnicity, gender, sexuality, nationality, class, neurodiversity. It may also include other specific aspects such as political beliefs, work activities/profession, sport and leisure interests and familial relations.

Identify your personal biases

Write about a time when you became aware of:

- a personal bias or prejudice you held towards others. How did you address it, and what did you learn from the experience?
- another person's biased, prejudicial behaviour towards you. How did you react, emotionally, behaviourally and psychologically?

Top takeaways

The following points are a selection of quotations and definitions that we believe support, articulate and reinforce the values and perspectives introduced in this chapter. Each statement or quotation is followed by a brief explanation for further context.

> Be kind whenever possible – it is always possible (The Dalai Lama, n.d.)

The above quotation underpins the importance of the psychological climate of care, compassion and empathy that is required in discussions and explorations of difference and diversity.

> Multicultural work is more than an intellectual exercise; it involves opening the self up to potentially painful, distressing and growth-enhancing intrapsychic and interpersonal experiences (Robert Carter, cited in Buckley et al., 2004, p. 23)

Courses dedicated to the exploration of difference and diversity dare to delve beneath everyday relationships and focus upon aspects of relational behaviour that can prove to be out of conscious awareness, extremely uncomfortable and indeed confrontational to one's own sense of self and how one relates to others in the world.

> The term 'disability' did not help me understand myself but was, instead a tool for deciphering the strange and disorientating moments when strangers would look at me and decide who I was and what I could do. People saw contrasts between their bodies and mine. They saw absence, lack. But I, having only ever been in my body, did not feel lacking. Going up the stairs feels like going up the stairs. Walking feels like walking. It looks strange, I guess, to those who watch me. It looks lesser. That would require lessons, for which I had many willing teachers... People make spaces I cannot enter, teaching me how forgotten I am, how excluded I am from 'real' life. I was stared at but not observed. I was both in and above the world, seeing from a distance, my consciousness forming in remove (Cooper Jones, 2022, p. 36)

In the above quotation, Chloe Cooper Jones pointedly reminds us of the impact of others' behaviours upon us and how difference and diversity is perceived and defined by others. Being subjected to negative perceptions and projections is painful, has an impact upon self-worth and confidence, and is traumatising.

> We must recognise and understand that counselling is an act of social justice (Khan, 2023, p. 13)

The above quotation by Myira Khan is a pertinent reminder of the philosophical and political aspirations underpinning psychotherapeutic approaches. To pay deep attention and empathically respond to a person's story relieves their suffering and facilitates that person's deeper understanding of themselves and their experiencing. This, in turn, has the capacity to inform their future way of being in the world. This is truly an act of social justice.

> However, we often tend to conceal the fact that no other profession involves a greater inequality of power than the psychotherapist's, in which one of the two poles is always, by definition, psychologically weaker than the other. For reasons intrinsic and structural to the psychological field, when a person is overwhelmed by suffering or convinced that his/her rational dimension (which up to that point had qualified him/her as a human being) has failed, asks someone stronger than he/she is to save him/her, s/he places that person in a position of power and superiority. This could also be why we undertake this profession: it is the only one that allows us to deal with weaker individuals, in partial identification with the omnipotent figure of saviour offering a hand to the suffering (Carotenuto, 1992, p. 51)

Aldo Carotenuto's words graphically remind any counselling practitioner of the power they can hold in the client's life, and when this component is added to power differentials in and between social groupings (e.g. prejudice, oppression, racism, sexism, disablism and so on), the necessity of therapist sensitivity, humility and comfort with difference is of paramount importance.

> At any moment, the world, in the shape of other people, can enter the therapy room (Lago, 2011, p. 5)

In this contemporary world, it is critical to appreciate that clients hail from a complex variety of backgrounds, ethnicities, cultures and experiences, and this quote substantiates just how critical it is for therapists to continually work on their knowledge of, and sensitivity to understanding of diversity in all its forms.

Questions for reflection

- Who am I? List as many aspects of your identity that you can and reflect upon or discuss these multiple perspectives with fellow course participants.
- How do others see me? Does my perception of myself accord with how others see me? What is it I might project, as perceived by others, which surprises or discomforts me?
- Consider a prospective client of a different and challenging identity entering your therapy office. Why might you find them challenging to work with? What emotions do they evoke in you? What aspects of continuing professional development might be helpful to you in addressing your negative response to this client?
- How can I stay curious and engaged with others when I am feeling negatively judgemental about them?

Recommended reading and key resources

- Dominelli, L. & Soydan, H. (2004). Anti-oppressive social work theory and practice. *European Journal of Social Work*, *7*(1), 118–120.

A review of anti-oppressive social work theory and practice.

- Hill Collins, P. & Bilge, S. (2020). *Intersectionality* (2nd ed.). Polity Press.

This text provides a deep dive into intersectional theory, essential for understanding how multiple forms of oppression intersect and affect individuals.

- DiAngelo, R. (2018). *White fragility: Why it's so hard for white people to talk about racism*. Beacon Press.

This book addresses the challenges and dynamics of discussing race and racism, and is particularly relevant for understanding privilege and anti-oppressive practice.

- Watson, N., Roulstone, A. & Thomas, C. (Eds.). (2022). *The Routledge handbook of disability studies*. Taylor & Francis.

A comprehensive guide to disability studies that provides insights into anti-oppressive approaches to disability.

References

Arthur, N. & Collins, S. (2010). *Counseling international students: Clients from around the world.* Springer.

Buckley, J., Hardy, G., Buchan, L. & Lewis, K. (2004). *Cross-ethnic therapeutic relationships: A qualitative study of therapists' experiences* [Unpublished doctoral dissertation]. University of Sheffield.

Burnham, J. (2013). Developments in social GGRRAAACCEEESSS: Visible-invisible, voiced-unvoiced. In I. Krause (Ed.), *Cultural reflexivity* (pp. 23–35). Karnac.

Carotenuto, A. (1992). *The difficult art: A critical discourse on psychotherapy.* Chiron Publications.

Cooper Jones, C. (2022). *Easy beauty*. Virago Press.

Crenshaw, K. (1989). Demarginalizing the intersection of race and sex: A Black feminist critique of anti-discrimination doctrine, feminist theory, and anti-racist politics. *University of Chicago Legal Forum*, *1989*(1), 139–167.

Dalai Lama. (n.d.). *AZQuotes.com*. https://www.azquotes.com/author/8418-Dalai_Lama

Dhillon-Stevens, H. (2004). *Healing inside and outside: An examination of dialogic encounters in the area of anti-oppressive practice in counselling and psychotherapy* [Unpublished doctoral dissertation]. Middlesex University.

DiAngelo, R. (2018). *White fragility: Why it's so hard for white people to talk about racism.* Beacon Press.

Hill Collins, P. & Bilge, S. (2020). *Intersectionality* (2nd ed.). Polity Press.

Jackson, C. (2024). Why Rogers is still relevant. *Therapy Today*, *35*(5), 18–23.

Khan, M. (2023). *Working within diversity: A reflective guide to anti-oppressive practice in counselling and therapy*. Jessica Kingsley.

Lago, C. (2011). *The handbook of transcultural counselling and psychotherapy*. Open University/McGraw-Hill.

Lago, C. (2016). On becoming a person-centred therapist for these contemporary times: Suggestions for professional development in the context of diversity. In C. Lago & D. Charura (Eds.), *The person-centred counselling and psychotherapy handbook: Origins, developments and current applications* (pp. 288–299). Open University Press.

Lago, C. & Smith, B. (2010). *Anti-discriminatory practice in counselling and psychotherapy* (2nd ed.). SAGE Publications.

Moodley, R. (2014). *Counseling and psychotherapy with South Asian women: A culturally sensitive approach*. Routledge.

Patterson, C.H. (1977). *Foundations for a theory of interaction and educational psychology*. Harper & Row.

Piketty, T. (2022). *A brief history of equality*. Belknap Press of Harvard University.

Pope-Davis, D.B. & Coleman, H.L.K. (Eds.). (2014). The intersection of multiculturalism and social justice: Implications for counseling psychology. In D.B. Pope-Davis & H.L.K. Coleman (Eds.), *Multicultural counseling: A handbook for practitioners* (pp. 1–12). SAGE Publications.

Proctor, G. (2002/2017). *The dynamics of power in counselling and psychotherapy: Ethics, politics, and practice*. PCCS Books.

Steinmetz, K. (2014). A comprehensive guide to Facebook's new options for gender identity. *Time*. https://techland.time.com/2014/02/14/a-comprehensive-guide-to-facebooks-new-options-for-gender-identity/

Strack, F. & Deutsch, R. (2024). Reflective and impulsive determinants of social behavior. *Personality and Social Psychology Review*, *8*(3), 220–247. https://doi.org/10.1207/s15327957pspr0803_1

Sue, S. & Sue, D.W. (2022). *Counseling the culturally diverse: Theory and practice* (9th ed.). Wiley.

Whitney, M., Proctor, G., Charura, D., Denger, T. & Wade, K. (2024). Possibilities and limitations of anti-racist training within a counselling programme. *Psychotherapy and Politics International*, *22*(1), 1–32. https://doi.org/10.24135/ppi.v22i1.05

7.

Assessment, formulation and therapeutic engagement

David A. Lane and Sarah Corrie

Introduction

Assessment and formulation are arguably the most important phases of any therapeutic engagement, as they establish the direction for the work, any aims or goals, what the therapeutic process might entail and who else might need to be involved (e.g. family members or other health care professionals). Assessment and formulation are also central in deciding whether therapy is suitable at all, and whether the therapist is best placed to deliver the needed service to a particular client at a particular point in time.

The aim of this chapter is to consider how to approach assessment and formulation from the perspective of the person rather than the theory, regardless of how valuable a theoretical perspective can be. We introduce a framework that can scaffold assessment and formulation without providing a misleading simplification of therapeutic work. While it can feel more comfortable to jump into 'doing something' under pressure from clients or service settings, without a clear understanding of the client's needs, therapists are at risk of reacting rather than having a thought-through approach. Undertaking a careful assessment and developing a formulation provide the compass and the map that can increase the likelihood of a better therapeutic outcome.

Scope of the chapter

The key topics that we consider in this chapter are:

- holistic assessment – why do we undertake it?
- what is the context for the assessment?
- what are the different types of assessment information?

- how do we know when to involve others in the assessment process?
- formulation – what is it and why does it matter?
- formulation concepts – a 4P framework: positionality, purpose, perspectives and process in formulation
- therapeutic engagement and building relationships.

These will be followed by a case study and questions for reflection, which end the chapter.

Holistic assessment – why do we undertake it?

There are several ways to approach assessment, but essentially, this task is a collaborative process of information-gathering to understand the factors that may be implicated in the issues with which the client presents. When a client approaches a practitioner for help or is referred by someone else, they have a tale to tell. They often have a sense of what concerns them and they or others have decided that professional assistance is needed. That tale might be a single issue or a more complex account involving multiple questions or participants who are part of the story. The client presumably believes that the professional with whom they are consulting brings knowledge from psychology and psychotherapy and has the skills to apply that knowledge in systematic ways to help them unravel the puzzle that they face. In this sense, the assessment is concerned with engaging the client in a sense-making process, and a decision needs to be made concerning what type of information is needed to develop a stance towards the work that is meaningful. It is not possible to predict exactly what will need to be discussed (although a referral letter or intake form might provide clues), so the first duty of the practitioner is to listen and explore in a way that enables the client to feel fully heard.

The main function of the assessment then, is to develop an approach for hearing the client's story and to collect information that will support an understanding of the client's needs. The need to develop that understanding is partly why it is important to avoid jumping straight into therapy. It is not possible to be certain at the outset if your offer makes sense for the client or even if a psychological intervention is the most appropriate for the challenges they face.

What is the context for the assessment?

To understand the client it is important to understand the context for the work that is to take place. Who is asking for this referral and why? The nature and purpose of the assessment will vary as a function of whether the client has sought out therapy themselves or has been referred by a third party. A broad issue to consider is the extent to which the client has agency in the process and perceives the referral as their choice or something recommended or perhaps prescribed by another.

A client comes to therapy with a view of themselves, their relationships and their world. They also have their own perspectives on what is involved in seeking help from a therapist. Similarly, the therapist will have their own sense of their position in the world and a view of themselves as a person and a professional. While therapists train within particular traditions of work, they do so from the position of their own values and beliefs about human nature, and a feature of counselling psychology (and some forms of psychotherapy) has been the acceptance and embracing of that subjectivity. However, therapy is also an engaged process where each party gradually develops a relational narrative. This becomes part of how the client's story comes to be understood in sufficient depth to be able to assist them in the changes they want to make.

Engaging the person using a systematic approach to information gathering can inform any therapeutic offer subsequently made and take the form of a process that is empowering for the client. It also enables consideration of risk and allows reflection on whether it makes sense for this client to engage with this practitioner at this time.

Any approach to assessment needs to begin with being clear about what needs to be assessed. There is a balance between getting enough information to be useful and fit for purpose and being overwhelmed by information that may be interesting but not necessarily relevant. Working collaboratively with the client, the assessment can consider key areas of a client's life context, personal history, current circumstances and needs (see Corrie et al., 2016). The focus is on hearing the story the client wants to tell and exploring its coherence to understand how the client sees themselves in the world, and the relationship between that and the experiences they currently face. Corrie and Lane (2010) outline different approaches to eliciting client stories. In doing so they seek to address the fundamental issue that faces practitioners of how to balance the generic understanding that they derive from our evidence base with the particular circumstances of the client.

What are the different types of assessment information?

An important starting point in balancing the generic and the particular in the client's story is to consider the potential contribution of two distinct forms of assessment: the nomothetic and the idiographic. The nomothetic approach to assessment classifies the features of particular disorders (diagnoses) that have been identified through large-scale, population-based studies. Arriving at a diagnosis will occur through exploration with the client but is often supported by the use of standardised, disorder-specific, self-report measures. An important point to note about diagnostic systems is that they classify disorders and not people. For different perspectives relating to people and not pathology, see Sanders and Tolan (2023).

In contrast to a nomothetic approach, an idiographic approach to assessment seeks to understand the factors that are of relevance to the individual client in their unique context. Thus, the therapist might seek to create a shared understanding of relevant background factors, current circumstances, a diagnosis if there is one, factors that enable and constrain the client's choices, strengths and resources, and factors that might play a role in maintaining the client's concerns. Self-report questionnaires and other rating scales might be used but are likely to be bespoke to the client (see Corrie et al., 2016, for a review of these different approaches).

It is important not to polarise the nomothetic and the idiographic, as professional practice often requires both, and each approach has strengths and limits.

While the idiographic approach is essential to the person-centred values that underpin counselling psychology (and some other forms of therapeutic practice), there are increasing demands facing all practitioners in health settings to deliver services that are evidence based. For practitioners, and clients, too, the skilled combination of both nomothetic and idiographic approaches can provide benefit. For example, the ability of the nomothetic approach to identify features that are relevant to a client's distress can more swiftly guide therapist and client towards an evidence-based process that is likely to prove beneficial. Moreover, clients can find a profile or diagnosis helpful; something now makes sense to them that did not before. Nonetheless, if poorly used, professionals can begin to fit clients to models. Likewise, if poorly used, the risk with the idiographic approach is that relevant wider information is overlooked. For the practitioner, the key to using this information lies in gaining a sense of what it means to the client. To what extent does any information speak to them, and is it seen as useful?

How do we know when to involve others?

It can be appropriate to seek support from others in generating assessment information. This can occur when, for example, incorporating the guidance of a spiritual leader in making sense of someone's spiritual crisis, or seeking the view of a medical practitioner concerning apparent psychological difficulties that could indicate an underlying physical condition, or where safety, safeguarding or other risk issues arise.

It is also important to consider who else might have an interest in the conclusions of any assessment and formulation that is undertaken. This can raise ethical–legal issues (e.g. others requesting your notes or seeking reports for the purposes of guiding decisions about compensation or sentencing) as well as cultural issues (e.g. psychological perspectives are not well received by all cultures). Contextual matters may also raise issues (e.g. who owns any information and to what use it can legitimately be applied) along with questions of inclusivity and diversity (services provided within the framework of dominant cultures that marginalise different views or may challenge the values of the practitioner).

Formulation – what is it and why does it matter?

Once the therapist and client have accumulated the information from the assessment process, it needs to be synthesised in a way that has implications for the next steps. The importance of formulation has been emphasised within psychology as a key competence (see Lane & Corrie, 2006, for a review). Yet, there are different ways to approach formulation. Originally, clinicians were expected to define their work in terms of psychiatric categorisations (Bruch, 2015). Subsequently an emphasis was placed on the scientist-practitioner model to guide practice (see Lane & Corrie, 2006). In the UK, Meyer (see Bruch, 2015) developed the idea of an individualised formulation of the client's issues shared with them, rather than imposed as a diagnosis from outside. Separately, from 1975 onwards Lane (1990) developed an individualised formulation model for working with children and schools. Lane later worked with Meyer to create a structured approach to case formulation (see Bruch, 2015, for a review of this work).

The information provided by clients is often complex. Making sense of it is, therefore, a process that involves constructing a shared sense of meaning out of the wealth of data obtained. As Corrie and Lane (2010) propose, formulation serves as a framework for clarifying the questions that drive the inquiry forward. It helps to identify those areas that need to be prioritised and those areas of risk that might need referral elsewhere or discussion in supervision. Moreover, formulation is an aid to understanding challenging aspects, since the story emerging can be reflected upon or changed. This helps to protect against premature decision-making and a rush to judgement.

Formulation can also represent a form of professional communication in that ideas can be shared with colleagues. However, formulation is not without its critiques (see the debate in Corrie & Lane, 2010, on accuracy and utility) and there is no one way to create a formulation. For some it is a process of building and testing hypotheses, whereas for others it is the application of particular theoretical perspectives. For the purposes of this chapter, however, formulation can be usefully understood as a particular type of story informed by the context in which it is created in order to meet specific client needs at a particular point in time.

Formulation – what concepts help to guide the approach?

In their work on formulation, Lane et al. (2025) developed a framework that can support practitioners in considering the impact of four critical areas that influence how they think and practice and that help to conceptualise the journey with a client. Their 4P framework encourages us to consider the following:

- **positionality** – our own schema or narrative as self and as a therapeutic practitioner and how we create space for the client to be

able to explore their own sense of self, their role as client and for both parties to consider who they are in relation to each other
- **purpose** – our shared sense of the work we will be doing together and what makes it worthwhile
- **perspectives** – our different perspectives on ourselves in relation to others and the world around us and beliefs about factors that will enable change
- **process** – the details of how we will work together, including agreeing a direction, how we will relate to each other, how we will know that the journey is progressing, and our point of conclusion.

Each element of the 4P framework is considered below.

Positionality

For therapists educated within the humanistic tradition, the starting point is an emphasis on a person-centred approach that honours the subjective nature of experience. Understanding the self is, therefore, the starting point. We need to seek to understand how we see ourselves and are seen by others and how that sense of our positionality affects the way we work. Similarly, we have to create the space in which our clients feel able to explore their own understanding of themselves and their place in their world. We each bring those positions to the encounter.

Purpose

Therapy can be considered a transactional or a relational process. As a transaction, client and therapist make an offer to each other to work on a specific issue using a defined process to reach an agreed outcome. As a relational process, they explore together how the journey might unfold and are both open to learning from the experience. How the purpose for the work is defined is part of that initial contracting to determine what type of journey they will undertake together. It could be a transaction whereby therapist and client agree to work, for example, to address a phobia that is causing distress and interfering with life (a situation to be addressed), or it could be a relational endeavour in which they explore patterns of behaviour that have an impact on core aspects of the client's sense of self (a person to be encountered). These different approaches can be conceptualised as working at the level of situation, pattern or person/case (Corrie & Kovacs, 2019). Working to agree the purpose of the work is the essential starting point for any therapeutic alliance, so that there is clarity concerning the direction of the work and why this direction is meaningful.

Perspectives

We all bring our own sense of self and our role to the therapeutic encounter. However, as we work together those reflections are shared and we gradually evolve a new relational narrative that encapsulates our sense of our presence in this shared journey. This may bring about a small change in our ways of seeing, particularly in a transactional encounter, or a more profound revisiting of beliefs in a relational encounter. Having agreed the purpose of the work, it is then necessary to explore factors that we believe will help us to construct the story to be told, to deconstruct unhelpful aspects of that story and reconstruct a new story that enables change. For some practitioners their knowledge of specific modalities provides guidance on perspectives that may be useful to understanding the issues the client presents – for example, Beck's (1995) CBT longitudinal formulation; Gilbert's (2010) compassion-focused therapy; Malan's triangles (1979); and person-centred formulation (Simms, 2011; Uphoff & Charura, 2016). As therapists we bring perspectives from our training to inform that work. Our client brings their expertise on their own life. Both parties bring a sense of self. Our perspectives might include the use of a scientist-practitioner model to provide an evidence base to inform our perspectives. We may draw upon different theoretical assumptions to help the process of unravelling the dilemmas faced. Whatever we draw upon, this is a shared space in which to address what we think is happening, why it is happening and how it might be changed to ensure problems are resolved and new possibilities are generated.

Process

The process we use will very much be influenced by our own therapeutic beliefs about the nature of human experience and how change occurs. If we see ourselves as a cognitive behaviour therapist we will explore questions differently than if we are psychoanalytically trained. There are advantages and disadvantages from taking theoretical stances. A single stance enables the development of a high degree of skill in that approach to the work. It can also lead to a narrowness in the areas explored, and some questions that might be helpful will not be explored, as they do not fit within the theoretical framework that is preferred. There are many suggestions for ways to explore the process. Many books on therapy will have a section on theoretical approaches that ask different questions and draw varying conclusions on the role of predisposing, precipitating, perpetuating and protective factors having an impact on the client's thoughts, feelings and actions. There is no one way to use the information from the assessment to create a formulation.

Therapeutic engagement and building relationships: what does the alliance look like?

Practitioners have always privileged the therapeutic relationship. However, this is not a simple matter, as relationships can be positive but also present challenges. They can also present dangers in over-identification and are multi-dimensional. Therapists are present for their clients' pain, joy or anger and may need to repair that relationship as difficulties emerge. Clients may have very different ideas about our role and expect us to act in certain ways that may not be consistent with our preferred stance or the expectations of our professional bodies. A client might understand the relationship as one of expert doctor and patient or one of a shared journey of discovery.

An alternative approach is to focus not on the idea of a therapeutic relationship but one of an alliance, whereby therapist and client choose to work together for a defined period to achieve a purpose and decide between them the nature of that alliance, although there are boundaries. That alliance is not set but changes over time and has to be constantly revisited and maintained. In studies of the working alliance, Bordin (1983) focused on the notion of collaboration in relation to goals (and the extent to which therapist and client can agree on these), tasks (the extent to which there is agreement on the tasks necessary to achieve the goals) and bond (the affective ties that develop a process of working towards the goals or a bond based on shared emotional experience). It becomes possible to consider both how the alliance is built and potential areas that might create resistance and ruptures. These can be because of misunderstanding in any of the three areas above or as a result of not understanding feedback on something, which may lead to resistance. We focus not just on the words spoken, but what is present but not yet articulated. We are open to our own process as well as what it is like to be with the experience of the client.

Case study

You are working as a therapist for a mental health charity that offers a service for a broad spectrum of mental health difficulties. Prospective clients are referred or can self-refer to the service, where a range of interventions are provided. All the therapies provided are time limited and can vary between 6 to 20 sessions. Clients' preferences are discussed during an initial assessment consultation to ensure that there is a good match between the service offer and the client's needs.

Sarina has been referred to the service by her GP with a diagnosis of mixed anxiety and depression. She discloses how difficult she finds living with such high levels of anxiety and that she feels permanently low in mood. However, what troubles her most is her inability to get out of bed in the morning, which worries her, as she is the single parent of two young children and the sole breadwinner for the family. Sarina says that what she most wants from therapy is to be able to get out of bed in the morning so she can get to work. As an example, she describes what happened the previous morning, when she woke up at 3.00am and then dozed until the alarm went off at 6.00am. She said that she 'just couldn't face the day' and lay in bed with 'a huge knot in my stomach', ruminating on how difficult life is and what a terrible parent she is to be unable to provide for her family if she cannot get herself out of bed and off to work. Yet, Sarina confirms that there are days when she can get out of bed and that these occasions usually coincide with her children needing her in some way.

Several things strike you. First, Sarina is able to get out of bed when there is an immediate need to do so. However, when that need is absent she retreats into a process of rumination and self-recrimination that appears to increase her anxiety and lower her mood. She responds to this escalating cycle by withdrawing from the world further, which reinforces her sense of failing to provide for her family, as she is not going to work. You also wonder if her withdrawal makes her anxiety and low mood worse by preventing her from having experiences that could be empowering (e.g. getting to work and taking pride in her ability to provide for her family) and even rewarding (e.g. enjoying the company of her colleagues).

Sarina agrees that getting some help with breaking the pattern you describe would be helpful. She tells you that the feelings are at their worst in the morning and ease a little by the end of the day. You ask what makes them easier at the end of the day and anything she might be doing to cope. She hesitates before disclosing that, 'I am drinking more alcohol than I should'. You sense her discomfort and invite her, therefore, to say more just at a level she feels comfortable with to begin with.

Sarina explains that over the last few months she has increased her alcohol consumption to a bottle of white wine each evening. She cries at this point – she recognises that relying on alcohol is not a solution (she had a father with alcoholism) and she is worried about the impact this could have on her children.

You are familiar with how clients often turn to alcohol to self-medicate and how this exacerbates anxiety and low mood, even though the person experiences short-term relief. You are also conscious that Sarina seems to be disclosing feelings of shame and that she seems to be engaging in experiential avoidance in which uncomfortable internal states are avoided through distracting herself, or ruminating, or numbing (drinking alcohol).

You acknowledge that this has taken courage to disclose and thank Sarina for her willingness to do so – it gives you the information you need to work with her to decide how to proceed. You wonder out loud whether her alcohol use could be connected to the difficulty she experiences with getting out of bed. Sarina would like some individual therapy, and working directly on tackling the cognitive and behavioural obstacles to getting out of bed appeals to her. Her own preferences, along with the evidence base, suggest that in this case a cognitive behavioural approach might be helpful. However, as a first step, you talk with Sarina about meeting with her doctor to talk about her alcohol use and to agree a coordinated plan with her GP (based on what she has told you, she is unlikely to meet the threshold criteria for referral to the local alcohol service). Sarina is at first reluctant to speak with her

GP, but after discussion about the potential benefits of doing so, agrees to make an appointment. At Sarina's request, you also confirm that you will contact her GP surgery to explain the current situation.

Top takeaways

- Assessment and formulation are key aspects of the encounter between client and therapist to build an understanding of the work they need to do together.
- Collecting information about the client's challenges, experiences and their context forms the basis for the assessment of need and the decision to offer a service.
- Formulation provides the shared account of all the information to create an intervention plan.
- The more collaborative the process of building the formulation, the more effective the working alliance will be.

Questions for reflection for trainees and throughout their career

- What is your own approach to assessment and formulation?
- How does your own approach relate to the ideas in this chapter and the case study?
- What ideas have supported or challenged your current thinking?
- How does the setting in which you work or the context in which you train have an impact on your approach to assessment and formulation?
- How do you know if you have done a good job of assessment and formulation?

Recommended reading and key resources

- Bruch, M. (2015). *Beyond diagnosis case formulation in cognitive behavioural psychology*. Wiley.

This book considers the origins of individualised formulation and provides several case examples.

- Corrie, S. & Lane, D.A. (2010). *Constructing stories telling tales: A guide to formulation in applied psychology*. Karnac.

This book explores formulation as a narrative encounter with the client and provides a detailed account of different approaches.

- Lane, D.A., Corrie, S. & Kovacs, L. (2025). *A guide to formulation in coaching*. Routledge.

This book provides a detailed account of formulation and how to approach it. It is part of a series on coaching but covers the key areas that also apply in counselling psychology and psychotherapy.

- Uphoff, A. & Charura, D. (2016). Person-centred futures: Surveying the landscape. In C. Lago & D. Charura (Eds.), *The person-centred counselling and psychotherapy handbook: Origins, developments and current applications* (pp.313–323). Open University Press.

This chapter outlines and exemplifies how to use a person-centred formulation.

References

Beck, J.S. (1995). *Cognitive therapy: Basics and beyond*. Guilford Press.

Bordin, E.S. (1983). A working alliance model of supervision. *The Counseling Psychologist, 11*, 35–42.

Bruch, M. (2015). *Beyond diagnosis case formulation in cognitive behavioural psychology.* Wiley.

Corrie, S. & Kovacs, L. (2019). The functions of formulation in coaching psychology. *The Coaching Psychologist, 15*(1), 66–75.

Corrie, S. & Lane, D.A. (2010). *Constructing stories, telling tales: A guide to formulation in applied psychology*. Karnac.

Corrie, S., Townend, M.J. & Cockx, A. (2016). *Assessment and case formulation in cognitive behavioural therapy* (2nd ed.). Sage.

Gilbert, P. (2010). *Compassion focused therapy*. Routledge.

Lane, D.A. (1990). *The impossible child*. Trentham Books.

Lane, D.A. & Corrie, S. (2006). *The modern scientist practitioner: A guide to practice in psychology*. Routledge.

Lane, D.A., Corrie, S. & Kovacs, L. (2025). *A guide to formulation in coaching*. Routledge.

Malan, D.H. (1979). *Individual psychotherapy and the science of psychodynamics*. Butterworth.

Sanders, P. & Tolan, J. (2023). *People not pathology: Freeing therapy from the medical model*. PCCS Books.

Simms, J. (2011). Case formulation within a person-centred framework: An uncomfortable fit? *Counselling Psychology Review, 26*(2), 24–36. https:doi.org/10.53841/bpscpr.2011.26.2.24

Uphoff, A. & Charura, D. (2016). Person-centred futures: Surveying the landscape. In C. Lago & D. Charura (Eds.), *The person-centred counselling and psychotherapy handbook: Origins, developments and current applications* (pp.313–323). Open University Press.

8.

Reading, writing, speaking and finding your voice in therapy training

John McLeod

Introduction

Within the pathway from deciding on therapy as a career, through to working as a qualified practitioner (e.g. psychologist, counsellor, psychotherapist), the phase of engaging in training typically comprises a three- to five-year block of intensive, focused learning. A central dimension of that learning process is a continual cyclical interplay between reading, writing and speaking, held together by personal reflection and meaning-making. This chapter explores the significance of these communication skills as key areas of therapist competence.

Scope of the chapter

This chapter discusses the following issues:

- what happens when we read, write or speak as therapists?
- how reading, writing and speaking skills can make you a better therapist
- learning to read, write and speak from a therapist perspective
- broadening one's reading, writing and speaking repertoire
- using writing within client work
- advocacy
- contributing to professional knowledge
- issues and dilemmas arising from developing competence in reading, writing and speaking.

Reflective questions are provided throughout this chapter to facilitate engagement with each of these key topics.

What happens when we read, write or speak as therapists?

There is a basic paradox, in the field of psychotherapy training and practice, between text (the written word) and conversation. Although there are some situations in which a client and a therapist may communicate in writing, the experience of counselling or psychotherapy is at its heart a conversational and relational process, typically described as *talking* therapy or the *talking* cure. The distinction between text and talk is generally an unremarkable and taken-for-granted aspect of everyday life that we all learn to cope with. However, in the context of therapy training and practice, it is potentially enormously significant.

In terms of the historical evolution of the human species, conversation and storytelling came first. Speaking is an embodied experience, in which the talker communicates from a felt sense of the moment and is able to finely adjust what they say in response to their perception of the listener's response. Talk occurs at a specific time and pace, and constantly makes reference to that shared context. The meaning of what is being said is only partially conveyed through words, which are overlaid and nuanced through breath patterns, voice quality, gesture, gaze, movement, rhythm, musicality, and many other embodied and sensory channels of communication.

By contrast, literacy emerged very recently in human history. The written word is a decontextualised, disembodied and predominantly linear form of communication. A writer generally produces text alone, still, and with their hand. A reader generally reads text alone. In an attempt to overcome the distancing effect of written text, this handbook has been conceived as a companion (and conversation partner) rather than as a reader.

While both text and conversation are means through which people can share information, knowledge and experience, they work in different ways. Essentially, literacy introduced a new way of being in relation to the world (Ong, 1982).

The tension between oral and literary ways of knowing permeates all aspects of therapy training. Students and trainees are expected to spend a lot of time reading books, clinical case studies and research studies, and writing essays, case reports, clinical notes and research dissertations. Even seminar discussions tend to be grounded in textual material such as a seminar paper or PowerPoint slides. At the same time, learning about an approach to therapy, such as psychodynamic or CBT, necessarily involves immersion in an oral tradition in which the student or trainee begins by listening to how more experienced practitioners talk about the work, gradually learns the language, and eventually joins in the conversation. The experience of working with a client is almost entirely embodied, contextual and conversational. In the early phase of learning to be a therapist, it is not unusual to come away from a session with a client with a sense that very little of what happened bore much resemblance to textbook theory. It can take a long time, and good supervision, to learn to see the lived process of therapy through the lens of formal theory.

Why does this matter? Surely, over time, text and talk come together in a productive and synergistic manner? The main reason why it matters is the status and authority attributed to the written word in both contemporary society as a whole, and the domain of therapy in particular. The concept of *epistemic justice* offers a valuable means of making sense of this phenomenon (Fricker, 2017). For any therapist who takes social justice seriously, it is necessary to learn how to be responsive to how issues presented by clients may reflect intersecting dimensions of structural adversity associated with aspects of contemporary social life, such as racism, gender violence and poverty (Winter & Charura, 2023). It is also necessary to be able to address the existence of inequality of power and control in the actual client–therapist relationship itself. Some of this inequality is linked to tangible aspects of power, such as who has the key to the therapy room, or control of the appointment diary. However, a therapist also exerts power through being able to claim superior knowledge that is based in theory and research. In the therapy relationship, such privilege rests on the mutual understanding that the therapist has studied textual sources for several years (and has the diploma on the wall to prove it), while the client – usually – only has knowledge from lived experience to fall back on. This situation replicates and reinforces a colonialist form of relating that disregards and suppresses the oral cultural knowledge and tradition from which the person lives their life (Mika et al., 2020). An over-reliance on textual knowing, therefore, not only distances a therapist from the everyday reality of the client, but has the additional effect of perpetuating hierarchical power relations that almost certainly played a major part in the development of the client's problems in the first place.

Personal reflection exercise 1

Take a few minutes to reflect, and make notes, on your experience of reading, writing and speaking during your therapy training. What have you learned so far about how you are able to use these core communication skills? In what ways has the capacity to read, write and speak, which you brought into training – and stretches back to your time as a child and at school – been challenged and stretched, or even upended, by your involvement in training? What have been the key moments in training, where you have needed to consciously and purposefully reflect on these competencies? What kinds of feedback and support have you received, from tutors or learning partners, in these areas?

How reading, writing and speaking skills can make you a better therapist

The following paragraphs explore some of the ways that reading, writing and speaking skills can be developed, and how these capabilities can both contribute to you being a more resourceful and facilitative therapist, and help you play an active and constructive role within the profession. An assumption that underpins all of these suggestions is that it is helpful to become able to move between the different vantage points associated with reading, writing and speaking (and also listening). For example, the aphorism 'how do I know what I think until I see what I say?' implies that deeper and more creative understanding can be achieved by writing down what one has said, or talking out loud about what one has written (Swedberg, 2020).

Learning to read, write and speak from a therapist perspective

Undergoing therapy training almost certainly involves learning new reading, writing and speaking skills and strategies. A significant proportion of therapy discourse consists of an interweaving of third-person description and analysis, with first-person subjective and reflexive information, alongside ethically sensitive material about therapy clients. This mix turns up in books, articles and talks. A further dimension of complexity within therapy discourse and published literature is the existence of a variety of genres of writing and reporting, which is associated with quantitative studies, qualitative studies, single-case analyses, theory papers and autoethnographic reports. There are also contrasting ways of talking and writing about therapy associated with different therapy traditions. For example, psychoanalysts and CBT therapists have quite different styles of writing and presenting talks. Learning how to handle this kind of genre fluidity is not straightforward. Many trainees bring with them ways of writing and talking in which they have been socialised in a primary discipline such as psychology or theology, only to receive tutor feedback that what they have produced is not appropriate. Trainees whose use of written language has been shaped by personal experience of neurodiversity, visual impairment, deafness, cultural identity and social class, may encounter many challenges around developing competence in professional communication.

There are many sources that are available to support the development of writing skills. A wide array of books and articles explain how to write up a statistics-based study or a qualitative investigation, how to structure an article according to the APA style manuals (e.g. APA, 2020; Levitt, 2020) and how to write an article for publication (Finlay, 2020). General guides to academic writing are available (e.g. Murray & Hughes, 2008), and many university student support services are willing to offer individual tutorial help around writing skills.

It can also be useful to be open to different ways of reading. Schools, and most university courses, tend to teach students to read in a distanced, analytic manner that enables critical analysis of the validity of the source that is being studied. Although such skills are necessary for anyone engaged in professional work, the specific demands of being a therapist mean that it is also essential to learn how to read for implicit and emotional meaning. Kuecker (2024) offers a highly accessible account of what is involved in 'reading differently', by taking time to imaginatively and emotionally enter the experience and world of the author, as well as – for instance, in a research study or case report – that of the clients or research participants being written about (McLeod, 2015, 2016, 2024).

The skill of speaking encompasses a range of situations in which one presents one's ideas, experience or knowledge to a professional or community audience, or facilitates a workshop or other kind of event. Speaking skills are also involved in psycho-education – teaching clients individually or in groups about therapy ideas and techniques that may be relevant to their recovery (Slade & Longden, 2015). All of these types of speaking can be contrasted with the ways of talking and engaging in dialogue and conversation that occur in therapy sessions.

As it entails continually reading, writing for essays and other assignments, and making seminar presentations – and receiving feedback on all of these activities – being a member of a training community provides many opportunities to develop communication skills that will stand one in good stead over the rest of one's career. For example, although editors of case study journals such as *Clinical Case Studies* and *Pragmatic Case Studies in Psychotherapy* are always keen to publish case reports from new authors, they are hampered by the fact that few therapists get to the end of their training with sufficient skills and competence to embark on writing up one of their cases – and do not have the time at that point in their life to acquire such skills. In this instance, gaining experience in collecting, analysing and writing up case material in a systematic manner, during therapy training, makes it possible to take advantage of a meaningful and career-enhancing activity at a later stage.

Personal reflection exercise 2

An activity that is frequently used in training to develop counselling skills is for one trainee to play the part of a client, while another acts as counsellor (typically focusing on the use of a specific skill), while another student and perhaps a tutor are observers. A means of gaining direct experience of some of the differences between talking and writing in a therapy context is to arrange to begin a skills practice session by talking, and then at the halfway point to continue the dialogue through email without any visual contact. Then change the order – begin with email dialogue before moving to face-to-face talking therapy. What difference do these modes of connection and communication have in the way you feel in yourself (as counsellor or client) and the type of therapeutic process that unfolds?

Broadening one's reading, writing and speaking repertoire

When asked about activities that have made a significant contribution to being an effective practitioner, many senior and experienced therapists highlight the importance for them of literature and the arts (Råbu et al., 2016). The value of reading and learning beyond the professional literature, to include novels, poems, theatre drama, movies, art, history, philosophy and studies of cultures, has been widely recognised within the therapy professions (Erikson et al., 2020; Holmes, 2014). To highlight just one aspect of contemporary therapy, it would be very difficult to make any sense of the notion of decolonising therapy by reading only books and articles published within the counselling and psychotherapy literature itself (McLeod, 2025). Most therapy training programmes design their curriculum to meet the accreditation criteria required by professional and governmental licensing bodies, and as a result rarely have space to encourage students to read beyond the mainstream therapy literature, for example novels and ethnographic studies. Similarly, although oral presentations in training contexts by tutors and students are generally structured along conventional academic lines, there are many examples of creative and personally involving talks and presentations available online or offered at conferences and workshops. During training, it can be useful to take opportunities to broaden one's own reading, writing and speaking repertoire along these lines. Such activities not only nurture and feed the therapeutic imagination (Holmes, 2014), but also help to develop a skill set that may be relevant to future employment opportunities.

Personal reflection exercise 3

What are some of the novels, movies, theatre plays, art works, events, performances, podcasts and talks that have most inspired and enlightened you in terms of understanding yourself and your capacity to offer a productive therapy relationship to someone who needs help? How have you used these experiences to enrich and expand how you communicate with clients and colleagues? What might you do to make more use of such sources?

In your training you may also come across the ethical and academic integrity debates and institutional guidance relating to the use of AI. What are your personal reflections on the use of different AI tools? For further discussion on the use of AI in reflective writing, please also see Chapter 11.

Using writing within client work

There are many ways that writing skills are relevant not only to producing academic essays and reports about aspects of therapy, but also for using *within* the process of therapy itself (McLeod, 2025).

A widely used approach using writing for therapeutic purposes is to keep a reflective diary, journal or log. One of the best ways to gain confidence and competence in supporting a client to engage in journal writing is to have had the experience of keeping a journal to facilitate one's own personal and professional development. Many training programmes encourage or require students to keep a journal throughout the course, or in relation to specific topics, as a means of developing self-awareness and a capacity to reflect on practice. However, this learning activity can also be regarded as preparation for using journalling in work with clients.

Another type of therapeutic writing is to write a letter or note to a client, either on a regular basis (Paré, 2016) or at specific points in therapy (Slettevold et al., 2024). A further mode of therapeutic writing involves working with a client to construct a letter to a third party – for example, when a transgender person is applying to be considered for a medical intervention (Brown et al., 2020; Budge, 2015). Both of these types of therapeutic writing can be quite challenging and anxiety-provoking for therapists, due to the fear of committing something to paper that might be insensitive or inaccurate. Therapists are more likely to be willing to try these techniques, and to be able to use them effectively, if they can draw on previous experience of successfully adapting their writing style, during training, to accommodate different purposes and contexts.

Advocacy

A significant shift has occurred within the field of counselling and psychotherapy in recent years, in the direction of an appreciation of the importance of engaging with a social justice agenda and being responsive to clients' socio-political concerns. Many therapists have found that, to do effective work around these issues, it is necessary to develop relationships and networks in local communities, and function from a position of solidarity and activism in terms of supporting oppressed individuals, families and groups to stand up for their rights (Ashley & Domínguez, 2021; Doherty, 2020). Within such an approach, *advocacy* skills can be identified as a key element of practitioner competence. Advocacy builds on meeting and dialoguing with people affected by inequality, and reading research and policy literature relevant to their needs. The active side of advocacy can range from working with individuals to support them in their negotiations with housing and social care providers (Goodman et al., 2009; Sullivan & Goodman, 2019), through formulating and presenting policy proposals to funding bodies and legislatures (Singh et al., 2023). In some circumstances it can also entail supporting groups of clients to protest against inappropriate forms of therapy (Chapman & Bovell, 2022). An increasing proportion of therapy training programmes provide advocacy skills courses for their students (Alexander & Allo, 2021).

Personal reflection exercise 4

In terms of your experience with particular issues and client groups, and the personal life experience and values that led you to want to develop a career as a counsellor or psychotherapist, identify *one* area in which you might wish to engage in advocacy. Alternatively, if you are already doing therapy-related advocacy, focus on *one* specific episode within that aspect of your work. What are the skills and personal challenges that you associate with this dimension of practice? How might you develop (or have you developed) such skills and overcome such barriers?

Contributing to professional knowledge

The topic of professional knowledge refers to the massive repository of insight and practical understanding developed by therapy practitioners around their work with particular client groups, presenting problems or therapy approaches. Sharing professional knowledge supports the existence of communities of practice through which practitioners are able to learn with and from each other, by offering and receiving collective solidarity, and sharing examples of good practice (McLeod, 2022). While such sources need to be read alongside evidence from formal research studies, professional knowledge articles and studies comprise a significant proportion of the overall counselling and psychotherapy published literature. Although most professional knowledge pieces are based on the accumulated experiences of senior practitioners, there have also been many influential articles produced by trainees and early-career therapists – for example, in journals such as *Clinical Psychology Forum* and *Counselling Psychology Review*. Autoethnographic writing represents an increasingly popular means of sharing professional knowledge (Råbu et al., 2021). Some trainers and lecturers view supporting students to publish such work as part of their responsibilities as role mentors. As well as through published articles, professional knowledge may be disseminated through talks at conferences and local networks. Granek and Nakash (2016) describe how they have used talks to professional audiences to generate synergy between their research and its relevance for practice.

Personal reflection exercise 5

How might you contribute to professional knowledge? What are the areas of personal knowledge and insight that have emerged from your experience of training, supervision and practice? How might you share this knowledge through talks and articles? What kinds of support might help you to accomplish these goals?

Issues and dilemmas arising from developing competence in reading, writing and speaking

It is important to recognise that the areas of competence development discussed in this chapter may entail a significant degree of emotional and ethical learning, and behaviour change. In these respects, it may be valuable to reflect on how this facet of the overall experience of training might need to be explored within supervision, personal therapy, experiential groups and informal support networks. A recurring theme in professional writing and speaking is sharing stories about work with clients, or about one's own life. Both of these areas are ethically sensitive. For example, writing or speaking about oneself may involve mentioning family members. Strategies for handling these ethical dilemmas have been established within the profession (Winship et al., 2024). However, even when great care is taken around preserving the confidentiality of clients or family members, there can still be a residual sense of guilt at personally gaining from sharing information about them.

In conclusion, this chapter has offered several examples of areas in which focused attention to reading, writing and speaking during training might be valuable groundwork for later career activities. However, this list is not comprehensive. Among the many other domains that could have been discussed are teaching, running training or psycho-education workshops, writing case notes, creating podcasts, blogs and social media outputs, writing in the popular press, or being a public intellectual. In a survey of Australian counsellor job advertisements, Beel (2023) found that the majority of employers expected applicants to be able to fulfil an array of functions in addition to providing therapy for clients, including psycho-education, community education, outreach, networking, interdisciplinary and collaborative teamwork, advocacy, administration and paperwork, programme evaluation, prevention and leadership.

At a time of great uncertainty in respect of the sustainability and social cohesion of the Western civilisation and culture of which psychotherapy is an integral element, it is essential for counsellors and psychotherapists to move beyond the boundaries of individualism, and learn how to operate more from a position of solidarity in relation to our clients and with each other (i.e. in our professional community) (McLeod, 2025). This can only happen if we are willing to write and speak in authentic ways that express our sense of the world as we experience it and participate in it.

Top takeaways

The core message of this chapter is that a key aspect and outcome of therapy training should be to enable students to find their own voice as writers and speakers, as well as learning how to be critically appreciative and responsive to other writers and speakers in ways that support them to communicate in their own voice and from their own place in the world.

Recommended reading and key resources

Further exploration of themes introduced in this chapter can be found in the following resources:

- Giffney, N. (2020). A new case study pedagogy for teaching psychoanalytic theory. In S. Frosh, M. Vyrgioti & J. Walsh (Eds.), *The Palgrave handbook of psychosocial studies* (pp. 1–25). Springer International Publishing.

An innovative and inspiring exploration of how engagement with different types of cultural activities and sources can support trainee therapists to deepen their understanding of theory and practice, and find their voice as practitioners.

- Lynne-Joseph, A. (2023). As a clinician, you have to be passionately involved: Advocacy and professional responsibility in gender-affirming healthcare. *Social Science & Medicine, 321*, 115788.

A compelling personal account of how one therapist discovered that working effectively with clients from a disadvantaged group required being willing to speak up on their behalf within a range of community contexts.

References

Alexander, A.A. & Allo, H. (2021). Building a climate for advocacy training in professional psychology. *The Counseling Psychologist, 49*(7), 1070–1089.

APA. (2020). *Publication manual of the American Psychological Association* (7th ed.). American Psychological Association.

Ashley, F. & Domínguez, S. (2021). Transgender healthcare does not stop at the doorstep of the clinic. *The American Journal of Medicine, 134*(2), 158–160.

Beel, N. (2023). More than just counselling: Australian counsellor job advertisement trends. *Psychotherapy and Counselling Journal of Australia, 11*(1). https://doi.org/10.59158/001c.77591

Brown, H.M., Rostosky, S.S., Reese, R.J., Gunderson, C.J., Kwok, C. & Ryser-Oatman, T. (2020). Blessing or BS? The therapy experiences of transgender and gender nonconforming clients obtaining referral letters for gender affirming medical treatment. *Professional Psychology: Research and Practice, 51*(6), 571–579.

Budge, S.L. (2015). Psychotherapists as gatekeepers: An evidence-based case study highlighting the role and process of letter writing for transgender clients. *Psychotherapy, 52*(3), 287–297.

Chapman, R. & Bovell, V. (2022). Neurodiversity, advocacy, anti-therapy. In J.L. Matson & P. Sturmey (Eds.), *Handbook of autism and pervasive developmental disorder: Assessment, diagnosis, and treatment* (pp. 1519–1536). Springer.

Doherty, W.J. (2020). My journey as a citizen therapist. *Journal of Humanistic Psychology, 60*(4), 477–487.

Erikson, M., Erikson, M.G. & Punzi, E. (2020). Reading fiction as a learning activity in clinical psychology education: Students' perspectives. *International Journal of Teaching and Learning in Higher Education, 32*(2), 171–179.

Finlay, L. (2020). How to write a journal article: Top tips for the novice writer. *European Journal for Qualitative Research in Psychotherapy, 10*, 28–40.

Fricker, M. (2017). Evolving concepts of epistemic injustice. In I.J. Kidd, J. Medina & G. Pohlhaus Jr (Eds.), *Routledge handbook of epistemic injustice* (pp. 53–60). Routledge.

Goodman, L.A., Glenn, C., Bohlig, A., Banyard, V. & Borges, A. (2009). Feminist relational advocacy: Processes and outcomes from the perspective of low-income women with depression. *The Counseling Psychologist, 37*(6), 848–876.

Granek, L. & Nakash, O. (2016). The impact of qualitative research on the 'real world': Knowledge translation as education, policy, clinical training, and clinical practice. *Journal of Humanistic Psychology, 56*(4), 414–435.

Holmes, J. (2014). *The therapeutic imagination: Using literature to deepen psychodynamic understanding and enhance empathy.* Routledge.

Kuecker, E. (2024). A closer kind of reading. *International Journal of Qualitative Studies in Education, 37*(6), 1577–1584.

Levitt, H.M. (2020). *Reporting qualitative research in psychology: How to meet APA style journal article reporting standards* (revised edition). American Psychological Association.

McLeod, J. (2015). Reading case studies to inform therapeutic practice. *Psychotherapie Forum*, 20, 3–9.

McLeod, J. (2016). *Using research in counselling and psychotherapy.* Sage.

McLeod, J. (2022). *Doing research in counselling and psychotherapy* (4th ed.). Sage.

McLeod, J. (2024). Reading with love: Developing therapeutic imagination through purposeful engagement with qualitative research. *European Journal of Psychotherapy and Counselling, 26*(3–4), 444–458.

McLeod, J. (2025). *An introduction to counselling and psychotherapy: Theory, research, practice and social purpose* (7th ed.). Open University Press.

Mika, C., Andreotti, V., Cooper, G., Cash, A. & Silva, D. (2020). The ontological differences between wording and worlding the world. *Language, Discourse & Society, 8*(1), 17–32.

Murray, N. & Hughes, G. (2008). *Writing up your university assignments and research projects: A practical handbook.* McGraw Hill.

Ong, W. (1982). *Orality and literacy: The technologizing of the word.* Methuen.

Paré, D.A. (2016). Writing therapeutic notes to young persons. In C.F. Sori, L.L. Hecker & M.E. Bachenberg (Eds.), *The therapist's notebook for children and adolescent* (2nd ed.) (pp. 270–275). Routledge

Råbu, M., McLeod, J., Haavind, H., Bernhardt, I.S., Nissen-Lie, H. & Moltu, C. (2021). How psychotherapists make use of their experiences from being a client: Lessons from a collective autoethnography. *Counselling Psychology Quarterly, 34*(1), 109–128.

Råbu, M., Moltu, C., Binder, P.E. & McLeod, J. (2016). How does practicing psychotherapy affect the personal life of the therapist? A qualitative inquiry of senior therapists' experiences. *Psychotherapy Research, 26*(6), 737–749.

Singh, M.N., Roberts, M.C., McKinney, W.S., Kelly, S., Ortega, A., Doyle, R. & Tampke, E.C. (2023). Advocacy as a professional competency in psychology. *Training and Education in Professional Psychology, 17*(4), 414–422.

Slade, M. & Longden, E. (2015). Empirical evidence about recovery and mental health. *BMC Psychiatry*, *15*, 285. https://doi.org/10.1186/s12888-015-0678-4

Slettevold, E., Fisher, P. & Leddy, A. (2024). Reformulation letters in cognitive analytic therapy: The practitioner's experience. *Counselling and Psychotherapy Research*, *24*(1), 308–316.

Sullivan, C.M. & Goodman, L.A. (2019). Advocacy with survivors of intimate partner violence: What it is, what it isn't, and why it's critically important. *Violence Against Women*, *25*(16), 2007–2023.

Swedberg, R. (2020). 'How do I know what I think till I see what I say?' An aphorism and its implications for creative theorizing. *Distinktion: Journal of Social Theory*, *21*(1), 1–18.

Winship, G., Scott, A. & Edgar, J. (2024). Towards a psychotherapy publishing ethics concordat. *European Journal of Psychotherapy & Counselling*, *26*(3–4), 411–427.

Winter, L.A. & Charura, D. (Eds.). (2023). *The handbook of social justice in psychological therapies: Power, politics, change*. Sage.

9.

Undertaking impactful psychotherapeutic research

Sofie Bager-Charleson, Alistair McBeath, Mary Atito and Alan McPherson

Introduction

This chapter links practical research skills to self-awareness and critical reflection to improve clinical practice. We focus on case studies from qualitative, quantitative and mixed-methods research, holding epistemic disruption, social justice and diversity in mind. Questions for reflection are included throughout this chapter.

Scope of the chapter

We cover the following key topics in this chapter:

- undertaking research journey(s)
- why do research – and how?
- types of research
- improving practice with research
- the importance of a literature review
- quantitative and qualitative research
- the need for epistemic disruption
- reaching out with your research
- you and your research.

Undertaking research journey(s)

We regard research as an invaluable form of lifelong learning. We also hope to communicate our enthusiasm for research. Our research on therapists' experiences of engaging with their own research has highlighted strong responses (Figure 9.1) (Bager-Charleson et al., 2018; Bager-Charleson et al., 2023).

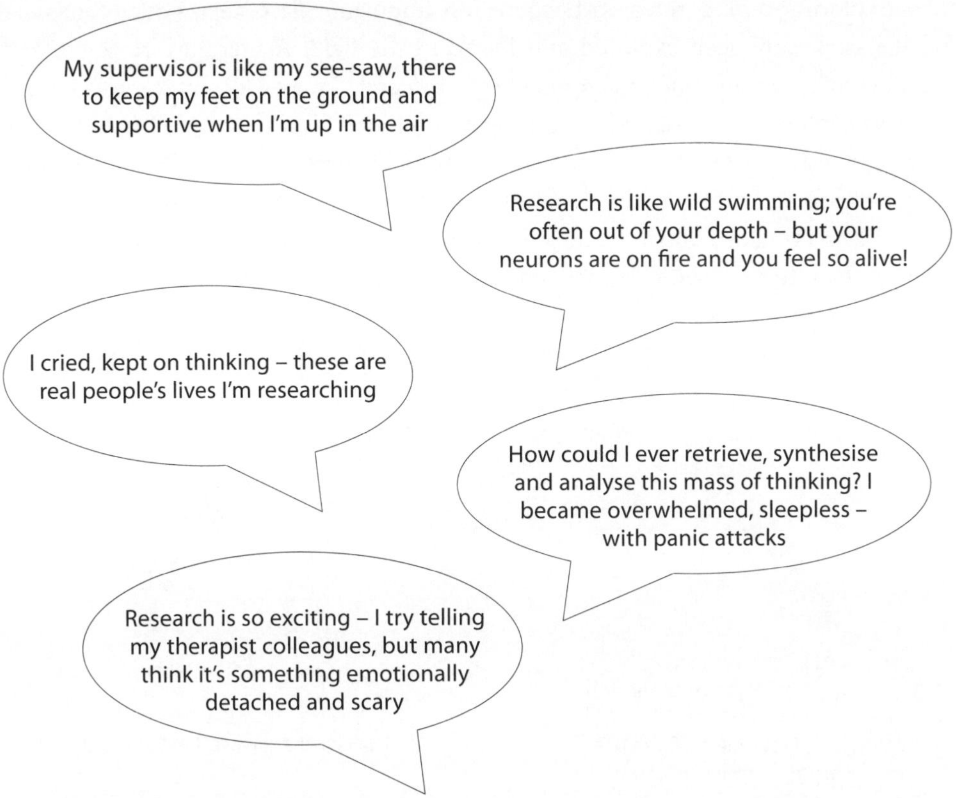

Figure 9.1 Therapists' experiences of research (Bager-Charleson et al., 2018; Bager-Charleson et al., 2023)

We also acknowledge that research 'journeys' often start with the desire to respond to a difficulty identified in therapeutic practice (see Figure 9.2).

Figure 9.2 Reasons for research (Bager-Charleson & McBeath, 2020, 2022)

Exploring others' research becomes an important first step, which considers what has already been explored and found in the field. A literature review offers insight into the many different approaches in research. We will look at some examples in this chapter. Literature reviews can help you to decide what approach suits your question best. Are you, for instance, interested in lived experiences? Or do you hope to generalise and draw on large quantities of data – for instance, to have an impact on policymaking or contribute in other ways on a wider scale? These are questions that can help to guide your chosen approach, as expanded on in Figure 9.3.

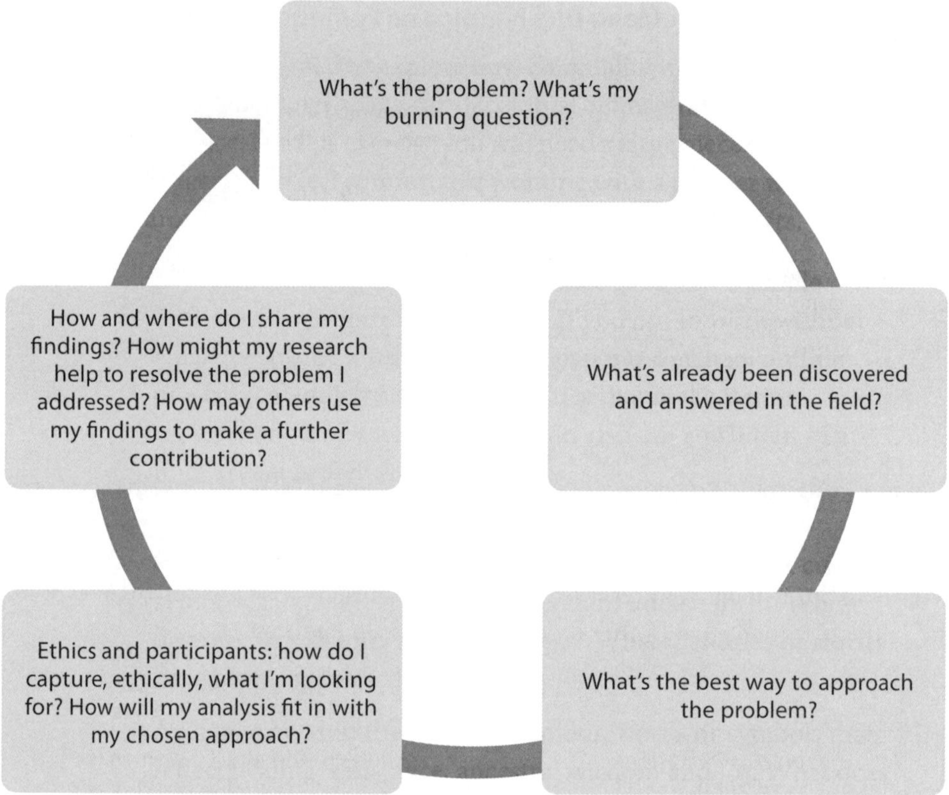

Figure 9.3 Engaging with a research life cycle from question to outcome

Why do research – and how?

We have already described research as lifelong learning. The importance of *knowing about* research is increasingly emphasised. The recently reviewed UKCP Standards of Education and Training (SET) states, for instance, that 'all trainings must encompass principles of psychotherapeutic counselling and psychotherapy research in order to enhance the student/trainee's own practice' (UKCP SET, 2017). The SCoPEd framework for counsellors and psychotherapists also emphasises an ability to 'understand, assess and apply' research to one's own practice as part of the required knowledge and skill competences (SCoPEd, 2022). Therefore, regardless of which psychological therapy professional training path you follow, understanding research and research processes are essential parts of becoming an ethical, evidence-based practitioner.

Types of research

There are, of course, many types of research. An often referred to distinction is made between quantitative and qualitative research. In brief, quantitative research can be described as reliant on measurable data, with a statistical, correlational or hypothesis-testing focus, while qualitative research typically helps to understand how people experience and make sense of the world. Within quantitative research we find, for instance, 'efficacy' research, which seeks to produce clinically measurable effects under 'ideal' conditions, often by testing hypotheses under conditions that are as similar as possible. Rosqvist et al. (2011) describe the goal of efficacy research to establish cause-and-effect relationships between independent (e.g. intervention) and dependent variables (e.g. symptoms), for instance, by testing 'behavioural interventions for sleep' on 'number of hours of sleeping each night'. The study relies on 'reasonable certainty' that other variables, for example antidepressant medication, are not responsible for the change. To avoid both random and systematic errors, the study relies on laboratory-like conditions with close control across all stages. 'Effectiveness' research aims, in turn, to examine interventions in more real-world settings (Rosqvist et al., 2011). It can be either quantitative or qualitative, but seeks to examine outcomes – such as to what extent therapy achieves intended results, under as normal circumstances as possible within wider contexts. 'Practice-based' research reflects, in turn, a broad research domain (Barkham et al., 2024), which also can include both quantitative and qualitative research. Instead of controlling variables, it aims to reflect everyday clinical practice. Co-produced, 'participatory' research develops this further based on what people with a lived experience can advise to improve services. For an overview of different approaches within qualitative, quantitative and mixed-method, please see the recommended reading at the end of the chapter. In this chapter we will expand on practice-based research as an umbrella approach for research aimed to evaluate and develop practice.

You and research

A surprising number of therapists are 'fearful' of research. Our studies (Bager-Charleson & McBeath 2021a, 2021b; Bager-Charleson et al., 2018, 2023, 2024) into how therapists experienced research highlighted a sense of the research being emotionally detached or removed from key aspects of their therapeutic practice. We instead approach research as an invaluable form of lifelong learning through its capacity to:

- address and potentially improve practice-based problems
- stimulate researchable questions and produce new knowledge
- consider and evaluate ongoing research in counselling and psychotherapy
- critically review the use of methodologies and methods in research
- value participants and promote ethical sensitivity in research
- engage with and critique research to heighten sensitivity to power, diversity and social justice
- reflect on the impact and usefulness of research.

The above points need to be considered as a way to inform and improve your research-based practice.

Questions for personal reflection

You will have your own special reasons for doing research, which may be personal, professional, or both. You may therefore want to ask yourself the following questions before embarking on a research study:

- How do you perceive research? What is a researcher, to you; and how do you fit into that perception?

Please also consider the following questions:

- What is your experience of research so far?
- Think of a problem in your practice that you might consider doing research to learn more about and improve upon.

Examples of research to improve practice

Two of the co-authors of this chapter, Mary Atito and Alan McPherson, will share some of their doctoral research experiences as part of their own research journeys. You will read about Mary's Afrocentric-constructivist grounded theory study into Black British men's perceptions of therapy, and about Alan's mixed-methods study into how therapists experience research.

We have focused on some of the early stages of their research life cycle, which include:

- addressing a practice-based problem

- formulating a researchable question
- reviewing others' research in the field
- epistemological and methodological decision-making.

Mary's case study illustrates both how counselling and psychotherapy never exist in a vacuum, and how practice-based problems often have personal and socio-political angles, sometimes calling for innovative methodologies.

Research about unique meanings or generalisable so-called facts?

A common distinction is often made between quantitative and qualitative research, with each having a focus on different outcomes and knowledge claims. The objective, scientific basis of quantitative research may, for instance, involve hypothesis testing, which typically needs large numbers of participants to offer statistical confidence in research findings, and the ability to generalise from those findings. In contrast, the exploratory and interpretative nature of qualitative research methods focuses on understanding the lived experience of individuals within different and/or changing social realities. Like in our clinical practice, we aim to understand more about each person's unique meaning that they attach to events – with an interest in the complex web of lived experience – with the individual's overlapping personal, gender, socio-political and cultural contexts in mind. The richness often lies in the complexity of individuals rather than in high numbers of participants. This means that fewer research participants (Smith & Osborn , 2008) are required for 'validity'. A contrast is sometimes described between nomothetic research (focusing on general principles and patterns applicable to groups) and idiographic research (focusing on understanding individuals in their unique context). Your research interest, coupled with the methodology, will help you decide what approach fits best.

In their research, both Mary and Alan combine subjective and unique individual data with generalising knowledge. Mary's study illustrates, further, the need for methodological innovation and epistemic disruption to explore and understand neglected lived experiences. Alan, too, illustrates a move beyond traditional methodological boundaries, to understand our research participants and share their experiences.

Case studies

Case study 1 (Mary): Black British men's perceptions of therapy – an Afrocentric-constructivist grounded theory study

As a Black British practitioner working in public and private psychological services, I noticed that the engagement in therapy was especially infrequent for Black men. Many who presented emotional trauma around racism collectively felt negative about interacting with psychological services. With the highest number of knife crime offences reported in London in 2019/2020, before the lockdowns introduced during the Covid-19 pandemic, and with the negative media attention surrounding Black men during this time, I found myself increasingly concerned about the wellbeing of the Black community, particularly men.

Case Study 2 (Alan): The silent practice – a mixed-methods exploration of the absence of practising counsellors, psychotherapists and counselling psychologists' contributions to research

How do practising therapists experience being a researcher and engage in the creation and publication of research? Some of the reported challenges in engaging in research include being too busy, managing imposter syndrome, fear of rejection and being good enough. This proposed doctoral research is split into two phases. The first builds on an online survey exploring how therapists engage with research, drawing together quantitative demographic and contextual information, such as modality and research experience, alongside qualitative data pertaining to beliefs in the value of research. The second phase explores the themes identified in phase one, using focus groups and interviews to examine both individual experiences and collective narratives from practising therapists and their engagement with research.

Alan's study provides a helpful context for therapists' engagement in research. Mary and Alan both illustrate how research can start with the acknowledgement of a problem and that something 'is missing'. The next step is, how to approach the problem?

The importance of a literature review

Your literature review describes, summarises or evaluates work already published in the field – and is a crucial step of your study. Are there perhaps already answers out there: what is already researched in this field? The literature review helps to shape the research question and form decisions around methodology and methods.

There are many approaches, including systematic or evidence-based literature reviews, with clear search question(s), and explicit methods for selecting, identifying and critically evaluating relevant research – documented so that others can follow (and evaluate) your search. There are also narrative literature reviews and variations decided by your research approach, as in Mary's example below.

A good literature search should always be methodical, rigorous and transparent. There are powerful search engines such as PsycINFO, PubMed and EBSCO that can deliver a wide range of material if queried correctly. Single words can be searched (e.g. 'depression'), but more powerful and effective is to search on combinations of words such as 'depression' and 'race'. In this case, search engines will only return material containing both linked words.

Grant & Booth (2009) illustrate 14 'review typologies', which are different methods that can be used to review and conduct research. PROSPERO (National Institute for Health and Care Research, 2025) is another helpful source for an overview of research and reviews. A further effective and transparent approach to doing a literature review is to follow the PRISMA (2020) process: PRISMA stands for 'Preferred Reporting Items for Systematic Reviews and Meta-Analyses'. The PRISMA process can generate clear flow charts, which record the process of an increasingly focused and selective search of the literature and show an eventual number of literature sources that are considered to be directly relevant to the key research question of your research. It is also important to note that there are emerging approaches that use AI-based automation tools to assist with systematic searching. It is worth noting, however, that different academic and research institutions have guidelines and policies to inform good academic integrity and ethical practice when using these tools.

We can now see how literature reviews helped to shape Mary's and Alan's research.

Case studies

Case study 1 (Mary)

My research is about Black men's perceptions of therapy, which grew from my literature review. My early literature search highlighted Black men suffering from racial stress due to living in a hostile environment, and yet were typically reluctant to seek assistance for emotional or physical problems. Also identified from the literature was that the Black male population was under-represented in therapy, while overrepresented in psychiatric services.

I decided to use constructivist grounded theory (CGT) as my research method, which allowed me to develop (construct) a theory on Black men's perceptions of therapy. CGT typically approaches the literature review as an ongoing, iterative process. My literature review developed throughout the interviews and the focus group. Especially at the start, I struggled to find appropriate literature through regular online libraries. I searched the literature and found studies on men's health and wellbeing, the way they manage and deal with it, and how this differs from that of women, and found that not a lot is known about Black British men in comparison to their white counterparts in this context. I also found research regarding identity and masculinity and how this plays a part in help-seeking for men in general, and research around depression in men that acknowledged that symptoms of depression need to be defined and considered differently for men in general. This tends to be a core debate linked to male undiagnosed depression and high rates of male suicide. I looked at help-seeking behaviours and coping of Black men and found research on spirituality as a recurring theme. I also found a UK-based study that used grounded theory analysis to explore men's consideration of therapy, but this did not include the narratives of Black men.

Considering the wellbeing of Black men and potential therapeutic support, I looked further at the NICE guidelines and did not find any specific model of therapy for practitioners to utilise when working with Black men. Also, the majority of the research about Black men was American based, outdated, used predominantly with children and adolescents and lacked the voice of participants themselves. What I noticed particularly during my literature search was that the literature did not ask what I believed to be important questions, for example, 'What are Black men's thoughts around therapy as a whole, and do they consider therapy a suitable intervention?'

Alan approached the literature review in a different way to Mary. The section below provides a sense of what his literature review involved. (Note that the references cited in Alan's case study are not listed at the end of this chapter.)

Case study 2 (Alan)

The literature review has been significant in the way the research question and methodological choices have developed. An iterative, hermeneutic process of discovery and rediscovery took place, drawing on Onwuegbuzie and Frels' (2016) seven steps approach. Using databases such as EBSCO, the search began with keywords such as 'practitioner-initiated research', 'research practice gap', 'therapist researcher' and 'scientist researcher'. From the fields of psychotherapy and psychology, the initial search identified the problem of a therapist–researcher gap, without in-depth exploration. Introducing the keyword of 'experience' deepened the review, drawing out more narrative explorations of the lived experiences of practitioners and researchers. The role of research is often mentioned; [therapist] member organisations assert, for instance, that 'the future of psychotherapy is reliant on research' (UKCP 2022), with research having a tangible potential in changing people's lives (BPS, 2018). The Higher Education Academy, however, identified research methods training as 'a weak area in the academic counselling community, as many came into teaching via practice' (Rutten & Hulme, 2013, p. 8). Research argues that training in, and engagement with research should be introduced from the inception of a therapist's training so that research becomes a natural part of a therapist's professional self-definition.

The literature review suggests, in turn, that psychotherapy research typically falls into two camps – either adopting the scientist-practitioner model now connected to evidence-based practice using quantitative methods to analyse therapeutic outcomes, or practice-oriented research drawing on authentic clinical experiences. Research stated how the gap between these two approaches to therapy research has been recently noted. The UK government's preference for evidence-based practice suggests that scientist-practitioner methods are favoured, contributing to a perpetuation of this divide. The search suggested an undeniable therapist–researcher gap within counselling, psychotherapy and counselling psychology clinical practice.

Quantitative and qualitative research

Mary and Alan's choice of methodology for their studies can be considered in the context of a longstanding dispute within research. The dispute starts with what constitutes reality and subsequent relevant knowledge in the field of mental health and emotional wellbeing. These key issues are fundamental to choices and reflections around ontology (the nature of reality), epistemology (the philosophy of knowledge) and methodologies (theoretical approaches to research). See chapters 2 and 3 for more about ontology, epistemology, methodology and theory in psychotherapeutic research.

Critical review of ontological and epistemological considerations for methodologies

An important aspect of choosing a methodology is explaining and critically reviewing our own personal and philosophical positioning in research. As Scotland (2012) asserts: 'It is impossible to engage in any form of research without committing (often implicitly) to ontological and epistemological positions' (p. 10). Figure 9.4 illustrates how each step in research is informed by this process, starting with ontology, epistemology and available pool of data – and progressing to conclusion, beliefs and actions. The reflexive loop invites us to consider this critically.

Philosophical research positions

In brief, some commonly cited epistemological positions derived from different ontological distinctions are positivism, post-positivism, interpretivism and critical theory (see Chapter 2 for more detail). As described earlier in this book, a positivist stance approaches reality as fixed, objective and accessible through measurement and observation (empiricism). In contrast, an interpretivist stance subscribes to a belief in multiple realities, where knowledge is fluid, subjective and constructed through language and social dynamics. We expand on epistemology and methodology in two textbooks (Bager-Charleson & McBeath 2020, 2022) that cover qualitative, quantitative and mixed methods. Some of the qualitative research approaches referred to include phenomenology, interpretative phenomenological analysis (IPA), narrative inquiry, reflexive thematic analysis, auto- and duoethnography and CGT. Mary's CGT study is an example of a co-produced and participatory research project, drawing on multiple perspectives and influences and based on working with people using mental health services in equal (i.e. shared) partnership with those providing them.

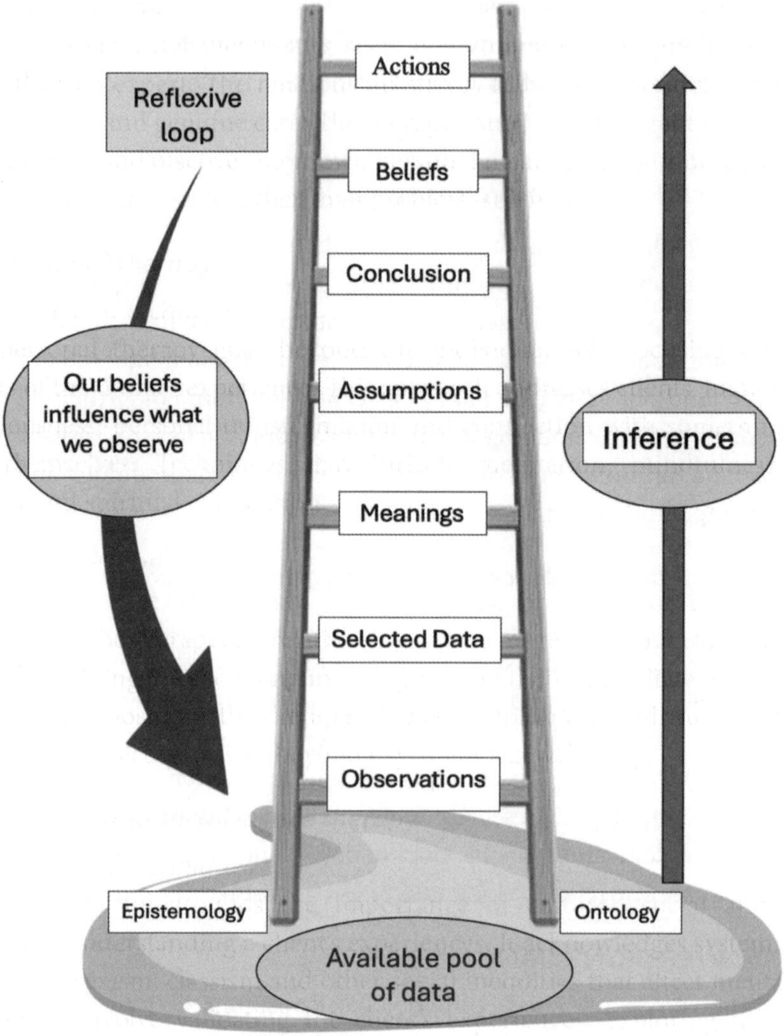

Figure 9.4 Ladder of inference

The need for epistemic disruption

> If we cannot give voice to all in research, how will we meet needs of clients in practice? (Bager-Charleson et al., 2024, p. 15)

Conventional theoretical epistemologies within counselling, psychology and psychotherapy are increasingly criticised for bias and marginalisation, because they leave certain socio-cultural and geopolitical histories positioned 'outside the sentence' (Moodley, 2009).

Charura and Wicaksono (2022) address the need for 'decolonisation' of our research culture, which remains Eurocentric and largely unrepresentative of diversity across many important dimensions of society, with significant effects on clinical practice. This resonates with Moodley's (2009) assertion of the lived experience of people being ignored in research due to their 'gender, ethnicity, sexuality/sexual orientation, disability, social class, religion/faith, age or neurodiversity' (Moodley, 2009, p. 297). In line with this, Ramirez (2021, p. 477) gives an example with specific reference to women from diverse communities, stressing a need for 'resistance and epistemic disobedience' to transgress and transcend 'fixity and binaries' imposed by 'categorizations of ethnic minority academic women' as if 'bodies out of place'.

Examples of epistemic disruption

Both Mary and Alan chose research approaches that sought deep knowledge about individual lived experiences, while also hoping to make some forms of claim about both potentially shared and different experiences among their participants.

Alan explains his research approach as follows:

> I regard psychotherapy as both an art and science, and my research approach reflects this stance. My research aims and questions have been formulated to draw from qualitative, quantitative and mixed-methods paradigms. Mixed-methods research can be inherently difficult… while also presenting opportunities through its dynamism, flexibility and scope. Pragmatism is often cited as a suitable paradigm for mixed-methods research…. There is much flexibility in this paradigm, drawing on the benefits of mixed-methods research in following research questions… without being constrained by an adherence to traditional research philosophies.

Mary's research is aligned with a social constructivist view, with an important focus away from Eurocentric to Afrocentric epistemology. Alan and Mary can both, in this sense, be described as supporting an epistemic disruption of traditionalist research paradigms to improve our therapeutic theory and practice.

Reflexivity plays a significant role here. Reflexivity refers to how our own positioning influences and constructs the collection, selection and interpretation of research data. Finlay and Gough (2003) suggest 'multiple routes' to a 'reflexive journey'. Their concept of 'reflexivity as social critique' (Finlay & Gough, 2003) focuses, for instance, on how socio-economic, gender and sexuality-related aspects affect our positioning in research, as Mary describes in her research. Her case study below shows the role of memo writing in CGT.

Case study 1 (Mary) continued: Black men and therapy – a neglected area

CGT aims to 'discover' a theory that reflects a construction of a shared reality (Charmaz, 2014). I used CGT to construct a theory embedded in an Afrocentric framework, reflecting a shared cultural and historical experience of people of African descent. There is a need for constructivist researchers to acknowledge and address possible power imbalance in the research. With biases in mind, it has been important for me to also be self-aware of my own stereotypes about age, race, gender and socio-economic status, as well as the correlation of those and further demographic factors. To harness the skills of theoretical sensitivity in this research, I first had to explore my own feelings around Black men, together with my beliefs around therapy and my perceived competence around being a novice CGT researcher. As a Black woman, it has thus been important to reflect over my own interest in the therapy among Black men. Growing up in South London I witnessed struggles that my community and I faced, and it was difficult to process and find language to communicate this. Becoming a therapist myself, I found myself concerned about the wellbeing of the Black community, particularly men, as their engagement in therapy was infrequent, but overrepresented in psychiatric services.

I felt impelled to explore this and attempt to adequately address it. I felt a need for significant qualitative understanding for appropriate therapeutic interventions to be developed. This co-produced an alignment that aids the agenda for liberation through therapy with Black men. My study involved in-depth interviews with five men who have, and five who haven't, had previous engagement of therapy, and the themes from that were then explored across two focus groups.

Memo writing

CGT is a qualitative approach that allows researchers to co-construct theory grounded in data and focuses on meaning given to social processes, experienced by participants. It is a fluid process that supports the conceptualisation of themes, codes, properties and categories, where the findings are literally created as the iteration process proceeds. Memo writing is an important part of this, as it forms a written record of the researcher's own thinking and analytical process strategy. Seeking to research within an Afrocentric framework has meant being guided by an African-centred worldview, which has grown out of shared cultural and historical experiences of people of African descent. This view places an emphasis on:

1. the centrality of community and collaborative living
2. acknowledgement and respect for African traditions and cultures
3. a high level of spirituality and ethical concerns

4. harmonious co-existence with nature
5. deep respect for one's elders and the veneration of one's ancestors
6. lastly, the emphasis on education and learning to liberate oneself, to challenge social inequality, and to humanise the world.

The key theoretical frameworks that further help to develop Afrocentricity were agency, centredness, location and orientation, humility, humanity and social justice theory.

Utilising the practice of memo-like notes to record reflections and annotations of the data, this practice was further employed to track the overall milestones and processes in the research progress to date. Therefore, some of those memo-like notes were used to construct this reflexive evaluation.

I followed guidance on memo-like notes as a continual process, which helped me to identify what triggered my lack of confidence. I discussed this with my supervisory team, and I was supported with taking time out of my studies. I used the support of a coach, who supported me with my self-esteem and confidence. We explored themes around trauma, co-dependency, saviour complex, toxic defence mechanism, self-acceptance and self-care, which helped me understand, work through and improve my perception and mindset around myself, and Black men. These steps have enabled me to work through current challenges and continue to reflect on the emotional process of my research.

I recall feeling hopeless and struggled to engage with my research. I felt like an imposter, using my time to support men in the wider community when I had my own young man in need of support. This affected my focus, and as time went by, I couldn't immerse myself in the research. Memo writing helped me to understand this better, (in terms of my positioning in the research). In addition to this, I have a learning difference, which requires me to take more time to process my thoughts and writing. These two combined affected my confidence and relationship with the research.

CGT directs, in this sense, researchers to bring analytical precision to their work, by combining personal reflection and developing theoretical sensitivity.

Reaching out with your research

Getting published in peer-reviewed academic journals is not for the fainthearted. Prepare for rigorous scrutiny and welcome new angles.

Where?

Your literature review will likely guide you towards journals open for your type of questions and chosen methodology. Keeping the mentioned 'ladder of inference' in mind can be useful when exploring options: What kind of epistemological reasoning guides the different journals? Where on the scale between positivist and interpretivist approaches are the journals – and how does your study fit into these? Each approach will use different language and ways to expand on aspects relating to reliability and validity. Across most journals, there is, however, often a shared value applied to what in Figure 9.3 is described as 'research life cycle(s)'. Many journals require articles that follow a prescribed structure: *introduction* with a research question and literature review, followed by a *methods* section where methodology and methods are clearly explained, followed by ethics, data gathering and data analysis before the *results, discussion* and *conclusion* sections (see Figure 9.5).

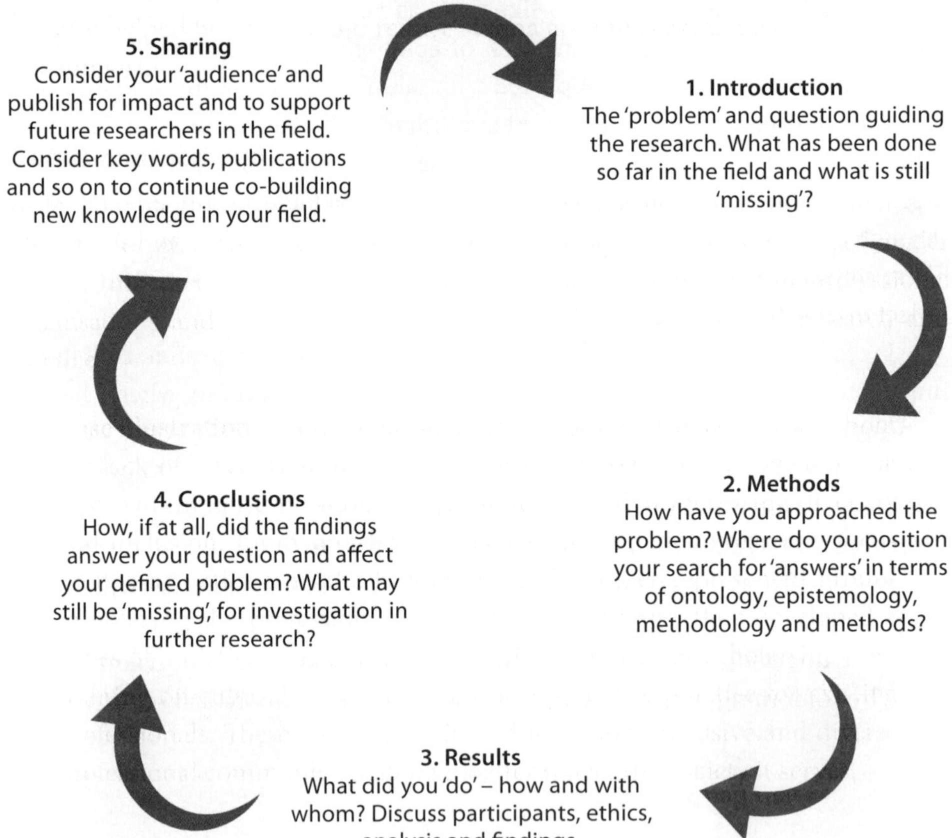

Figure 9.5 Examples of the research life cycle in journal articles

There are various additional ways of disseminating your research to a wider audience – for example, posters, conferences, presentations, podcasts, blogs, interviews, discussions, networking, or promoting your research on social media.

You and your research

We now encourage you to return to a practice-based problem, bearing the examples of Mary's and Alan's research in mind. Divide, if possible, into pairs to discuss the following stages of your own potential research.

How to address a practice-based problem

- Formulate a researchable question for that problem.
- Do a literature review to inform you of research already done in the field.
- Critically review others' and your own choice of methodology and methods.

The items above will have an impact on the considerations and questions later in your journey, namely:

- Consider your participants and ethics.
- How might you choose to analyse your data – what does your methodology suggest?
- What support might you need? What do you hope to gain from your research supervisor? How might you best communicate that?
- Reflect on the impact and usefulness of research.

Top takeaways

This chapter has approached research as valuable lifelong learning, through its capacity to:

- address and potentially improve practice-based problems
- stimulate researchable questions and produce new knowledge
- consider and evaluate ongoing research in counselling and psychotherapy
- critically review the use of methodologies and methods in research
- value participants and promote ethical sensitivity in research
- heighten your sensitivity to power, diversity and social justice within research
- reflect on the impact and usefulness of research.

Recommended reading and key resources

We hope this chapter helps to inspire you about the value of making research part of your practice. Some recommended reading for your journey is listed below.

Quantitative, qualitative and mixed-methods research

- Bager-Charleson, S. & McBeath, A.G. (2022). *Supporting research in counselling and psychotherapy: Qualitative, quantitative and mixed methods.* Palgrave MacMillan.

This book includes practical examples of reflexive thematic analysis, auto- and duoethnography, large- and small-scale surveys and different forms of mixed-methods research. Decolonisation and bridging traditionally opposing approaches in research are significant themes.

- Bager-Charleson, S. & McBeath, A.G. (2020). *Enjoying doing research in counselling and psychotherapy: Qualitative, quantitative and mixed methods.* Palgrave MacMillan.

Guided by the idea that research can be enjoyable, this book builds on the work of experts in approaches like IPA, CGT, narrative inquiry, outcome research, creative use of survey and other research examples.

Research supervision

- Bager-Charleson, S., McBeath, A.G., Charura, D. & Symons, C. (2024). The importance of diversity and inclusion within the research supervision relationship: The views of research students and supervisors. *Counselling and Psychotherapy Research 25*(1), 1–15. https://doi.org/10.1002/capr.12776

This article highlights findings and suggestions for diversity and inclusion in research supervision, including addressing power imbalances and expanding on the terms decolonisation and epistemic disruption.

- Bager-Charleson, S., McBeath, A.G. & Challenor, J. (2023). The relational 3C model for research supervision for counsellors, psychotherapists and counselling psychologists. *Counselling and Psychotherapy Research, 25*(1). https://doi.org/10.1002/capr.12680

This article expands on a study with 250 supervisors and supervisees around experiences of and suggestions for effective, helpful research supervision in therapy-related research.

Academic writing

- Finlay, L. (2020). How to write a journal article: Top tips for the novice writer. *European Journal for Qualitative Research in Psychotherapy, 10*, 28–40.

We wish you all the best on your research journey!

References

Bager-Charleson, S., du Plock, S. & McBeath, A.G. (2018). 'Therapists have a lot to add to the field of research, but many don't make it there'. A narrative thematic inquiry into counsellors' and psychotherapists' embodied engagement with research. *Journal for Language and Psychoanalysis, 7*(1), 4-22. https://doi.org/10.7565/landp.v7i1.1580

Bager-Charleson, S. & McBeath, A.G. (2020). *Enjoying doing research in counselling and psychotherapy: Qualitative, quantitative and mixed methods.* Palgrave MacMillan.

Bager-Charleson, S. & McBeath, A.G. (2021a). Containment, compassion and clarity. Mixed methods inquiry into supervision during doctoral research for psychotherapists and counselling psychologists. *Counselling and Psychotherapy Research, 22*(3), 689-707. https://doi.org/10.1002/capr.12498

Bager-Charleson, S. & McBeath, A.G. (2021b). What support do therapists need to do research? A review of studies into how therapists experience research. *Counselling and Psychotherapy Research,* 1(3), 555-569. https://doi/10.1002/capr.12432

Bager-Charleson, S. & McBeath, A.G. (2022). *Supporting research in counselling and psychotherapy: Qualitative, quantitative and mixed methods.* Palgrave MacMillan.

Bager-Charleson, S., McBeath, A.G. & Challenor, J. (2023). The relational 3C model for research supervision for counsellors, psychotherapists, and counselling psychologists. *Counselling and Psychotherapy Research, 25*(1). https://doi.org/10.1002/capr.12680

Bager-Charleson, S., McBeath, A.G., Charura, D. & Symons, C. (2024). The importance of diversity and inclusion within the research supervision relationship: The views of research students and supervisors. *Counselling and Psychotherapy Research 25*(1), 1–15. https://doi.org/10.1002/capr.12776

Barkham, M., Charura, D., Cooper, M., Gabriel, L., Hanley, T., McLeod, J., Moller, N., Reeves, A. & Smith, K. (2024). The role of BACP in maximising the potential of counselling and psychological therapies research in the UK: Benefitting clients, communities, and societies. *Counselling and Psychotherapy Research, 24*(4), 1–8. https://doi.org/10.1002/capr.12777

British Psychological Society (2018, November 26). *Planning for research excellence.* bps.org.uk/blog/planning-research-excellence

Charmaz, K. (2014). *Constructing grounded theory.* Sage.

Charura, D. & Wicaksono, R. (2022). Doing arts-based decolonising research. In S. Bager-Charleson & A.G. McBeath (Eds.), *Supporting research in counselling & psychotherapy: Qualitative, quantitative and mixed methods* (pp. 39–55). Palgrave MacMillan.

Finlay, L. & Gough, B. (2003). *Reflexivity: A practical guide for researchers in health and social sciences.* Wiley.

Grant, M.J. & Booth, A. (2009). A typology of reviews: An analysis of 14 review types and associated methodologies. *Health Information & Libraries Journal, 26*(2), 91–108. https://doi.org/10.1111/j.1471-1842.2009.00848.x

Moodley. R. (2009). *Outside the sentence: Readings in critical multicultural counselling and psychotherapy.* CDCP.

National Institute for Health and Care Research. (2025, September). *What is PROSPERO*? https://www.crd.york.ac.uk/PROSPERO/#aboutpage

Onwuegbuzie, A.J. & Frels, R. (2016). *7 steps to a comprehensive literature review: A multimodal & cultural approach*. Sage Publications.

PRISMA. (2020, September). *PRISMA 2020 checklist*. https://prisma.shinyapps.io/checklist/

Ramirez, C.C. (2021). Epistemic disobedience and grief in academia. *Education Science, 11*(9), 477. https://doi.org/10.3390/educsci11090477

Rosqvist, J., Thomas, J.C. & Truax, P. (2011). Effectiveness versus efficacy studies. In J.C. Thomas & M. Hersen (Eds.), *Understanding research in clinical and counseling psychology* (2nd ed., pp. 319–354). Routledge/Taylor & Francis Group.

Rutten, A. & Hulme, J. (2013, September). Learning and teaching in counselling and psychotherapy. *The Higher Education Academy*. https://documents.advance-he.ac.uk/download/file/document/1927

SCoPEd (2022). A shared framework for the scope of practice and education for counselling and psychotherapy with adults. https://www.bacp.co.uk/about-us/advancing-the-profession/scoped/scoped-framework/

Scotland, J. (2012). Exploring the philosophical underpinnings of research: Relating ontology and epistemology to the methodology and methods of the scientific, interpretive and critical research paradigms. *English Language Teaching, 5*(9), 9–16.

Smith, J.A. & Osborn, M. (2008). Interpretative phenomenological analysis. In J.A. Smith (Ed.), *Qualitative psychology: A practical guide to research methods* (pp.53–80). Sage.

United Kingdom Council for Psychotherapy. (2017, September). *UKCP standards of education and training (2017): The minimum core criteria psychotherapy with adults*. https://www.psychotherapy.org.uk/media/52glceaa/ukcp-adult-standards-of-education-and-training-2017.pdf

United Kingdom Council for Psychotherapy. (2022). *Research*. https://www.psychotherapy.org.uk/policy-and-research/research/

10.

Clinical placements, supervision and safeguarding

Ariana Jordan

Introduction

I knew I wanted to help people…

This chapter focuses on placements, supervision and safeguarding, which are key aspects of your training as a counsellor, counselling psychologist or psychotherapist. Included in this chapter are key questions that I wish I had known in my training as a counselling psychologist, so that you might feel better equipped for the journey ahead. Also included are *quotes from current trainees* (shown in italics throughout the chapter), so you can learn from their experiences.

We'll begin with what can feel like a less helpful companion on your learning journey: anxiety. You may or may not be aware of what has brought you to want to train in your chosen profession. For many people, they know they want to help people, but underlying, deeper motivations will also affect your learning journey and your experiences and responses on the course, on placement, and in supervision. It would be useful to explore this in personal therapy from the outset, so that you can be prepared and supported on the psychological and emotional aspects of your training.

Your personal and professional development is the foundation of your progression, and so you will be continually assessed on your readiness for the profession. For most people, this continual assessment triggers all kinds of thoughts and feelings of judgement by others, imposter syndrome being a common one. This anxiety can then be expressed in a variety of ways and can affect your relationships with tutors and colleagues. Your course tutors will expect you to learn how to accept the inevitable anxiety on your learning journey and to manage it so that you behave in a professional manner at all times. This includes on placement, at your learning institution, and on social media.

You will read more about self-care and professionalism in chapters 12 and 13, respectively. However, one way of managing anxiety in relation to your performance on placement, is in preparation. A key aspect of placement learning, indeed all your learning on your training course, is organisation. It is your responsibility to meet training institution deadlines and no one else's; this means allowing extra time when progress reports and paperwork are due, in case of supervisor holidays and any unforeseen circumstances.

Scope of the chapter

This chapter addresses the following key questions:

- How do I find a suitable placement that will complement my learning and provide me with the necessary challenges and support?
- How can I make the most of the placement experience in order to equip myself with the necessary tools for my chosen field?
- How do I handle difficult situations, such as the risk of falling short of the client hours requirement?
- What is the importance of supervision and what makes a beneficial and enriching supervision experience?
- What is meant by safeguarding and what are the key points I need to know as a healthcare practitioner, including when and how to take action, when needed?

Placements

Be clear about the trajectory and timelines of various placements over the years. Don't necessarily rule out specialist services at the beginning.

Placements offer a unique opportunity to apply theory into practice and make all your classroom learning come alive. Placements also enable you to consolidate your decision to follow this profession – coming away from a 'good' session with a client, where you felt you were able to support them at a time of distress or confusion, is what makes the intensity of the training worthwhile.

In addition, placements are an ideal opportunity to gain experience working with the client groups and areas in which you are interested. If you want to work with children, consider placements like Place to Be or an organisation that uses creative arts therapies. Once you are more experienced, you might want to apply to a child and adolescent mental health service (CAMHS). Likewise, you might have a special interest in working in prisons, schools, or with a particular difficulty, such as eating disorders. Be mindful of qualification requirements – some courses require experience in multiple settings. The key is to plan your placement pathway carefully so that you can explore as many opportunities as possible ahead of graduating and establishing yourself in a particular field.

In your placement you will follow professional and ethical guidelines set by accrediting bodies like the Quality Assurance Agency (QAA) and organisations such as the BACP, UKCP and HCPC (also see Chapter 15). Your training should equip you to become a 'self-reflective, evidence-based, ethical practitioner' (QAA, 2022). Throughout your training, you'll integrate theory with practice and work towards specific placement learning outcomes.

Plan for NHS placements

While not essential for all programmes, an NHS placement is extremely valuable. You will be well supported and offered experience in a multidisciplinary team, with group facilitation, ongoing training, and insights into wider systems affecting client work. You can choose to work in various departments and with various client groups, thereby gaining specialist knowledge. It also means the possibility of being offered a permanent role in the NHS once you graduate.

Finding a placement

Finding a suitable placement can feel overwhelming, especially if you are not certain what to look for. Some institutions allocate you a placement and you have little choice in the matter. Other courses will expect you to find your own placement. This process can sometimes be disappointing because either you are not given the placement you would like, or one you have chosen is not approved by your institution. As a rule, placement providers have to have suitable policies and procedures in place, offer an induction to introduce you to these policies and procedures, and have suitably qualified and experienced counsellors/psychotherapists/psychologists or placement educators running the organisation. These components are important to ensure that you will be adequately supported in your placement experience and that they mitigate any potential risk. It is important you keep an open mind as you embark on this process – other people's experiences are not necessarily going to be your experiences. Of course, if you do have a concern over a placement, then do bring this up with your tutor or placement coordinator.

Start a shortlist of possible placements early, especially if you live in a rural area, and check your training institution's placement criteria. Contact local mental health charities, for example MIND or CRUSE Bereavement, as they often accept trainees. Be sure to have an updated CV, which includes all relevant helping experience. You may then be invited in for interview. It is then very much a matter of 'fit' – whether your professional manner and way of working aligns with the organisation's main modality and ethos.

Meeting clinical hours requirements

> *Find a placement that can offer a steady flow of clients.*

Training institutions often require a set number of client hours, including both in-person and online work. Regularly track your hours, and if you're falling short, seek a second placement. Your flexibility with finding a second placement will, of course, vary from trainee to trainee: for those with children or caring responsibilities, or those who need to allow more time for paid work, you might want to consider having an online placement, if your training institution allows this.

> *Attending peer support groups and regular meetings with the clinical placement onsite manager [helped]. The experience of being offered free CPD and regular placement training helped significantly to stay up to date with psychotherapy practice.*

Do remember it is not all about gaining clinical hours, and that professional practice and clinical skills can be developed by engaging with non-clinical work, for example, in meetings with colleagues, group facilitation and further training.

If things go wrong

Occasionally, challenges may arise on placement; for example, you might not feel comfortable with something said by your placement supervisor, or maybe you have been at the placement for several months and are still waiting for clients, or a safeguarding challenge arises and your placement supervisor disagrees with your external supervisor on the best course of action. If you feel uncomfortable or encounter issues, raise concerns with your supervisor. They can then support you in raising the matter with the placement directly. Sensitive matters should always be approached in a non-judgemental, relational manner, thereby enabling a progressive conversation to take place. Remember that you are looking to cultivate the core conditions of empathy, congruence and unconditional positive regard (Rogers, 1959) in every relationship – both personal and professional.

Paperwork

The paperwork often involved in placement experiences can seem like the bane of a trainee's life. However, it can be divided into key areas:

- approval paperwork (for self-found placements)
- client hour logs
- supervision hour logs

- progress report forms
- end-of-placement feedback.

This documentation ensures that you are meeting your training objectives and provides feedback for your development. It is also important for the placements team at your training institution, to ensure the quality of placement provision is maintained and monitored.

Mentoring

Some organisations, like the Black, African and Asian Therapy Network (BAATN) and BACP, provide mentoring services to help guide your professional development:

- https://www.baatn.org.uk/mentoring-programme/
- https://www.bacp.co.uk/about-us/mentoring-scheme/

Top tips for getting the most out of your placement

Your placement experience is fundamental to being able to apply your learning where it matters – in the therapy room – so take time to plan the whole experience, from beginning to end:

- **Initial preparation:** Shortlist possible placements and confirm they meet your institutional and own practical requirements in terms of travel time, location, length of commitment and life circumstances.
- **At the beginning of the placement:** Read through policies and procedures to increase knowledge and confidence. Have a pre-placement meeting to go through expectations of the placement – what is the dress code? How and when does supervision take place? How much flexibility is there in terms of the number of clients seen and the hours/days worked? Will someone more experienced be assessing clients first?
- **During the placement:** Stay on top of paperwork and prepare well for reviews and supervision. Track your hours and progress, and ensure you meet all requirements. Reflect regularly, using your logs and reviews to guide your learning.
- **Ending the placement:** Prepare for ending with clients, finalise outstanding paperwork and provide placement feedback to your institution.

By staying organised, seeking support and planning ahead, you will maximise the benefits of your placement experience.

Clinical supervision

I grew throughout the process.

Alongside the placement experience, clinical supervision is crucial in building your confidence and competence as a trainee in psychotherapy or counselling. Supervision provides both practical guidance and emotional support as you develop your clinical skills. It is important, therefore, to work with a supervisor who is experienced and qualified in your specific modality (e.g. psychodynamic, CBT) and who is familiar and aligns with your training requirements. It is also beneficial to experience different supervisors throughout your training to gain a range of perspectives and find what works best for you. These multiple perspectives and ways of working will all contribute to your own model of integration in your clinical practice. In addition, they will be beneficial if you go on to become a supervisor in the longer term after you have qualified and gained the necessary experience.

Supervision sessions should be planned carefully, with time dedicated to preparing key questions or challenges, bearing in mind the confidentiality of your clients. A useful tool to prepare for supervision is the client log for supervision (see Appendix 1). After each session, use this log to capture any key challenges or questions that arise in the session. As you prepare for supervision, you just need to look on your log, and the questions for supervision will be ready for you. You can also record your supervisor's guidance and keep track of which clients might be 'forgotten about' and brought to supervision less frequently.

Finding a supervisor

Be sure to allow plenty of time to find a suitable supervisor: you will normally have to have at least one or two supervision sessions before your first session with a client. It is important to establish clear expectations with your supervisor from the beginning, known as contracting, including practical details like meeting frequency, location (online or in person), fees (don't be afraid to ask if there is a trainee discount), and how and when to contact them in case of a critical incident with a client. How will you receive feedback and what is required from you in preparation for each session? (Some supervisors might require you to give a brief overview of all your clients before you focus on key questions/clients for the session.) Also, be clear on when your goals will be reviewed.

If in-person supervision is required by your training institution, bear in mind that some geographical areas are better resourced for supervisors than others:

Primary supervision was challenging to find. Not that many supervisors on the register where I lived at the time... I spent a lot of time travelling.

According to your training requirements, you may have a placement supervisor, an external supervisor (i.e. someone who works externally to the placement), or both. If you have both, consider having a three-way meeting at the start of your work together to introduce each other and to establish how risk and safeguarding processes will be managed between you. It is also important that your supervisor has been trained to at least the level of your training (e.g. if you are studying for a doctorate in counselling psychology, that the supervisor has a doctorate in counselling or clinical psychology), or has suitable experience and qualifications that are congruent with the modalities of practice. That way, they will have a clearer understanding of the demands of your training. Even if your placement supervisor is not approved by your institution, you will still need to attend placement supervision (otherwise referred to as 'secondary supervision'), which will often be held in a group. This will still be a valuable experience, even though you might not be able to count the hours:

> *Secondary supervision was always interesting. As an integrative trainee, it was very rich to hear and see so many different approaches from supervisors and fellow supervisees.*

Your supervisor will need to be approved by your training institution and aligned with your therapeutic modality, because this consolidates the theory and will greatly enhance your confidence and progress. There may be a list of approved supervisors that you can work from. Ideally, your placement, supervision and personal therapy would all align to support the focus of your course; so if you are currently studying CBT, you would be practising CBT in your placement, be supervised by someone experienced in CBT, and also be in therapy with a CBT-informed therapist. This is the ideal situation, of course, and it can be difficult to align all three elements in such a way.

Sometimes, it might be advisable to gain extra supervision, even if only one or two sessions, with a specialist supervisor who has expertise in a particular area. The specialist knowledge gained will be invaluable:

> *Additional access to supervision for special occasional circumstances was particularly supportive. We called it 'closing the loop' when dealing with a critical incident.*

What to expect from good supervision

Clinical supervision serves several important functions in your professional development: according to the BPS website, clinical supervision should 'offer Psychologists intellectual challenges enabling reflection, transformational learning and psychological support to maximise their responsibility for appropriate self-care' (BPS, 2024). You should feel able to explore a range of questions openly, without fear of judgement. The professional and regulatory bodies all publish their own guidelines for effective supervision. While this will be addressed on your course, it would be worth your while reading those that apply to your training programme. Here is a link to one example from the BACP supervision guidelines: https://www.bacp.co.uk/membership/supervision/

When you first meet your supervisor, you will be contracting about how you will work together and will discuss mutual expectations. This will be a good opportunity to share the course programme handbook and to discuss availability and any upcoming holidays, particularly around assignment deadlines. Three months before any progress reports are due, remind your supervisor of the upcoming deadline, so you both have time to prepare.

What do I take to supervision?

Of primary importance are any safety concerns – yours or your client's. The way clients are allocated to you varies from placement to placement, but you can expect an experienced counsellor to be carrying out the initial assessments until you are confident and competent to do so. Your clients will therefore be allocated to you. Upon receipt of the referral, read through the assessment notes and think about questions that might be useful to address with your supervisor; for example, thinking about safety first, does your client have a history of self-harm, or any present thoughts of self-harm or suicide? You should highlight any safety concerns with your supervisor as you talk through your first meeting with the client, and how you will approach this, given their family, medical and relational history. Please note that if you are a trainee with little experience, you should not be allocated any complex clients in the first stages of your placement experience. Your supervisor should be able to support you in reviewing the suitability of your client allocation, bearing in mind your level of experience, competence and the requirements of your training programme.

Risk assessments are not only carried out when first meeting a client, but should also be a regular part of your therapeutic work. As your skills in formulation (the client's 'story') develop, you will learn to use formulation to highlight potential risks and appropriate risk management and use supervision to guide you through this process (see more on assessment and formulation in Chapter 7). Your placement should have clear policies and procedures to support you in taking appropriate action when there are potential risk issues.

If any questions come up, or you feel any discomfort in your clinical practice, talk to your supervisor in the first instance. Although this may feel scary, it is an important and learned skill to be able to approach difficult questions, find your voice, and do so with respect and courtesy, while still making yourself heard. Taylor (2023) reminds us of the importance of creating a safe space for everyone's 'experiences and insights'. This is important not only for your own development, but also so you can learn to make space for the diverse experiences of your clients. Of course, it is a shared responsibility to provide the safe space for these conversations to take place (there is more on this in Chapter 6). If you need support in approaching your supervisor, turn to your personal tutor. In summary, effective supervision helps you develop and refine your practice, better understand clients and feel more confident in your role.

Top tips on making the most of supervision

- Your supervisor should initially contract with you so that you both have a clear understanding of expectations from both sides.
- You should leave supervision sessions feeling supported and held.
- You should feel safe enough to share questions and uncertainties without the fear of being judged or criticised.
- Supervision enhances your learning, helping you grow as a practitioner with confidence and competence.
- Supervision should also be a place where matters of equality, diversity, inclusion and reflections on identity, culture, language, values and worldviews can be explored.

Safeguarding

A key requirement from your placement learning is knowing the procedures in place when you have concerns over safety. Doing our best to provide safety for a client is our legal responsibility. Safeguarding means 'protecting a citizen's health, wellbeing and human rights; enabling them to live free from harm, abuse and neglect. It is… a collective responsibility' (NHS England, n.d.). You will recall that, in the placements section, I mentioned becoming familiar with the policies and procedures on your placement. Safeguarding should be the first area you cover. You want to make sure you are clear on the pathway before you are called to put it into action.

Case studies

Types of safeguarding challenges

Depending on your placement, various safeguarding challenges can arise. Here are two examples:

Example 1: You are allocated an adult client with a moderate learning disability who has a history of sexual and physical abuse from family members. She has been referred by her GP due to low mood. In the initial assessment, the carer (a family member) seems very obliging and keen to engage, and you arrange a suitable day and time for the therapy sessions. The client is also keen to engage, raising her head to answer your questions, but then lowering it and remaining quiet in between. However, the client is not brought to the first session. When you ring the carer, they tell you the client is unwell and so won't be attending. The next session, they do the same, and continue in this way, often sending you a message to reschedule just an hour before the scheduled session time. This continues for four further sessions. You remember that in the first session, the carer had turned to the client and acknowledged that they sometimes 'get stressed' with the client but that they 'don't mean it'.

In this first example, a vulnerable person is being neglected by not being brought to her healthcare appointments. Her low mood at initial assessment could be due to past trauma and/or present unsafe circumstances. The behaviour of the carer in this case – being very obliging and keen to engage in the first assessment and then avoiding sessions from then on – raises concern. As the care arrangements are unclear, and the client has a history of abuse, a review of the care package is necessary to ensure the client's needs are being adequately met. The review could also identify support needs of the carer.

Example 2: You are working with a young person who has been diagnosed with ADHD and autism. He has been referred to you due to behavioural challenges inside and outside of the home and verbal and physical aggression, mainly directed towards his family. Over time, the young man's behaviour becomes more dangerous and his parents are increasingly less able to keep him safe. On one occasion, they resort to locking him out of the house to protect his younger sister from his outburst.

In Example 2, there is potential harm not only to the young person, but also his parents, sister and anyone else affected by his behaviour. It is better in this case to discuss your concerns with the parents and let them know that you feel they should be supported in their role to ensure safety all round and that you will be sending a report to the local safeguarding team. Given their struggle and the stress they are likely to experience, they will hopefully be in agreement to refer their case.

As with all safeguarding concerns, it is important to discuss these with your placement supervisor in the first instance, so that you can be supported in following the correct procedure. You will also be supported by the laws and ethical frameworks of governing bodies. Some useful resources that will also help guide you are:

- BACP Ethical Framework (2018)
- UKCP Code of Ethics and Professional Practice (2019)
- National Counselling Society (NCS) Ethical Framework (2016) – now NCPS
- The Care Act (2014)
- The Children Act (1989, 2004)
- Human Rights Act (1998)
- Equality Act (2010)
- Mental Health Act (2007)
- Mental Capacity Act (2005)
- Corey at al.'s 8 steps of ethical decision-making (2018)
- safeguarding training for adults, which will normally be provided by your placement.

Top takeaways

- Ensure you make the most of your placement experience by exploring the types of placement you are interested in, in terms of client group and/or areas of presenting difficulty.
- Know the safeguarding procedures in place at your placement and what to do if you have concerns over a client.
- Carefully consider clinical supervision – what to expect from a supervisor – and what to do if you feel uncomfortable in any way.
- Always hold in mind that supervision should serve to offer you professional support, and enhance your personal and professional development and wellbeing.

Questions for reflection

- What questions do I have with regard to safeguarding challenges?
- What procedures and policies does my placement have in place to support me, and how familiar am I with these?
- Who and what are available resources for any issues arising in relation to my placement?
- How will supervision help me in relation to safeguarding challenges?

Further resources

Placement opportunities

In addition to your own training organisation, some professional bodies can put you in touch with other placements and job opportunities:

https://www.baatn.org.uk/jobs/#view
https://www.bacp.co.uk/careers/find-jobs-and-placements/

Support, funding and mentoring opportunities

Training to be a counselling psychologist or psychotherapist is a challenging but immensely rewarding experience. Further sources of support can be found in Appendix 2.

Recommended reading and key resources

On your placement, you will be working with diverse populations. In order to broaden your awareness of power and difference and strengthen your cultural competence, the following texts might be useful.

- Ade-Serrano, Y. & Nkansa-Dwamena, O. (2025). *Reimagining race in psychology: Challenging narratives and widening perspectives in training and practice*. Routledge.
- Charura, D. & Lago, C. (2021). *Black identities and white therapies*. PCCS Books.
- Hills, J., Christodoulidi, F. & Charura, D. (2023). A duoethnographic study of power and privilege in the psychotherapeutic space: Dialogical research as professional development. *International Journal of Qualitative Methods*, *22*, 1–11. https://doi.org/10.1177/16094069231199903
- Nerenberg, N. (2021). *Divergent mind: Thriving in a world that wasn't designed for you*. Harper Collins.

References

BACP. (2018). *Ethical framework for the counselling professions* [Online]. Lutterworth: BACP. https://www.bacp.co.uk/events-and-resources/ethics-and-standards/ethical-framework-for-the-counselling-professions/

British Psychological Society. (2024). *Supervision guidance for psychologists*. https://www.bps.org.uk/guideline/supervision-guidance-psychologists

Care Act 2014, c. 23. (2014). *Legislation.gov.uk*. https://www.legislation.gov.uk/ukpga/2014/23/contents/enacted

Children Act 1989, c. 41 (UK). https://www.legislation.gov.uk/ukpga/1989/41/contents/enacted

Children Act 2004, c. 31. https://www.legislation.gov.uk/ukpga/2004/31/contents

Corey, G., Corey, M.S. & Callanan, P. (2018). *Issues and ethics in the helping professions* (9th ed.). Brooks/Cole.

Equality Act 2010, c. 15. (2010). *Legislation.gov.uk*. https://www.legislation.gov.uk/ukpga/2010/15/contents/enacted

Human Rights Act 1998, c. 42 (UK). https://www.legislation.gov.uk/ukpga/1998/42/contents/enacted

Mental Capacity Act 2005, c. 9. (2005). *Legislation.gov.uk*. https://www.legislation.gov.uk/ukpga/2005/9/contents/enacted

Mental Health Act 2007, c. 12. (2007). *Legislation.gov.uk*. https://www.legislation.gov.uk/ukpga/2007/12/contents/enacted

National Counselling Society. (2016). *Ethical framework for the counselling professions*. National Counselling Society. https://ncps.com/about-us/code-of-ethics

NHS England. (n.d.). *About NHS England safeguarding*. NHS England. https://www.england.nhs.uk/safeguarding/about/

Quality Assurance Agency for Higher Education. (2022). *The quality code for higher education: Part A – setting and maintaining academic standards*. Quality Assurance Agency for Higher Education. https://www.advance-he.ac.uk/knowledge-hub/quality-assurance-agency-qaa-uk-quality-code-higher-education

Rogers, C.R. (1959). A theory of therapy, personality, and interpersonal relationships: As developed in the client-centered framework. In S. Koch (Ed.), *Psychology: A study of a science. Formulations of the person and the social context* (Vol. 3, pp. 184–256). McGraw Hill.

Taylor, F. (2023). *Unruly therapeutic: Black feminist writings and practices in living room*. Norton Professional Books.

UKCP. (2019). *Code of ethics and professional practice*. United Kingdom Council for Psychotherapy. https://www.psychotherapy.org.uk/media/bkjdm33f/ukcp-code-of-ethics-and-professional-practice-2019.pdf

11.

Becoming a reflective practitioner

Charlotte O'Brien and Divine Charura

Introduction

Reflective practice is a central tenet and core value of all counselling psychology and psychotherapeutic training pathways. In fact, all the psychotherapeutic professional bodies highlight the importance of reflective practice as part of ethical and professional practice. For example, the HCPC (2023) explicitly require reflective practice as a core competency for qualified therapeutic practitioners, deeming it essential for psychological practitioners to reflect on and review their practice in order to:

- support continuous professional improvement
- critically consider the 'use of self' in the therapeutic process
- critically evaluate their practice and consider alternative ways of working
- understand models used in supervision and their contribution to practice
- recognise the value of multi-disciplinary reviews, case conferences and other methods.

BACP (2018), in its ethical framework, highlights supervision as one of the forums in which therapists can reflect on how to sustain good practice throughout their working life, by providing practitioners with 'regular and ongoing opportunities to reflect in depth about all aspects of their practice in order to work as effectively, safely and ethically as possible' (BACP, 2018, p. 22).

Given that this chapter will be read by trainees and practitioners internationally, we also note that other professional bodies, such as the American Counseling Association (ACA) (2014), highlight the importance of therapists being aware of their own values, attitudes, beliefs and behaviours, and avoid imposing them on clients they work with. In line with this, the process of reflection and CPD facilitates the ongoing respect of clients' and research participants' intersectional aspects of difference and diversity. It also enables the identification of areas in which training can be undertaken to practise in a non-discriminatory manner and minimise the risk of imposing one's own values onto clients (ACA, 2014).

In this chapter we introduce you to the concept of reflective practice, exploring what it is, why we do it and how we can effectively use both traditional and contemporary models. We will provide a broad overview of reflective practice with a keen focus on helping you to identify the right reflective practice for you. We will also consider the concept of reflexivity and how we can use this as part of a reflective cycle to place our learning back into our therapeutic practice and research.

Scope of the chapter

In this chapter we will discuss the following:

- reflective practice – what it is and why we do it
- models of reflective practice – traditional, group and peer-to-peer, creative, contemporary, supervisory and therapeutic approaches
- a critique on how reflective practice is presently conceptualised and operationalised
- reflexivity – putting our reflective learning back into our work.

We present a case study as an example of reflective practice including negotiating complexities, challenges and learning that might emerge in the therapeutic relationship. We also highlight the importance of engaging with a transcultural and anti-discriminatory approach to reflective practice and provide an exercise to encourage you try out a model. At the end of the chapter, we provide several reflective questions for you to begin to explore and build your own unique approach to an authentic reflective practice.

Reflective practice – what it is and why we do it

A good introduction to the concept of reflective practice is provided by Linda Finlay (2008, p. 1) who defines it succinctly as:

> Learning through and from experience towards gaining new insights of self and practice.

Finlay (2008) notes that there are many different models of reflective practice, yet each aims towards the same goal – namely, to help us to unpick our learning and make links between what we *think* and what we *do* in therapeutic practice. This learning is then iteratively and reflexively put back into our work, with the aim of creating new enhanced therapeutic experiences and best practices for our clients, thereby completing a reflective cycle (British Psychological Society, 2024).

Cooper & Wieckowski (2017) propose that reflective practice in psychological therapy is a crucial process that is essential to intricately examine our own counselling sessions and techniques. In fact, it is common in many modalities, such as psychoanalysis, to record and review entire sessions with a supervisor, to explore what you did moment-by-moment in the session and why. This helps you to re-assess your practice retrospectively and consider alternative actions (see the case study later in this chapter). Reflective practice is also an essential process of self-examination, which enables us to enhance our own self-awareness, assist personal and professional growth and, perhaps most importantly, continuously improve the care we provide to our clients.

Newton (2025) argues that reflective practice is also fundamental for us to address our implicit biases, enabling a shift from passive awareness to an active commitment to social change. This means recognising and disrupting harmful systems, elevating marginalised voices, which are often left outside of the sentence, and implementing practices that promote inclusion and equity (Newton, 2025). It is also a vital part of ethical practice, helping us to develop the ability to manage our own personal values so that they do not unduly influence the therapeutic process. Kocet and Herlihy (2014) assert that by using reflective practice we can enable a process of *ethical bracketing*, whereby we can intentionally set aside our personal values, worldviews and belief systems, and mitigate their potential impact on the client or therapeutic process.

Models of reflective practice

In this section we present the most commonly taught traditional models of reflective practice in higher education. We also explore the value of group and peer-to-peer reflective models, creative approaches for reflection, and examine some contemporary ideas of reflective practice using new technologies, such as AI. Finally, we consider the benefits of reflective practice in both the supervisory and therapeutic relationships.

Traditional models

We begin by exploring the three core traditional models of reflective practice. Feel free to try them out as we go or choose one that you would like to explore in the future.

Gibbs's reflective cycle

This model was developed by Graham Gibbs in 1988 to help individuals learn from experiences by providing a structured approach to reflection. It commonly involves six main stages, and many templates and guidelines are available (e.g. York St John University, 2025):

1. Description – of the topic for reflection, including what happened, when it occurred, who was involved and the outcome.
2. Feelings – this stage asks you (the person reflecting) to explore your emotional response to the situation, how you felt and how others reacted.
3. Evaluation – in this stage, you assess both the positive and negative aspects of the experience, making objective judgements about what worked well and what didn't.
4. Analysis – this stage asks you to make sense of the situation, identifying what you think was going on, considering any contributing factors, and understanding the underlying reasons for your reactions and outcome(s).
5. Conclusion – here you are asked to draw conclusions from your experiences, identifying what you have learned, and what you might have done differently.
6. Action plan – based on your conclusions, you develop a clear plan for how you can approach a similar situation in the future and outline any specific actions you will take based on what you have learned during this reflective cycle.

The positive aspects of Gibbs's reflective cycle are that it encourages a deep exploration of a particular experience, including both the positive and negative aspects. It also identifies an explicit action plan and key areas for development, with clear steps on how to do it. However, the general critique of this method is that, as with all the traditional models of reflection, it relies heavily on a written approach and using cognitive and analytic functions, which some trainees may struggle with if they have physical disabilities, dyslexia or present with aspects of neurodivergence that they experience or voice as challenging. Others also argue that this process of reflection tends to be superficial, with a lack of focus on challenging assumptions, and neglect of external or group perspectives.

Schön's model of reflective practice

Donald Schön (1983) developed a framework for professional development that emphasised learning through experience and continuous improvement by reflecting on one's own *actions*. This has become commonly known as a model of *reflection-in-action* and *reflection-on-action*. Reflection-in-action occurs during an event or activity, and reflection-on-action happens after the event. This approach encourages the practitioner to become more aware of their therapeutic practice moment-by-moment, to adapt to new situations, and then subsequently to develop a deeper understanding of their work. In essence, Schön's model of reflective practice is a dynamic process of learning, adapting and growing through thoughtful engagement with one's professional experiences.

Exercise

Let's explore this approach together. Choose an activity or event that you would like to reflect on and follow these steps as you undertake that activity:

1. Reflection-in-action: what are you thinking while you are doing this activity? How are you adapting to any unexpected situations moment-by-moment? Are you making any on-the-spot adjustments? Are you present during this activity, thinking through the situation as it unfolds?
2. Reflection-on-action: looking back at this activity or event, can you understand what happened, why it happened, and how you could improve outcomes in the future? (This is a more deliberate and analytic type of reflection that takes place after the event.)
3. Learning through experience: this model highlights both the successes and failures of any experiences. Can you identify any areas for growth or refinement in your approach?
4. Critical thinking: this form of reflective practice encourages you to question your assumptions in the moment, challenge your actions, and develop a more critical perspective on your work. How might you challenge your actions in this event?
5. Continuous improvement: by using a process of ongoing reflection, you can begin to identify patterns, refine your skills and adapt to new challenges, which in turn lead to continuous improvement in your personal life and professional practice. What patterns do you notice during your reflections on and in action? How might you refine or adapt your skills based on your learning in this exercise?

How did you find this reflective experience using Schön's model? What were the positive and negative aspects of the process of reflecting in this way? What do you think you need from a reflective process? Jot down some top takeaway reflections from this exercise.

While Schön's approach could be seen to include more critical thinking and clear steps for continuous improvement than Gibbs's reflective cycle, common critiques of the model include concerns about its individualistic focus, its neglect of systemic and broader social and political contexts, and potentially overlooking the cognitive processes required before action. It may also be overly descriptive and hinder learning and creative development.

Kolb's experiential learning cycle

Kolb's (2015) model of reflective practice is rooted in experiential learning theory and is a cyclical model for learning through experience. It emphasises reflection as a crucial step in the learning process, guiding individuals to analyse past experiences and apply those insights into future actions. It can also be used as a basis for structuring reflective essays or as a way to structure your thinking.

The cycle comprises four main stages:

1. Concrete experience – in this first stage you describe an experience you have had and your thoughts at that time.
2. Reflective observation – next, you explore your reflections on the experience, what you were feeling, linking this to your skills, knowledge and any prior experience(s).
3. Abstract conceptualisation – this stage is all about learning from your experiences. Here you analyse and explain your reflections, focusing on the meaning and other possibilities. You acknowledge what went well and what did not, and identify any areas for further exploration.
4. Active experimentation – This final stage is concerned with putting your learning into practice, translating your analysis into action moving forwards. Here you set specific, measurable and achievable goals. This stage is also about circling back reflexively and applying your learning to new experiences.

Kolb's model of reflective practice is perhaps the most widely used in teaching, as it helps trainees to reflexively apply what they have learned, and iteratively apply it back into their therapeutic practice. However, common critiques include concerns about the lack of empirical evidence for its learning style, oversimplification of learning processes, and the neglect of social and cultural contexts. Others argue that this approach is too rigid and does not adequately address the complexities of real-world learning.

Both Kolb's experiential learning cycle and Gibbs's reflective cycle are ideal for individual reflection. The steps facilitate a scaffold for exploring how experience may have led to learning through concrete experience, reflecting on and evaluating the experience, exploring of one's feelings, and developing an action plan for the future. Of course, this individual reflection may also facilitate the supervision process or dialogue with peers.

Group and peer-to-peer models

Group and peer-to-peer models of reflection and supervision have grown in popularity on training programmes and in clinical practice settings, as they play an important part for both trainees and professional practitioners who are aiming to develop their reflective and supervisory approaches. Traditional group models such as personal and professional development groups are commonly used as they allow trainees to safely reflect and explore their learning and personal development within a zone of proximal development (Vygotsky, 1978) while supported by a tutor. There are many benefits to using a group model of reflection over the traditional individual approaches like the ones that we have just explored. These include an improved collective and collaborative approach to problem-solving, enhanced self-awareness in relation to others in the group, a stronger sense of support or team cohesion, and combined resilience. There is also benefit in becoming more culturally informed while sharing your reflections with others from a broader range of backgrounds, worldviews, professional experience and cultural contexts of origins. Group models of supervision and reflection can also provide *psychological safety* (Lee et al., 2022), enabling group members to feel psychologically safe and to engage in interpersonally risky behaviours, such as disagreeing, asking questions and reporting mistakes, without negative consequences.

We will now explore two key group approaches to reflective practice – namely, the Leeds group reflection model, which is commonly used in professional healthcare and education settings such as the NHS, and personal and professional development groups, which are commonly used in university training programmes.

The Leeds group reflection model

This model, designed by David Green (2008), is regularly used in therapeutic and healthcare settings. From our experience we have learned that the ideal size for a group supervision setting would ideally range from three to five participants. This allows for sufficient time for each supervisee to have space to bring material (over a period of time) or to respond to material being explored, and facilitates an optimum environment for peer interaction, discussion and learning. The model consists of five main phases and involves a facilitator as well as a group of participants:

1. Request for assistance (5–10 minutes). An individual talks for no more than 10 minutes about a dilemma from their therapeutic or professional practice. They choose a piece of work that others in

the group are not involved with. They spontaneously talk without any prior preparation. They begin by giving the reason for choosing this particular dilemma (e.g. due to it being interesting, worrying or unusual). The individual is not expected to give a comprehensive summary and can omit information if they desire. The individual then identifies one of three aspects for help with development:

- intervention skills
- personal insight
- integration of theory and practice.

2. Questioning period and identification of focus (5–10 minutes). This phase involves going around each group member to allow all to pose questions to the presenter (they are allowed to pass if they need more time to think). At the end, the facilitator identifies issues for focus in the discussion phase.

3. Reflective feedback and discussion (15–20 minutes). The presenter remains silent and may leave the circle, and is encouraged to take notes. Group members provide feedback in the first person (to avoid the presenter getting drawn back into question-and-answer dynamics). This may sound something like, 'While listening to what Bob shared, I think that discussing a safety plan with the client will be important'. Interactive discussion takes place where all discussants are encouraged to participate (some groups prefer to start by going around each group member to give their reflection). As noted in this example, suggestions need to be constructive, and the presenter is then addressed in the third person to show that they are included back into the discussion. The facilitator needs to be empathic to the presenter's perspective and check any statements that may be construed as judgemental (in reflective team mode).

Pause period of 5 minutes to allow the presenter to reflect and form response.

4. Presenter response (5–10 minutes). The presenter responds to peer suggestions, stating what was helpful and what might need further discussion. Discussants remain silent unless asked for more detail.

5. Optional discussion (timing to be agreed, e.g. 5–10 minutes). This is an opportunity for closure or further exploration. At this stage the facilitator may give input.

Group approaches to reflection such as this can be very powerful, and support individuals to think around their difficulties using all the lenses and perspectives in the group. It can also be effective in helping the individual presenting their dilemma feel compassionately and empathically supported by their peers. Challenges to this approach include the possibility that some participants, including those who feel vulnerable, stigmatised or oppressed, may feel excluded or stay silent, as they fear how their contribution may be received. It is up to the facilitator to make sure all voices are heard and encouraged.

Personal and professional development groups

A common approach to group reflective practice includes personal and professional development groups. These collaborative learning groups are often used on psychotherapy training programmes and aim to provide a supportive environment where individuals can share insights, learn collectively and engage in structured reflection led by a tutor (McKeown et al., 2024; Spencer, 2006). They often involve discussing issues relating to therapeutic work, considering topics of diversity, difference, prejudice and discrimination, and exploring important concepts in therapy such as power and social justice. They can also be creative spaces that engage trainees by using reflective postcards or pictures, cultural items, creative objects, books or experiential learning. However, they can be very exposing spaces, and it is essential that group members lean into self-care practices, personal therapy and tutor support to make the most of this experience. Group contracts are also helpful for all members to agree what safe reflective practice looks like for them.

Peer-to-peer duoethnography

Duoethnography is a research method that can also be understood as a dialogic way of reflecting, bringing together elements of autoethnography, autobiography, self-study, life history and more (Breault, 2016; Norris & Sawyer, 2004). We have found that duoethnographic dialogue between peers facilitates a wonderful depth of reflective process as they interrogate and reconceptualise their existing beliefs and perspectives through conversations. It also enables an exploration of complex feelings and lived experiences over time. We have found in our own duoethnographic experiences together that it disrupts our personal beliefs and meta-narratives and, as posited by Norris and Sawyer (2012), juxtaposes personal, solitary voices with the voice of another, through which 'neither position can claim dominance or universal truth' (2012, p. 15). Duoethnography differs from other group and peer-to-peer models in that participants take turns speaking and writing over time and can share a diversity of resources, including drawing from literature, poetry and their lived experiences.

For more on duoethnographic perspectives, including examples of reflections and noted conversations that are written in a playscript format, please also see:

- Charura and Bushell (2023) for an exploration of difference and diversity from a Jungian psychoanalytic perspective
- Hills et al. (2023), who showcase reflections between three practitioners on power and privilege in therapeutic practice
- Charura and Smith (2024), who explore reflective practice while working with trauma
- O'Brien and Charura (2024) for our own work reflecting on psychotherapeutic integration in practice
- Chapter 16 in this handbook, in which Robin Shohet and John Wilson engage in a duoethnographical dialogue on their own professional reflective journeys.

Creative approaches

Creative approaches to reflective practice can be truly beneficial, as they allow each individual to idiosyncratically apply their own way of being and form(s) of expression. The use of creative metaphor is a key competency required by the HCPC (2023) and can provide a great depth of self-expression and learning. By integrating creative methods such as art, journalling, storytelling, scrapbooking or poetry, or by engaging with creative spaces such as museums, art galleries or nature, individuals can often delve more deeply into their experiences, leading to more profound insights and understanding. These approaches also foster a growthful, creative mindset that is open to innovation and experimentation, which can be particularly helpful to trainees in creating transferrable employability skills. We will now explore some creative approaches to reflection.

The tree of life

The tree of life is a reflective approach that is rooted in narrative therapy (Ncube, 2016) and Indigenous storytelling. It is designed to help individuals to explore their life stories and build a stronger sense of self. This exercise can also be used therapeutically with clients, or on team away days, where individuals can explore their own roots and aspects of self before sharing reflectively with the team to explore differences and diversities within the team and each other's worldviews.

Each person begins the reflective process with a large sheet of paper and access to coloured pens of their choice. They are then asked to draw freestyle in any way of their choice (no particular artistic skills are required!). The key elements of the tree of life are as follows.

- Roots: these represent where a person comes from, their origins, ancestry and cultural background.
- Ground/soil: represents the person's current place of residence and

the environment in which they live.

- Trunk: symbolises the person's skills, talents and values.
- Branches: represent the person's hopes, dreams and aspirations for the future.
- Leaves: represent important people in the person's life who offer support and connection.
- Fruit: represent the gifts and positive experiences the person has received from others.
- Compost: represents experiences or problems that the person wishes to leave behind or no longer be defined by.
- Flowers: represent positive aspects of the self, team, work environment or professional practice that they value.

This creative approach links to narrative therapy by enabling the individual to re-author their life story, externalise problems, build resilience, identify strengths and resources, increase cultural sensitivity, and aid reflection on the self, team dynamics or professional practice. Critiques of this approach, however, include the potential for re-traumatisation and the need for self-care and grounding processes. Some also argue that it is problem-focused, and narratives in mental health services can perpetuate a cycle of negative self-perception. However, this collaborative and community-based approach can be particularly beneficial to vulnerable populations, provide a sense of belonging and support during training, or help to build rapport in professional teams.

Other examples of creative approaches include:

1. Creative journalling – this can involve writing, poetry, drawing, doodling, using collage, textiles, chalks, inks or paints to express your thoughts and feelings.
2. Discovery maps – creating messy maps (which Charlotte O'Brien used to help her reflect on her doctoral thesis), or visual representations of challenges, areas of strengths and potential solutions using strategic thinking.
3. Storytelling – sharing personal narratives verbally or through written accounts, which can help individuals to process their experiences and understand their impact.
4. Using creative materials – at a conference we attended recently, we engaged in a collective creative workshop, expressing our feelings and emotions in a freeform style using Lego, clay or materials of our choice. We then joined our item onto a net to symbolise our collective support and self-discovery.

In conclusion, creative reflective practices offer a dynamic and engaging way to learn from experiences and foster personal and professional development. They embrace the core HCPC (2023) competencies of artistry in the use of language and metaphor and have the potential to help us engage more deeply with our own non-verbal emotions and inner wisdom. There is no one-size-fits-all in reflective practice, and it is therefore vitally important to encourage creativity and self-expression using the wealth of contemporary tools and spaces available to us. Creative reflective practice can greatly benefit the development of our professional practice and skills, as it not only helps us to uniquely and idiosyncratically solidify our learning (Trigwell et al., 1999), but also helps us to gain additional employability skills in communicating ideas and experiences, promoting adaptability, and working creatively in a diverse range of environments (University of Oxford, 2024).

Contemporary approaches

With the rise and popularity of AI, there is a wealth of new ways to explore and reflect at our fingertips. While it is essential that we never share any confidential client material, we can make good use of tools such as ChatGPT for reflective practice. For example, one way might be to write a reflective letter to yourself on a topic that you are finding difficult, and ChatGPT can write you a letter back. This can creatively help to prompt ideas and offer an alternative perspective that you haven't thought about, generate thought-provoking questions, summarise information to facilitate a deeper analysis, or give you ideas or a new lens to think with. The opportunities are endless.

Many universities and institutions worldwide are exploring the use of AI for reflective practice. For example, Stanford University (Britos Cavagnaro, 2023) recently presented a classroom teaching resource on enhancing reflective practices with AI. They suggest the use of tools such as 'Riff' – an inquisitive chatbot powered by generative AI that is designed to ask you reflective questions and help you make sense of your experiences. However, there are important rules of engagement when using such tools (e.g. understanding that they have limits to what they can and cannot do, and recognising they are meant as tools to further the stimulus of our thinking and reflection rather than offer advice). Another AI tool that is now being commonly used in academia is NotebookLM, a product made by Google. This tool is multifaceted and could be used, for example, to keep a reflective diary and provide you with summaries of your reflective practice each month. It could also give you an audio overview of your reflective practice to help you gain perspective on what you have written, or how you could move your practice forward. It can also highlight trends and connections between your entries to give you insight into your learning and practice.

Other contemporary approaches to reflection can benefit trainees and professionals alike, including helping individuals who experience physical, cognitive, mental health or language differences, or have neurodiversity requirements. For example, the NHS (2025), in their *Transformative Reflection Resource Guide*, suggest using audio diaries, creative and expressive vlogs, blogs, or freeform prose using dramatic art or imagery. They also suggest the use of creative inquiry using encounters with artistic or creative practices or spaces. In our own teaching, we have often taken trainees to local museums or galleries to reflect on topics such as social justice. By giving trainees time and space for reflection in inspiring locations, it enables them to reflect in their own way with free association without censorship or editing.

Supervisory and personal therapeutic approaches

The British Association for Counselling and Psychotherapy (2018) informs us in its *Ethical Framework for the Counselling Professions* that supervision is essential to good practice. Reflection in the supervisory relationship provides practitioners with regular and ongoing opportunities to reflect at depth on all aspects of their practice in order to work as safely, ethically and effectively as possible. The supervisory relationship can be seen as key to helping each practitioner take a 360-degree look at their practice, helping them to find any blind spots they may have due to their own worldview. It also helps trainees and practitioners to delve more deeply into their practice, to see what they are doing and why, and how to make any continuous improvements (see Chapter 10 for more information on how to use supervision). In the case study that follows, Divine provides an example of how he has used a psychoanalytic approach to supervision to assess his practice, improve his learning and develop his skills.

Case study

This case study offers an example of working with a client in which I (Divine) learned a great deal about reflective practice and its importance in facilitating a relational and anti-discriminatory therapeutic stance. My reflective practice was informed by Wilfred Bion's (1962) psychoanalytic work *Learning from Experience*. This way of reflecting facilitates a process of staying with the experience of uncertainty and not rushing to quick certainties and conclusions about the client's process (Mintz, 2016). I hope that my reflections and the questions I engaged with will aid your own reflective process.

Working with Valentina

Valentina was referred to me for trauma therapy. In the assessment process, I learned that she had been in and out of the local psychiatric hospital, had been diagnosed with borderline personality disorder and had a long history of self-harming. As the session progressed, I learned that she was a mother of three, and following multiple violent relationships, the children had been taken into care. We both realised the challenges that we were faced with in this new therapeutic encounter. As the sessions progressed, I continued to be authentic, open, non-judgemental and did my very best to communicate my empathy with her experiences. I took a trauma-informed approach of 'what has happened to you?', rather than a pathological one of 'what's wrong with you?'. We initially contracted to 24 psychotherapy sessions. As the sessions progressed, Valentina became more open, and it emerged that she had been sexually abused in childhood. Understandably as a child, she had struggled, and her psychological distress had continued into adulthood. During our sessions, she would often become very angry with me and let me know how much she 'hated men', and six months into our work she disclosed multiple traumatic experiences she encountered perpetrated by three different men, one of whom was Black. I learned so much about working with complex trauma presentations and about myself, and my process in relation to how I managed my emotions, feelings, masculinity, my power as a man and as a therapist, and matters relating to difference and diversity.

My learning and reflective practice

My supervisor drew on psychoanalytic theoretical perspectives, including learning from experience (Bion, 1962), and he encouraged me to engage in a reflective process that included challenging my own desire to avoid my anger. This included writing detailed process notes, and in reflective supervision, I would engage with, for example, a range of reflective questions including:

1. What was being communicated and meta-communicated between us?
2. What was the 'contact-barrier' (Bion, 1962) and the things that got in the way of me being able to 'contain' Valentina's process?
3. How could we name and explore issues of race, culture, difference, diversity and embodied felt experiences in our therapy encounters?
4. What were the developmental needs, transferential dynamics between us, fantasies and unconscious phantasies?
5. What was I going to do differently in the next session?

During our therapeutic relationship together, which lasted a year, we worked through Valentina's experiences. I engaged in my own reflective practice, personal therapy, journalling and supervision, and worked on my personal difficulties in processing my own experiences of the impact of racism. I also attended continuing personal development classes, psychoanalytic lectures and inter-cultural psychodynamic psychotherapy seminars and these enabled me to link theory and practice. Furthermore, I found that by engaging in a dialogical duoethnographical process supported by Jungian theoretical perspectives, it challenged me to face parts of myself that I was psychologically defending against. These included my own prejudice towards this client, and my own shame of what I had introjected about whiteness, Blackness and matters relating to gender and discrimination (Charura & Bushell, 2023). My learning from working with Valentina highlighted the importance of shifting from reflective practice as just an introspective process, to an externalised and actionable process by which we can directly face and address our prejudices, thereby actively take an anti-discriminatory and decolonised stance.

Having read the case study, what reflections will you take away from Divine's powerful experiences? What thoughts, emotions and bodily sensations do you notice within yourself? Are there any actionable changes that you will make as a result of what you have read?

Supervisors can also help you to explore reflectively in your sessions by providing a safe supervisory relationship and environment where you are able to ask any questions that may help improve your own professional development. They may use techniques such as Socratic questioning, ask you to complete Gibbs's cycle on a particular topic you are struggling with, or explore your practice together using a model of supervision. For example, the seven-eyed model of supervision (Hawkins & Shohet, 2000) can be used with your supervisor to help you to reflectively consider your client, interventions, therapeutic relationship, therapeutic process, supervisory relationship, supervisory process and the wider context and systems at play in your therapeutic work. For more guidance on reflective practice in supervision, please see the *Reflective Supervision Resource Pack* (Earle et al., 2017).

It is also important to understand that supervisors are not personal therapists. Therefore, alongside your professional development in supervision it is essential that all psychotherapeutic practitioners engage at depth with a personal reflective process that can be supported by a personal therapist. In fact, most training programmes require trainees to undergo at least 40 hours of personal therapy for just this reason. The reflective questions at the end of this chapter may also help you to begin to think about your own self-concept and intersectionality of experience, and how this may differ from your clients. It is important that we engage in a continuous process of reflection for the purposes of self-awareness, and to ethically bracket our own values and worldviews to mitigate any negative impacts on our clients.

A critique of models for reflective practice

We have highlighted and championed a range of reflective models in this chapter. However, we also recognise the numerous critiques of the way that reflective practice is presently conceptualised and operationalised. We concur with Lilienfeld and Basterfield (2020), who noted several poignant points, including that reflective practice models presume that the activities they outline can enhance practitioners' capacities to think critically about their practice and make them more discerning and effective clinicians. We agree with the challenge that there is an assumption that reflective practice enables individuals to overcome their biases, which is problematic, as this may not always be the case. For example, there are a number of theories from the field of cognitive psychology that assert that we tend to have limited direct access to our higher-order cognitive processes, such as the causes of our behaviours (Nisbett & Wilson, 1977) and that we have a propensity to perceive others, but not ourselves, as susceptible (bias blind spot) (Pronin et al., 2002).

This idea can be understood through the concept of 'introspection illusion', whereby individuals erroneously believe that their introspections facilitate valuable insight into their biases (Hansen & Pronin, 2012). Over-valuing of personal introspection occurs in a variety of domains, including in making clinical judgements and decision-making, personal and therapeutic relationships, or in relation to stereotyping and prejudice (Pronin, 2009). For example, we can all reflect on an encounter and remain convinced we were right, even after having used a reflective model. Yet over time, with more experience, through new information or as a result of learning, we may subsequently realise we were wrong or biased.

As therapeutic practitioners, we know that it can be painful to face our own prejudices, feelings of inadequacy or biases, and there is a diversity of therapeutic models that also suggest that these may be unconscious/at the edge of our awareness, and therefore may be denied or distorted to our awareness. In line with this, some research suggests that when individuals attempt to detect bias in themselves through reflection, the process they engage in is introspective in nature as they search inwardly for evidence of such bias (Lilienfeld & Basterfield, 2020; Pronin, 2009). However, this may inadvertently exacerbate mistaken impressions that they do not have biases and prejudices, and thus an opportunity for change and growth is missed (Pronin & Kugler, 2007).

Another important point is that newly qualified and early-career therapists and practitioners generally start with a basic level of therapeutic skills. We draw here on Dunning's (2011) work that showed that people with low-level skills and knowledge tend to overestimate their skills and knowledge, a phenomenon termed the Dunning–Kruger effect. In line with this, Lilienfeld & Basterfield (2020) suggested that when applied to reflection in therapeutic practice, practitioners who are the least skilled at reflection may be those most likely to fail to detect their knowledge and skills gaps, and are more likely to perceive themselves as adept (Lilienfeld & Basterfield, 2020; Pronin, 2009). Put simply, Dunning (2011) argued that an individual is often ignorant of their own ignorance. We see this as akin to being unconsciously incompetent. To address these challenges, practitioners need, therefore, to use activities that facilitate engagement with others, including, for example, supervision, in which the supervisor (or indeed their peer learning group, where appropriate) can hear an actual recording of their therapeutic sessions. That is, reflection needs to be more than an introspective activity by the individual in which they use one of the traditional models of reflection that involves self-reflection only.

We value Lilienfeld and Basterfield's (2020) assertion of the importance of engaging with reflective practice model exercises that encourage cognitive debiasing, that is, a process in which the influence of cognitive biases is reduced. Using this process, trainees and seasoned practitioners alike are invited to consider perspectives that differ from their own introspective conclusions. Croskerry et al.'s (2013) 'consider the alternative' is one such example. In the light of this important critique, we invite you to consider reflective processes and models that facilitate this shift and truly enable you to face your own biases and prejudices, thereby enhancing your learning and personal professional development.

Reflexivity – putting our reflective learning back into our work

Reflexivity, in our own experience, is often a new concept for trainees. It is defined by Finlay (1998) as examining your own judgements, beliefs and best practices. It involves questioning our own assumptions, attending to them, noticing their impact and accepting that we are inherently part of the research or therapeutic process.

Reflective practice is a wonderful tool, as we have seen, to learn and improve our therapeutic mastery. However, reflexivity is vital for critically applying what we have learned back into our practice. Finlay (2008) notes that there are three fundamental processes of reflexivity, namely:

1. retrospection – thinking back about a situation or experience
2. self-evaluation – critically analysing and evaluating the actions and feelings associated with the experience, using theoretical perspectives
3. re-orientation – using the self-evaluation results to influence future approaches to similar situations or experiences.

Reflexivity helps us to remain alert to new and alternative ways of thinking, and to help us to iteratively and continuously consider the ways in which we personally affect what emerges between ourselves and our clients as a result of our own life story, culture, class, gender, sexuality and so forth (Hedges, 2010). It is a key skill to develop in therapeutic practice and in our research, as we consciously explore the impact of our own lens, values and worldview on others.

We hope that you have enjoyed this whistle-stop tour of the different types of reflective practice, and hope that you will use this brief introduction, questions for reflection, and recommended reading to deeply engage with the process of finding a reflective approach that works for you. Here are some top takeaways from this chapter.

Top takeaways

- Take time to find your own authentic reflective practice. Try out many models and styles of reflective practice and identify one (or more) that suits you.
- Use a reflective practice that promotes psychological and theoretical safety. Feeling safe is vital to providing the right environment for reflection, where you can have an open, questioning stance, and where innovative suggestions and creativity are encouraged.
- Be a learner. Allow yourself to lean into your position as a learner over your training journey. It is okay to get things wrong, reflect on them, and transform your practice with the help of your peers and supervisor.
- Be creative. A creative mindset enables innovation, new solutions and strengthens resilience, adaptability and employability skills. Allow your mind to wander and your own creativity to emerge.
- Be reflexive. Maintain an open curiosity about yourself as you develop and change across your trainee and professional journeys. Remain curious and observe any potential impact on your clients from your own positionality and lens. Put your learning back into your practice to experience the full impact of the reflective and reflexive learning cycle.

Questions for reflection

1. Having read this chapter, what reflective practice models are you drawn to and why?
2. Of your chosen model(s), how can you ensure that you address matters relating to intersectionality, diversity and anti-discriminatory practice?
3. What other reflective practices (e.g. supervision or peer-to-peer activities) do you engage with to ensure that your biases and prejudices are authentically challenged?
4. How do you best express yourself (perhaps through writing, art, creative methods or using technology)?
5. What are you currently finding challenging in your training or professional practice?

We encourage you to choose a reflective model or two of your choice to try out over the next month, take your findings to supervision or peer group reflection, and reflexively put your learning back into your practice.

Recommended reading and key resources

- Bager-Charleson, S. (2024). *Reflective practice in counselling and psychotherapy.* Sage Publications Ltd.

This is an excellent core text, which provides best practices and a solid practical and theoretical underpinning for reflective practice in counselling and psychotherapy. It takes the reader through a step-by-step history of reflective practice, considers ideas of knowledge and power, and explores how we deal with issues of the self.

- Finlay, L. (2008). Reflecting on 'reflective practice'. Practice-based Professional Learning Paper 52. *The Open University.* https://oro.open.ac.uk/68945/1/Finlay-(2008)-Reflecting-on-reflective-practice-PBPL-paper-52.pdf

This is an excellent paper, which explores ideas and debates relating to reflective practice.

- Health and Care Professions Council [HCPC] (2025). *Reflective practice.* https://www.hcpc-uk.org/standards/meeting-our-standards/reflective-practice/

This is an excellent guide to creating space to reflect on your practice by yourself, with colleagues or as part of a group. It provides useful videos of examples of reflective practice.

References

American Counseling Association. (2014). *2014 ACA code of ethics as approved by the ACA Governing Council,* 1–24. American Counseling Association.

Bion, W.R. (1962). *Learning from experience.* Karnac Books.

Breault, R.A. (2016). Emerging issues in duoethnography. *International Journal of Qualitative Studies in Education, 29*(6), 777–794. https://doi.org/10.1080/09518398.2016.1162866

British Association for Counselling and Psychotherapy. (BACP). (2018). *Ethical framework for the counselling professions.* https://www.bacp.co.uk/events-and-resources/ethics-and-standards/ethical-framework-for-the-counselling-professions/

British Psychological Society. (2024). *Reflective practice.* https://doi.org/10.53841/bpsrep.2024.rep178.7

Britos Cavagnaro, L. (2023). *Enhancing reflective practices with AI.* https://teachingresources.stanford.edu/resources/enhancing-reflective-practices-with-ai/

Charura, D. & Bushell, S. (2023). A duoethnographic exploration of colonialism in the cultural layer of the objective psyche. *Journal of Analytical Psychology, 68*(1), 27–47. https://doi.org/10.1111/1468-5922.12878

Charura, D. & Smith, P. (2024). A duoethnographic exploration of relational psychotraumatology: Research, training and practice considerations. *Counselling & Psychotherapy Research, 24*(3), 972–981. https://doi.org/10.1002/capr.12749

Cooper, L.D. & Wieckowski, A.T. (2017). A structured approach to reflective practice training in a clinical practicum. *Training and Education in Professional Psychology*, *11*(4), 252–259. https://doi.org/10.1037/tep0000170

Croskerry, P., Singhal, G. & Mamede, S. (2013). Cognitive debiasing 2: Impediments to and strategies for change. *BMJ Quality & Safety*, *22*(Suppl 2), ii65–ii72. https://doi.org/10.1136/bmjqs-2012-001713

Dunning, D. (2011). The Dunning–Kruger effect: On being ignorant of one's own ignorance. In J.M. Olson & M.P. Zanna (Eds.), *Advances in experimental social psychology* (Vol. 44, pp. 247–296). Academic Press.

Earle, F., Fox, J., Webb, C. & Bowyer, S. (2017). *Reflective supervision: Resource pack*. https://www.researchinpractice.org.uk/media/2d2dxwrn/reflective_supervision_resource_pack_2017.pdf

Finlay, L. (1998). Reflexivity: An essential component for all research? *British Journal of Occupational Therapy*, *61*(10), 453–456.

Finlay, L. (2008). *Reflecting on 'reflective practice'*. Practice-based professional learning paper 52. The Open University. https://oro.open.ac.uk/68945/1/Finlay-(2008)-Reflecting-on-reflective-practice-PBPL-paper-52.pdf

Gibbs, G. (1988). *Learning by doing: A guide to teaching and learning methods*. Further Education Unit. Oxford Polytechnic.

Green, D. (2008). *Structured peer group supervision*. [Video]. https://mymedia.leeds.ac.uk/Mediasite/Showcase/default/presentation/497b1e52ed0249cda505b175e8b1e3d71d

Hansen, K.E. & Pronin, E. (2012). Illusions of self knowledge. In S. Vazire & T.D. Wilson (Eds.), *Handbook of self knowledge* (pp. 345–362). Guilford Press.

Hawkins, P. & Shohet, R. (2000). *Supervision in the helping profession* (2nd ed.). Open University Press.

Health and Care Professions Council [HCPC] (2023). *Standards of proficiency*. https://www.hcpc-uk.org/standards/standards-of-proficiency/practitioner-psychologists/

Hedges, F. (2010). *Reflexivity in therapeutic practice*. Palgrave.

Hills, J., Christodoulidi, F. & Charura, D. (2023). A duoethnographic study of power and privilege in the psychotherapeutic space: Dialogical research as professional development. *International Journal of Qualitative Methods*, *22*, 1–11. https://doi.org/10.1177/16094069231199903

Kocet, M.M. & Herlihy, B.J. (2014). Addressing values-based conflicts within the counselling relationship: A decision making model. *Journal of Counseling and Development*, *92*(2), 180–186.

Kolb, D.A. (2015) *Experiential learning: Experience as the source of learning and development* (2nd ed.). Pearson Education.

Lee, E.H., Pitts, S., Pignataro, S., Newman, L.R. & D'Angelo, E J. (2022). Establishing psychological safety in clinical supervision: Multi-professional perspectives. *The Clinical Teacher*, *19*(2), 71–78.

Lilienfeld, S.O. & Basterfield, C. (2020). Reflective practice in clinical psychology: Reflections from basic psychological science. *Clinical Psychology Science & Practice*, *27*(4). https://doi.org/10.1111/cpsp.12352

McKeown, U., Coulter, S. & Mooney, S. (2024). The 'four selves' framework for facilitating personal and professional development (PPD) in qualifying-level systemic psychotherapy training. *Journal of Family Therapy*, *46*(3), 306–321. https://doi.org/10.1111/1467-6427.12465

Mintz, J. (2016). Bion and Schön: Psychoanalytic perspectives on reflection in action. *British Journal of Educational Studies, 64*(3), 277–293. http://www.jstor.org/stable/43896344

National Health Service. (2025). *Transformative reflection resource guide.* https://www.hee.nhs.uk/our-work/enhancing-generalist-skills/enhance-learning-resources/handbook/cross-cutting-themes/transformative-reflection

Ncube, N. (2016). *The tree of life project: Using narrative ideas in work with vulnerable children in Southern Africa.* https://narrativetherapycentre.com/wp-content/uploads/2020/12/Tree-of-Life-by-Ncazelo-Ncube-2006.pdf

Newton, C. (2025). What I bring to the room: A reflective practice for addressing implicit bias in trainees and practitioners. *Reflective Practice*, 1–13. https://doi.org/10.1080/14623943.2025.2494328

Nisbett, R.E. & Wilson, T.D. (1977). The halo effect: Evidence for unconscious alteration of judgments. *Journal of Personality and Social Psychology, 35*(4), 250–256. https://doi.org/10.1037/0022-3514.35.4.250

Norris, J. & Sawyer, R.D. (2004). Null and hidden curricula of sexual orientation: A dialogue on the curreres of the absent presence and the present absence. In L. Coia, N.J. Brooks, S.J. Mayer, P. Pritchard, E. Heilman, M.L. Birch & A. Mountain (Eds.), *Democratic responses in an era of standardization.* (pp. 139–159). Troy.

Norris, J. & Sawyer, R.D. (2012). Toward a dialogic methodology. In J. Norris, R.D. Sawyer & D. Lund (Eds.), *Duoethnography: Dialogic methods for social, health and educational research* (pp. 9–40). Left Coast Press.

O'Brien, C. & Charura, D. (2024). 'Integration by immersion': A contemporary model of integration for psychotherapeutic and pedagogical practice. *Counselling and Psychotherapy Research, 25*(2). e12833. https://doi.org/10.1002/capr.12833

Pronin, E. (2009). Chapter 1 The introspection illusion. *Advances in Experimental Social Psychology, 41*, 1–67. https://doi.org/10.1016/S0065-2601(08)00401-2

Pronin, E. & Kugler, M.B. (2007). Valuing thoughts, ignoring behavior: The introspection illusion as a source of the bias blind spot. *Journal of Experimental Social Psychology, 43*(4), 565–578. https://doi.org/10.1016/j.jesp.2006.05.011

Pronin, E., Lin, D.Y. & Ross, L. (2002). The bias blind spot: Perceptions of bias in self versus others. *Personality and Social Psychology Bulletin, 28*(3), 369-381. https://doi.org/10.1177/0146167202286008

Schön, D. (1983). *The reflective practitioner.* Basic Books.

Spencer, L. (2006). Tutor's stories of personal development training – attempting to maximise the learning potential. *Counselling and Psychotherapy Research, 6*(2), 108–114.

Trigwell, K., Prosser, M. & Waterhouse, F. (1999). Relations between teachers' approaches to teaching and students' approaches to learning. *Higher Education, 37*, 57–70.

University of Oxford. (2024). *Develop your employability skills.* https://www.careers.ox.ac.uk/develop-your-employability-skills

Vygotsky, L.S. (1978). *Mind in society: The development of higher psychological processes.* Harvard University Press.

York St John University. (2025). *Reflective writing: Gibbs model of reflection.* https://www.yorksj.ac.uk/media/content-assets/document-directory/documents/Reflective-Writing-Gibbs-Model-of-Reflection-Factsheet.pdf

12.

Self-care, personal therapy and practical survival tips

Gerrie Hughes

Introduction

Self-care for therapists is the equivalent of training sessions for football teams, or daily class for dancers. Personal therapy offers a basis for a practice of self-care, and it is discussed here along with other practical suggestions for how to develop an understanding of what self-care involves for you, as a student or at any stage of your career.

The self is what we use to become aware of what clients are communicating in their words or silences, their bodies and breath, the emotional mood and ambience that co-emerges from the exploration, or the spontaneous responses that arise almost mysteriously from our attitude of being present to what is taking place. Attending to self-care keeps practitioners responsive, resourced and resilient during sessions with clients.

Fitness to practice involves being physically and psychologically robust and flexible and is the foundation for an ethical approach. Self-care is likely to be as individual as each practitioner is, although routines will probably cover the various aspects of being human: body, mind, emotions, spirituality and creativity. Professional background and the context of the work are also relevant. This chapter explores aspects of self-care, and the activities suggested at the end of it are offered as a framework for building your own approach.

Scope of the chapter

In this chapter I explore the following key topics:

- what self-care means
- the impact of training on the self and personal relationships
- the professional self in different contexts
- a conceptualisation of self

- identifying personal vulnerabilities and responses to stress
- the role of personal therapy.

I also provide some exercises and questions for reflection at the end of the chapter.

What is self-care?

'Self-care' is a term that seems to be so commonly and casually used that it is in danger of becoming a cliché. I want to begin this chapter by shaping a concept of self-care that is relevant, robust and relational, and by proposing a definition of it that involves resourcing people to grow towards achieving their potential. This handbook is written for those who are undertaking initial training or pursuing CPD, supporting them in the formation of a potentially lifelong profession. Malinowski (2014) summarises the work of Goncher et al. (2013, p. 14) by affirming that 'when self-care is taught early in one's educational training and new techniques are learned and practised later in one's career, the quality of life can be much improved'. The ability to change and grow is necessary for achieving those goals. Coincidentally, the profession itself requires the ability to support growth and change in others. So, by resourcing ourselves, to the extent that we are able, we become ready to support and facilitate others in their change process too.

The impact of training on the self and personal relationships

Meaningful change is achievable only in the context of relationship, and from being situated within a wider personal and professional environment. While you are in training, your relationships in the training group provide an important 'playing field' for deepening learning about other people and, at least as significantly, about yourself. Your trainers impart knowledge of theory, tell stories about their own professional experience to bring the theory alive, and provide feedback on how they perceive you as an individual and on the dynamics of the group as a whole. You will have the training ground of personal therapy and, as your training proceeds, you will experience supervision on your client work (see Chapter 10). Such profound experiences are likely to have an impact on close family relationships and friendships too. 'Families and close, intimate relationships are fundamental components in the therapist's life' (Bager-Charleson, 2012, p. 162), and attending to these renegotiations is an important aspect of caring for ourselves and those who are important to us.

The professional self in different contexts

Therapy is a collaborative process. Even if, like me, you work from home, the ethical principles of the 'profession' are present in the traditions and structures that inform your day-to-day practice. Being embedded in our training and professional organisations, adhering to ethical frameworks and codes of conduct and being subject to complaints procedures, all create accountability and maintain high standards (see Chapter 5 and Chapter 15). They are also stalwart supports for our robustness, confidence and wellbeing. Personal relationships, particularly those we have with our supervisors and other professional colleagues, are supportive and enabling (Hawkins & Shohet, 1989). In addition, we are required to obey the laws of the land and be familiar with statutory mental health provision. These practices hone our ability to make effective choices, supporting us to care for ourselves and our clients, as well as contributing towards a culture of care in the profession.

Attending to self-care is an acknowledgement of our inter-connectedness with other humans and with the non-human world, as we live on the planet that provides us with oxygen, water and food, and so much more. Self-care is the foundation of a process that enables us to contribute towards a culture of care for our clients, in our families and personal and professional communities and, potentially, wider society (Parry, 2017).

A conceptualisation of self

Who am I? Asking myself this simple question, as I'm writing this now, I experience a rush of possibilities. I feel the metal of my laptop under my wrists and the regular giving way of the keys as my fingers press down in various places. I am a body then, flesh and feelings. Yet the easy rhythm with which I select the keys to press, is organised by my mind. Distinct from the matter of the brain that sits inside my skull, my experience is of a mind that allows me to think and imagine, to recall the past and predict the future. My body sensations resonate with what my mind perceives, and I experience emotions, responses to the actuality of being alive that are at the same time both recognisably universal and uniquely personal. Still, there is more. I am creating something that has never existed until a minute ago; this activity is meaningful and matters to me, fulfils some deep yearning in my body, mind and emotions. Even more than this, I am aware of connecting with some power that exists both inside and outside my self, a source of mystery and awe. From all this, I construct a concept of what it means to be human, to be a self, to be me.

I acknowledge that condensing the vast, active experience of being alive in the world at this moment may seem reductionist. Nevertheless, in order to explore what it means to be one's self and to care for that self, I offer the following summary of aspects of the experience of being human, all of which operate within self and in response to relationships and encounters:

- body
- emotions
- mind

- creativity and imagination
- transcendence and spirituality.

Suggestions for taking care of each of these aspects of self follow, although it is important to remember that we are whole beings. Care (or not) for one aspect of self has an impact on all the others. After all, 'it is a whole human being who finds the beautiful path' (Wall Kimmerer, 2020, p. 47).

Body

We relate to the world by means of our senses. Our organs of sensing are situated in our bodies, for example in our eyes, ears, nose, mouth, skin and gut. We feel pleasure and pain in our bodies. We can also experience limitation, numbness and disconnection. The body has needs. Oxygen, water, food and sleep maintain life and support good functioning. Our bodies have evolved in response to our environment, so we need movement and flexibility, and also resistance, to build muscular strength. Excretion of waste matter and toxins is required. We also need touch, and other stimuli from the environment that are experienced through the senses; there is a connection between this and our emotional responses (Damasio, 2000).

Emotions

Our emotional state is very dependent on what happens in our bodies. We experience sensations, and language gives us names for feeling states that are familiar from day-to-day life, or responses to significant events. As a basis for life, we need to feel safe in our environment and to be able to meet our needs there. Emotional needs are wide ranging and can arise from feeling security, love, belonging, joy and awe. Most of us would perceive these as positive. Anger, fear, sadness, loss, hurt and humiliation are some of the emotions we might consider negative, because they cause us pain. Yet each emotion has evolved because it is necessary for a life that is secure, rich and meaningful. They are not inherently 'good' or 'bad', but open to how we interpret them. Many emotions have a body response connected with their expression and resolution: crying, shouting, sighing and laughing are all examples.

We can also think and imagine, relive conversations in our minds, wonder what will happen at the difficult meeting tomorrow, worry about paying the fuel bill… Our minds affect our emotions too.

Emotions are powerful. We learn how (or how not) to express them by experiencing others' reactions, particularly those of early carers. Some emotions may have become more permissible and acceptable than others, yet we need to be able to experience the full range. Otherwise, we may diminish the richness of our experience, or fail to take into account all aspects of our response in decision-making. Self-care involves the ability to bear, contain and express emotions. Understanding and accepting this process helps us avoid a sense of overwhelm or awkwardness when we experience them. Familiarity and comfort with our own emotions is important. Being understood and accepted by others in the fullness of our emotions is one of the supports that makes this possible.

Therapy can be the context for reconnecting with and releasing emotions that may have remained unexpressed for many years, as well as for honing the ability to experience the full emotional range gracefully and effectively, which is one of the reasons that personal therapy is a training requirement.

Therapy provides a context for experiencing emotional connectedness, although, of course, it is not the only one. Relationships with family and friends can support emotional expression too. Learning to become fully emotionally articulate in therapy can enrich and enhance personal relationships. Sometimes it leads to a renegotiation of them, and occasionally to their ending.

Mind

Our thoughts may complicate and intensify the emotions we experience. They can also help us to console ourselves and endure, or else make plans for moving on. Being aware of when thoughts are unhelpful, and having strategies for directing them more productively, is both an important life skill and a significant aspect of self-care. Some examples of activities that support self-care are discussed below:

- Mindfulness is a well-known practice for managing unhelpful thought processes, and any style of meditation has similar benefits.
- Yoga, tai-chi, dance and other sports also offer a productive method of escape from the grind of the mind's treadmill and bring physical advantages of their own.
- Simply directing awareness to the rise and fall of the breath in the body can help us return to ourselves in the moment.
- Discovering the beauty of a tree, birdsong or the salty sea-air, also offers a powerful route out of our minds and into our senses.

In my experience, directing thought is a process, rather than something that can be achieved once and for all. The practice itself is the most important thing. Just believing it is possible can sometimes be the route into developing the habit of regular practice.

Creativity and imagination: Stories

Our fertile minds enable us to imagine and plan, to create art, music and literature, and to conceive of the ineffable. For myself, I categorise these creations of the mind as stories. Human beings are storytellers and meaning-makers. We tell ourselves (and each other) tales about our experiences all the time, referring to our stories as philosophy, art, science, law, religion and even therapy.

Creativity seems to be an important part of being human, however it is expressed. Gardening, cooking, DIY and craft work, drawing cartoons with children and telling bedtime stories, journalling or writing poetry, singing, dancing and playing a musical instrument are all everyday expressions of this impulse, and are necessary for the care of the self (and of those close to us).

Transcendence and spirituality

We have names for incidences that we do not entirely comprehend, like beauty, wonder, awe, spirituality, transcendence, numinosity, God, the sublime… We may not fully understand these experiences, but we know we have need of them. Some people use the word 'soul' in relation to this aspect of self and connect it with ritual and prayer, devotion to deities or other sacred beings, perhaps adherence to a particular belief system or performing charitable and other good works. Recognising the sacredness of the more-than-human is a traditional approach to spirituality (see Chapter 2). However we might experience it, the presence of a spiritual or transcendent element can add depth and meaning to our lives.

The importance of caring for self in relationships and in different contexts

The richness and complexity of each individual self is created within and through our relationships with others. We care for ourselves among a network of relationships, from those that are most intimate and fundamental with partners, children and parents, through extended family, friends and community networks like neighbourhood groups, and with those who share our religious, faith or other beliefs.

Being embedded in such a variety of networks means that the therapeutic work we do with our clients reflects the concerns of the wider society and has the potential for helping us all address our common challenges (Bronfenbrenner, 1979). We are citizens of the nation we inhabit and, in this globalised, interconnected environment, also participants in developments that shape our world, like the recent Covid-19 pandemic, climate change, the colonisation of peoples, the development of space exploration and the impact and consequences of AI. The intersecting impact of being immersed in such a complex world requires us to continuously self-care if we are to maintain robust stamina for our work with our clients.

What are the risks of putting others first at the cost of self-care?

During the editing process of this book, while we were discussing this very topic, Charlie (Dr Charlotte O'Brien, co-editor) reminded me of how, in an aeroplane emergency, we are instructed to put on our own oxygen masks before helping others. Even when there is no emergency in a therapy context, it helps greatly if the practitioner's basic needs are met, as discussed later in this chapter. It occurs to me that keeping resourced is the best way of avoiding emergencies in the therapy room. Nevertheless, things can go wrong. Therapy is hard and some of the environments in which we work are demanding, and life happens.

Our work involves supporting people at their most vulnerable, when they may be feeling desperate. In some circumstances, the psychological challenges that clients present may make a deep impact and can at times even be potentially harmful. Other risks that come with the profession include when a client dies by suicide, when there are statutory enquiries like tribunals or court cases for which we need to provide evidence, and if complaints (formal or informal) are made to a professional association. We have only ourselves to use, so it is fundamental that we care for ourselves in order to be able to support our clients to become as resilient and resourceful as they are able. It is therefore essential that individual practitioners, professional associations, training institutes and workplaces create a culture of care, so that as professionals we can be compassionate to one another, as well as with our clients. We are not invincible, and we need time and support to recover from our hurts and disappointments.

Identifying personal vulnerabilities and responses to stress

Many of us are drawn to becoming therapists because we may have struggled with aspects of ourselves in the past. Even the therapist is not immune to experiencing mental health difficulties, having a psychological or neurodevelopmental diagnosis, or experiencing relational challenges. Without due self-care or reflection, personal vulnerabilities may have an impact on the therapeutic work or, at worst, even be harmful for clients. This implies that a lack of appropriate self-care can result in unethical professional practice. (See Chapter 5 for more about relational ethics in the psychotherapeutic professions.) Personal therapy is where we can discover any potentially challenging characteristics we may possess, find ways of ameliorating them when we can, and become sensitised to when they might negatively affect our work.

We can protect ourselves, our clients and those we love by understanding the markers that become present when we approach overload. For me, supervision is an essential part of self-care. At the beginning of my monthly session, I review what is happening in my life currently and outline it briefly to my supervisor. Such situations may involve death or losses, illness – my own or a family member's – house repairs, neighbourhood disputes, disappointments, recent successes, too much work or too little… Both of us can then hold the information in mind as we discuss what has been happening in my work with clients. Stress, burnout and vicarious trauma are all recognised as being hazards for therapeutic practitioners. For further information on these and other professional risks, see Malinowski (2014).

Stress

A certain amount of stress is inevitable and natural for those who want to live a life that is meaningful and fulfilling, yet it is important to be aware of the point at which energising stress tips into being debilitating or harmful, maybe with the potential to lead eventually to burnout. Each of us is different in our response to stress, so it is helpful if we become familiar with our own particular triggers. Mine tend to occur when I face challenging situations both at home and at work. Another significant marker for me is an increased desire for sweet foods, particularly cake.

Burnout

Burnout can be life changing. I am fortunate to have avoided it for myself (so far), but I have worked with many people who have endured challenging situations for extended periods. Often, there is a breaking point. Something snaps, and it is impossible to carry on any longer. Maybe they walk out of the workplace dramatically, have a car crash or suffer a physical injury, or perhaps a significant relationship breaks down. When this happens, it is as though the person has lost their sense of themselves and feels adrift and often worthless. There is a way back from these desperate situations. What seems to really help is when people begin to create a new sense of who they are and, consequently, make different choices around how they live their lives. For many people, this can open up new possibilities for the future. I have heard people say they are glad they experienced burnout because it brought out different aspects of themselves that they now value.

Vicarious trauma

Listening to people talk about traumatic events they have experienced, and being a witness to the despair and distress they are suffering, can result in second-hand trauma being absorbed. Practitioners who work with client groups among whom trauma is common, for example refugees or victims of domestic violence, seem to value being part of a supportive team where there is plenty of opportunity to talk about challenging sessions with clients very close in time to when they happened. Access to formal (and informal) supervision can also bolster resilience in this environment.

Personal therapy

The focus of this chapter is self-care. I believe that personal therapy is one of the foundations for caring for the self, and for contributing towards a culture of care in our personal and work environments. Becoming a therapeutic practitioner usually requires a substantial period of personal therapy. It seems reasonable enough for an aspiring professional to be expected to experience the treatment they will eventually offer. Some people choose to undertake training because they have had a positive experience of therapy previously. For others, starting their training is their first involvement. Your training establishment will provide support and information to help you negotiate this significant decision. You will be advised about practitioners who are appropriate and available, and the number of sessions required during the training period. Yet the final choice of therapist is yours. How can you be sure that you understand the aim of therapy and that you choose the right therapist?

Therapy, identity and society

Personal therapy is an important context for exploring our identity: gender, sexuality, heritage, class, physical impairment, neurodiversity and more. In our therapy, we sensitise ourselves to how these issues impact on our own lives, so resourcing us for exploring them later with our clients. Your choice of therapist may be influenced by aspects of your own identity (or theirs). Our personal explorations enable us to be more attuned to noticing inclusivity (or lack of it) in training groups, institutes and wider society. Chapter 6 explores issues of difference and diversity in greater detail.

Personal therapy is where you can expand insight, and understanding of your character traits, habitual responses and ways of engaging with the world. Your chosen therapist is your guide and companion in this process, just as you will become a guide and companion to your own clients later. Your training institute is likely to encourage you to choose a therapist who practises the theoretical orientation of your training, or an approach that is closely compatible, so that you can experience in action the principles you are studying.

A therapeutic relationship that facilitates self-care

Many approaches recognise the relationship between client and practitioner as the foundation for the therapeutic process. My own orientation is gestalt, so my concept of the therapeutic relationship is that of a dialogue that co-emerges between therapist and client. Dialogue involves becoming as authentic and transparent as I am able in the moment and being very alive to when and how that becomes smooth or difficult (Joyce & Sills, 2010).

The terms transference and countertransference are often used in describing one aspect of the therapeutic relationship. Our styles of relating carry echoes of past encounters, particularly those in our early lives, with parents and other significant people (Miller, 1995). Transference refers to the responses of the client and countertransference to those of the therapist. For myself, I prefer to use the term 'co-transferring', which seems to imply a greater sense of equality and is more in tune with a gestalt approach. Also, being a verb rather than a noun, it has a more dynamic feel.

Becoming aware of when either party is reacting in a way that was learned in a previous situation, rather than responding to what is happening in the room now, can be revealing of past hurts. Though it can happen at any time, in my experience, it is easy to fall into old patterns of responding when there is a controversy that needs to be resolved. I am very careful if I need to draw an infringement of the therapeutic contract to a client's attention. This could have involved habitual lateness, repeated attempts to rearrange session times or difficulties with payment. I want to avoid the least hint of 'telling off' in my manner (this probably reveals something of my relational history), but remain adult and open, to support an authentic response. I watch carefully for any sign of a defensive or aggressive attitude. Sometimes I may ask, 'Did you feel criticised when I said that?'

Unearthing painful past experiences of self-worth being diminished, or of being reprimanded or shamed can lead to the expression of long-held emotions that had been previously out of awareness. It offers the possibility for a more flexible response with me in the moment, and for communicating with others differently in the future too, thereby achieving more satisfying outcomes. Having had the opportunity to explore my own relational history in therapy is what equips me to be able to do it with my clients now and to continually monitor the need for my own self-care to do this challenging yet rewarding work.

Exercises for personal reflection

Reflect on how the following activities could facilitate your own self-care. Notice those to which you are particularly drawn and others that may seem irrelevant, and be curious about it:

- personal journalling
- engaging with creative methods such as drawing or painting, music, movement and so on
- discussions with family members, friends and colleagues
- personal therapy
- supervision and reflective practice
- physical exercise you enjoy such as sport, yoga, walking and so on
- cultural or spiritual practice.

Top takeaways

- Self-care is the foundation for being able and available to care for others because it is a relational practice that emerges from and within an environment of respect, insight and compassion.

- Self-care maintains health of body, mind, emotions and spirit, thereby increasing our capacity for creativity and transcendence.
- Self-care increases our ability to withstand challenging emotional encounters and remain effective in tough environments by increasing awareness of personal vulnerabilities and responses to stress. Attending to the balance between vulnerability and resilience is what makes us effective.
- Self-care forms a buffer against burnout, vicarious trauma and stress, so is a way of ensuring that we maintain longevity in our personal lives and are able to offer ethical professional practice.

Questions for reflection

Consideration of these questions is intended to increase insight and understanding of your own assumptions and attitudes to self-care. All the questions are framed in the first person.

1. What does it mean for me to care for myself? What impact does my self-care (or lack of it) have for others?
2. How do I care for each aspect of my self – body, mind, emotions, spirit and creativity? Are any aspects easier/more difficult to resource? What are the reasons this may be the case?
3. Where are my support networks and who is involved? (This may include family, friends, colleagues and so forth.) Are there any gaps? Does anything surprise me?

Recommended reading and key resources

- Hughes, G. (2014). *Competence and self-care in counselling and psychotherapy.* Routledge.

My original book on the topic (second edition planned for 2026).

- Malinowski, A.J. (2014). *Self-care for the mental health practitioner.* Jessica Kingsley Publishers.

This book offers a detailed exploration of the hazards of being a therapist.

- Parry, S. (Ed.). (2017). *Effective self-care and resilience in clinical practice.* Jessica Kingsley Publishers.

This book offers personal accounts from practitioners.

- Spagnuolo Lobb, M. (2016). Psychotherapy in postmodern society. *Gestalt Today Malta, 1*(1), 97–113.

This journal article offers an analysis of common themes in society brought to therapy since the 20th century.

- Wotton, M. & Johnson, G. (2023). *A straight talking introduction to therapy: What it is, why it works, how to get it.* PCCS Books.

This book provides a simple, factual, objective explanation of what you get when you seek therapy, based on the latest research. It also tells you what works (and what doesn't work), how it works, what you should look for from therapy and your therapist, and what to do if it isn't helping.

References

Bager-Charleson, S. (2012). *Personal development in counselling and psychotherapy.* Learning Matters.

Bronfenbrenner, U. (1979). *The ecology of human development.* Harvard University Press.

Damasio, A. (2000). *The feeling of what happens.* Vintage.

Goncher, I.D., Sherman, M.F., Barnett, J.E. & Haskins, D. (2013). Programmatic perceptions of self-care emphasis and quality of life among graduates training in clinical psychology. The mediational role of self-care utilization. *Training and Education in Professional Psychology, 7*(1), 53–60.

Hawkins, P. & Shohet, R. (1989). *Supervision in the helping professions.* Open University Press.

Joyce, P. & Sills, C. (2010). *Skills in gestalt counselling and psychotherapy.* Sage.

Malinowski, A.J. (2014). *Self-care for the mental health practitioner.* Jessica Kingsley Publishers.

Miller, A. (1995). *The drama of being a child.* Virago Press.

Parry, S. (Ed.). (2017). *Effective self-care and resilience in clinical practice.* Jessica Kingsley Publishers.

Wall Kimmerer, R. (2020). *Braiding sweetgrass.* Penguin Books.

Section Three
Becoming a Practitioner and Beyond

13.

Professional practice and developing identity as a therapeutic practitioner

Peter Pearce

Introduction

Entering the psychological professions in the UK requires not only academic knowledge but also a deep understanding of professional practice and the development of a professional identity. This chapter explores key topics surrounding professional practice and identity formation for therapeutic practitioners. This includes ethical issues and practice, therapeutic models and how they position us, cultural humility, sensitivity and diversity, social privilege in therapy, community engagement, supervision and CPD. The chapter offers exercises, reflections and takeaways to guide you on your journey into and through this rewarding yet challenging profession.

Scope of the chapter

The key topics covered in this chapter are:

- ethical issues, practice and contemporary challenges
- the importance of the therapeutic model in professional identity
- cultural humility, sensitivity and diversity
- social privilege and anti-oppressive practice in therapy
- advocating for social justice, equity and community engagement
- supervision and CPD
- integrating personal and professional identities.

I also provide brief case illustrations throughout to help relate each aspect to real-world practice and end with an exercise and some questions for your own reflection.

Ethical issues and practice

Ethical practice is the cornerstone of therapeutic practice, ensuring that as practitioners we maintain professional standards and integrity in our work. The codes of ethics and conduct from professional bodies including the BPS, UKCP, BACP and BPC provide us with clear frameworks for ethical decision-making, emphasising principles such as respect, competence, responsibility and integrity. Similarly, the HCPC standards of proficiency outline the professional and ethical standards required for practice. These documents help guide us in our professional conduct, helping us to navigate complex ethical dilemmas and also helping to ensure the welfare of our clients. To maintain these standards, it is essential for practitioners to stay updated with the latest guidelines and engage in regular ethics training. Understanding and applying these principles in everyday practice not only protects our clients but also reinforces the credibility and trustworthiness of the profession. For more on ethical issues in practice please see Chapter 5.

Contemporary ethical challenges

Current ethical challenges are multifaceted, requiring our nuanced understanding and rigorous adherence to ethical guidelines. Some key contemporary ethical issues include confidentiality in the digital age, navigating dual relationships, managing boundaries in an interconnected world and using ethical decision-making models.

Confidentiality in the digital age

The rise of digital communication tools, online therapy platforms and the growing use of AI have introduced new complexities in maintaining client confidentiality. Data breaches, insecure communication channels, AI-driven transcription or note-taking tools and inadvertent sharing of sensitive information all pose significant risks in our work. Practitioners must therefore exercise caution, ensuring that any digital or AI-based tools they use comply with professional, legal and ethical standards for safeguarding client information.

> **Case illustration**: Maryam, a counselling psychologist, conducts a teletherapy session with a client, Aisha, using a video conferencing platform. After the session, she sends follow-up notes via email. While the video conferencing platform claims to be secure, recent news reveals a potential vulnerability in its encryption protocols. Additionally, Maryam uses her personal email account, which lacks robust security measures. Following reflection within supervision, Maryam consults the BPS and HCPC guidelines, which emphasise the importance of using secure, encrypted communication tools for therapy. She transitions to a HCPC-recommended platform with end-to-end encryption for video sessions

and sets up a professional email account with enhanced security features. Maryam also attends a workshop on digital ethics to stay updated on best practice for protecting client information online, including guidance on the safe and ethical use of AI.

Navigating dual relationships

Dual relationships can occur if, as a practitioner, we have another significant connection with a client outside the therapeutic context, which risks impairing objectivity and professional judgement.

> **Case illustration**: George, a psychotherapist, is approached by a long-term friend, Alfonso, seeking therapy for anxiety. For Alfonso, approaching George as an already known and trusted friend, might seem a logical and far easier step than seeking an anonymous professional. However, George providing therapy to Alfonso might blur the lines between their personal and professional relationships, potentially compromising the therapeutic process. George consults the ethical guidelines provided by UKCP, which advise against dual relationships that could impair professional judgement or increase the risk of harm to a client. He discusses the potential ethical conflict with his supervisor and decides to refer Alfonso to a trusted colleague. This decision helps maintain professional boundaries and ensures Alfonso receives uncompromised support.

Managing boundaries in an interconnected world

In an increasingly interconnected world, practitioners may face challenges in maintaining professional boundaries, particularly when clients attempt to engage with us on social media or in community settings.

> **Case illustration**: Leigh, a counsellor, receives a friend request on Facebook from a current client, Barry. Accepting the request risks blurring professional boundaries, while rejecting it might risk affecting the therapeutic relationship. Leigh reflects on the BACP guidelines regarding social media use and professional boundaries. They decide to discuss the issue with Barry in their next session, explaining the importance of maintaining clear boundaries to protect the therapeutic process. Leigh also reviews their privacy settings on social media to prevent future client interactions outside of therapy sessions. This conversation helps Barry to understand the professional necessity of boundaries and strengthens the therapeutic alliance.

Ethical decision-making models

Ethical dilemmas often require practitioners to make complex decisions that need to balance multiple ethical principles and professional responsibilities.

> **Case illustration**: Sangita, a counselling psychologist, works with a teenager, Lucy, who discloses engaging in risky behaviour that could harm herself or others. Sangita needs to decide whether to break confidentiality to ensure Lucy's safety, weighing the ethical principle of confidentiality against the duty to protect. Sangita applies an ethical decision-making model recommended by the BPS, which involves identifying the ethical issues, consulting relevant guidelines, considering potential consequences, seeking supervision and reflecting on her own values and principles. After consulting with her supervisor and considering the potential risks, Sangita decides to inform Lucy of the need for other people to know about the issues she has shared to keep her and others safe, and to think with Lucy about how this happens – whether Lucy would like to do this with Sangita alongside, or if she would prefer Sangita to share the necessary information with parents and appropriate authorities on her behalf. The conversation might go something like, 'You've shared this with me so you would like someone to know. Let's think together about who else might need to know to keep you and others safe and what might be our options for how best this should happen.' This approach helps balance the ethical imperatives of confidentiality and safeguarding.
>
> The range of contemporary ethical challenges we might encounter as practitioners demands our careful consideration and adherence to established guidelines. The application of ethical decision-making models, our continuing professional development and effective supervision will all support us as practitioners to navigate these issues and uphold the highest standards of professional ethics.

The importance of the therapeutic model in professional identity

Counselling and psychotherapy have evolved significantly over time, with different approaches (or 'forces') shaping the way practitioners engage with clients and their challenges. These forces each bring distinct philosophies, methods and perspectives that affect the therapist's professional identity as well as the therapeutic process. Each, in offering unique perspectives and techniques for helping our clients, also positions us differently as a therapeutic practitioner in relation to our clients, the relationship and the tasks and intentions of therapy. Familiarity with these approaches and how they position us as a practitioner, will enable us to make clear choices about professional identity, communicate our approach clearly to clients and colleagues, and adapt to each of our clients' unique needs. See Chapter 1 for an overview of the different forces.

Psychoanalytic/psychodynamic therapy

Perspective and techniques

This approach, rooted in the work of Sigmund Freud, focuses on exploring unconscious thoughts, early childhood experiences and the hidden dynamics that shape behaviour. Therapists using this model explore deep emotional conflicts and unresolved issues from the past that continue to affect the present. Techniques like free association, dream analysis and exploring transference (how the client projects feelings onto the therapist) are commonly used.

Therapist's position

As a practitioner, we position ourselves as an expert who helps clients uncover hidden aspects of their psyche. The relationship is often more formal, with the therapist maintaining some emotional distance to encourage deeper exploration. The goal is to bring unconscious material into awareness, leading to greater self-understanding and emotional healing.

Cognitive and behavioural therapies

Perspective and techniques

Cognitive behavioural therapies focus on the present, examining the link between thoughts, feelings and behaviours. Practitioners work with clients to identify negative thought patterns and behaviours that contribute to emotional distress. Techniques include cognitive restructuring, behavioural experiments and exposure therapy.

Therapist's position

Here, the therapist is more of a coach or teacher, helping clients develop practical tools to change their thinking and behaviour. The relationship is collaborative and active, with a focus on problem-solving. The task is to guide clients in developing healthier coping mechanisms and cognitive frameworks that lead to better emotional regulation and improved life choices.

Humanistic-existential therapy

Perspective and techniques

Humanistic and existential approaches emphasise the client's inherent potential for growth, personal meaning and self-awareness. These therapies focus on the present moment, personal responsibility and the client's subjective experience. Techniques often involve empathic listening, unconditional positive regard and encouraging self-exploration.

Therapist's position

In this approach, the therapist is seen as a compassionate guide or facilitator rather than an expert. The relationship strives to be non-hierarchical, based on deep empathy and genuine care. The therapist supports the client to explore their own potential and discover their own personal meaning, positioning therapy as a journey of self-discovery rather than problem-solving.

Transpersonal therapy

Perspective and techniques

Transpersonal therapy goes beyond the individual self, focusing on spiritual aspects of the human experience. This approach addresses clients' higher states of consciousness, personal transformation and connection with something greater than themselves. Techniques may include meditation, mindfulness, guided imagery and spiritual exploration.

Therapist's position

The therapist here serves as a spiritual guide or facilitator of transcendent experiences. The therapeutic relationship can be more open and exploratory, with a focus on helping the client find meaning beyond their immediate personal issues. This approach positions the therapist as a companion on a spiritual or existential journey, emphasising growth beyond psychological wellbeing.

Transcultural and social justice therapy

Perspective and techniques

This approach foregrounds the importance of cultural, social and political contexts in understanding a client's experiences. It acknowledges systemic factors like racism, sexism, classism and other social inequities that affect mental health. Techniques involve validating the client's experiences, exploring identity and addressing social justice issues directly within therapy.

Therapist's position

The therapist acts as an ally and advocate, acknowledging their own cultural positioning and bias while empowering clients to understand and navigate societal challenges. The relationship is built on mutual respect and collaboration, with a focus on affirming the client's cultural identity and working towards personal and social empowerment.

Each of these five forces in counselling and psychotherapy offers unique perspectives and techniques that shape not only the therapeutic process but also the practitioner's identity. For further expansion on these forces and relevant references, please see chapters 1 and 3.

Cultural humility, sensitivity and diversity

In a multicultural society like the UK, cultural humility and sensitivity is crucial for providing effective and inclusive psychological and therapeutic services. Recognising and valuing cultural diversity, including factors such as race, ethnicity, gender, sexuality and socio-economic status, is essential if we are to foster a therapeutic environment where all clients feel our efforts to understand and respect them.

Understanding cultural contexts

We must be aware of the cultural contexts in which our clients live and how these contexts influence their experiences and mental health. This involves ongoing education and self-reflection to challenge our own personal biases and assumptions.

> **Case illustration**: Ahmed, a British Muslim man of Pakistani heritage, sought therapy for anxiety. His therapist, Sarah, initially approached the sessions without considering Ahmed's cultural background. However, as she learned more about his life, she realised that his anxiety was partly related to his experiences of Islamophobia and pressure to conform to both his cultural traditions and British societal expectations. By educating herself about the cultural and religious aspects of Ahmed's life and understanding the impact of systemic discrimination, Sarah was better able to tailor her approach. This included acknowledging and validating Ahmed's experiences and exploring coping strategies that aligned with his cultural and religious values.

Adapting therapeutic practice

Cultural humility and sensitivity also require us to adapt therapeutic practice to meet the specific needs of diverse client populations. This might involve using culturally appropriate interventions, being mindful of language and communication styles, and considering cultural beliefs and values in our treatment planning.

> **Case illustration**: Chen, a Chinese woman, experienced depression and sought therapy. Her therapist, John, noticed that Chen often spoke about her family and community in their sessions. John adapted his therapeutic approach by incorporating culturally relevant interventions, such as family systems theory, which resonated with Chen's cultural emphasis on familial relationships. Additionally, John attended carefully to metaphors and analogies Chen used that were culturally familiar for her, enhancing her engagement and comfort in the therapy process.

Cultural humility and self-examination

Cultural humility involves a lifelong commitment to self-evaluation and self-critique, recognising the power imbalances in the therapeutic relationship, and developing mutually beneficial and non-paternalistic clinical and advocacy partnerships. For us as counselling psychologists and psychotherapists, this means continuously examining our own cultural inheritance and positioning, to support our anti-oppressive practice.

Case illustration: Seema, a woman of Indian heritage, felt misunderstood by her previous therapist due to cultural differences. Her new therapist, Emma, endeavoured to maintain cultural humility by acknowledging her own cultural limitations and bias. Emma openly acknowledged her lack of familiarity with Indian cultural practices and invited Seema to share insights about her cultural background, as well as Emma endeavouring to educate herself by reading widely around Indian culture and speaking at length with colleagues from an Indian heritage about differing cultural practices and considerations. This approach helped to establish a more trusted, collaborative therapeutic relationship where Seema experienced her cultural identity as respected and valued.

Attending to our cultural sensitivity and humility and striving for anti-oppressive practice through genuine broaching conversations, are essential contributions to the creation of an inclusive and effective therapeutic environment in our work with diverse client populations. As therapists we can help by continuously educating ourselves, reflecting on our own biases and adapting our practice. This can help, both to enhance our therapeutic relationships and to support our clients to feel more empowered to navigate their cultural identities and experiences with confidence and resilience.

Social privilege in therapy

As practitioners we must critically engage with our own social privilege to deliver truly competent care, carefully considering how we might consciously and subconsciously enact oppression within our therapeutic work. Only through striving to develop a deep understanding of our own privilege, can we hope to better appreciate the lived experiences of marginalised clients.

Case illustration: Derek, a white, middle-class therapist working with Charles, a Black client from a low-income background, may find himself inadvertently perpetuating harmful stereotypes or misunderstanding Charles's experiences due to a lack of awareness of his own privilege.

Through self-reflection and critical analysis, Derek might hope to identify his potential bias and work towards creating a more equitable therapeutic space for Charles.

Anti-oppressive practice

Anti-oppressive practice involves actively addressing and challenging systemic and structural inequalities that affect our clients' mental health and wellbeing. This approach emphasises advocacy, social justice and empowerment in our therapeutic work (Khan, 2023; Winter & Charura, 2023).

Case illustration: James, a Black British man, experienced racial discrimination in his workplace, leading to significant stress and low self-esteem. His therapist, Laura, recognised the impact of systemic racism on James's mental health. Laura integrated an anti-oppressive approach by recognising the broader context of James's experiences and supporting him in developing strategies to advocate for himself. With James's consent, she also connected him with community resources and support groups for Black professionals, fostering a sense of empowerment, allyship and solidarity.

Advocating for social justice, equity and community engagement

Our professional role in advocating for social justice and equity involves us actively challenging systemic barriers and discrimination that negatively affect mental health. This advocacy can take many forms, which may include policy work, community engagement and professional activism.

Policy advocacy

As counselling psychologists and psychotherapists, we can engage in policy advocacy to promote mental health equity. This can involve collaborating with professional organisations to influence public policy affecting mental health services and striving to address disparities in access to care.

Case illustration: Kasia, a psychotherapist, noticed a significant gap in mental health services for low-income communities in her town. She collaborated with other mental health professionals and community leaders to advocate for increased funding for mental health services in underserved areas. Through persistent lobbying and presenting data on the mental health needs of these communities, they successfully influenced local policymakers to allocate additional resources, resulting in the establishment of several new community mental health centres.

Community engagement

Engaging with the community is another vital aspect of social justice advocacy. This might involve our taking part in outreach programmes, public education campaigns and partnership with community organisations to help raise awareness about mental health issues and to reduce issues of stigma.

> **Case illustration**: Ali, a psychotherapist, observed a high rate of mental health issues among refugees in his community. Recognising the barriers people faced in accessing mental healthcare, he partnered with a local refugee support organisation to develop a series of workshops on trauma and mental health. These workshops were designed to be culturally sensitive and were conducted in multiple languages. Ali's efforts not only provided refugees with valuable information and coping strategies but also helped build trust and reduce stigma around seeking mental health support.

Professional activism

Professional activism involves using our professional platform and influence to advocate for systemic changes within the psychological professions and broader society. This can include advocating for diversity and inclusion within professional organisations and addressing systemic bias within psychological research and practice.

> **Case illustration**: Emily, a counselling psychologist, was concerned about the lack of diversity in the psychological professions. She joined a task force within her professional organisation aimed at increasing diversity and inclusion. Emily and her colleagues conducted surveys and focus groups to understand the barriers faced by under-represented groups in entering the profession. Based on their findings, they developed a series of initiatives, including mentorship programmes, scholarships and training on cultural sensitivity and anti-oppressive practice for existing professionals. These efforts contributed to a more inclusive and diverse professional community, helping it better reflect the society it serves.

Addressing systemic inequities

Addressing systemic inequities requires a comprehensive understanding of the cultural, historical and socio-political contexts affecting clients. This is particularly crucial when working with marginalised populations, such as refugees, who often face multiple layers of trauma and discrimination acting to intersect.

Case illustration: Amina, a refugee from Syria, sought therapy to cope with her experiences of war and displacement. Her therapist, David, offered a trauma-informed approach, acknowledging the complex layers of Amina's trauma. David also worked hard to recognise the socio-political challenges Amina faced in the UK, such as a language barrier, isolation and uncertainty about her asylum status. He strived to provide a culturally sensitive intervention, helped Amina navigate social services, and, with her consent, helped connect her with a local refugee support group. David's holistic approach helped enable Amina to address her mental health needs while also empowering her to navigate her new environment more effectively.

Advocacy and social justice should be integral components of our professional practice. By engaging in anti-oppressive practice, policy advocacy, community engagement and professional activism, we can contribute to working towards a more equitable and inclusive society. Such efforts will not only enhance our individual therapeutic outcomes but also contribute to broader systemic change, helping mental health services to become more accessible and responsive to the diverse needs of all communities.

Supervision and continued professional development

Engaging in regular supervision and CPD activities is vital for maintaining our professional competence and wellbeing as counselling psychologists and psychotherapists. Supervision provides a structured space for reflection, feedback and support, helping us as practitioners to navigate the complexities of our work and enhance our clinical skills.

By fostering self-awareness, resilience and a commitment to self-care, these practices can help us as practitioners maintain our wellbeing and passion for the profession and help to prevent burnout. Please see Chapter 12 for more about the prevention of burnout as well as self-care more broadly.

Professional identity formation

Developing a strong and authentic professional identity is an ongoing process that involves exploring our values, beliefs and personal attributes in relation to the roles of counselling psychologist and psychotherapist. This self-awareness can both enhance our professional effectiveness and help contribute to a sense of fulfilment and purpose in our work.

Reflecting on personal values and beliefs

Personal reflection is a key aspect of professional identity formation. As practitioners we must consider how our own values and beliefs align with the ethical principles and guidelines of the profession. This involves examining our personal motivation for entering the field as well as identifying our strengths and areas for growth.

> **Case illustration**: Hannah, a trainee counselling psychologist, found herself struggling with the ethical dilemma of maintaining confidentiality while knowing a client was engaging in harmful behaviour. Through personal reflection, she examined her own values around honesty, responsibility and care. Moreover, by discussing her concerns with her supervisor and reflecting on the ethical guidelines for the profession, Hannah was able to navigate the situation in a way that upheld her personal values and professional responsibilities, reinforcing her commitment to ethical practice.

Integrating personal and professional identities

A coherent professional identity integrates our personal attributes with our professional role and responsibilities. This involves finding a balance between our own personal authenticity and professional expectations, allowing each practitioner to bring their whole selves to their work while upholding ethical standards.

> **Case illustration**: Michael, a counselling psychologist who identifies with the LGBTQ+ community, initially felt the need to compartmentalise his personal identity and his professional role. Over time, through reflective practice and discussion with mentors, Michael learned to integrate his personal experience and identity with his therapeutic work. He found that being open about his identity, when appropriate, helped build trust and rapport with clients with similar lived experiences, enhancing his effectiveness as a therapist and his sense of authenticity in his work.

Contemporary challenges in identity formation

Trainees often face challenges such as imposter syndrome, balancing personal and professional identities, and adapting to the evolving demands of this field. Addressing these challenges through reflective practice, mentorship and peer support can be a crucial support for developing a resilient and authentic professional identity.

> **Case illustration**: Rachel, a counselling psychologist in training, frequently experienced imposter syndrome, doubting her competence

and fearing judgement from her peers. By engaging in reflective practice, she identified the roots of her self-doubt and worked on building self-compassion. With the support of her mentor and peer group, who shared their own similar experiences, Rachel gradually developed a stronger sense of self-confidence and professional identity. This support was crucial in helping her recognise her growth and capabilities as a competent practitioner.

The formation of a professional identity is a dynamic and ongoing process. It requires sustained reflection on personal values, alongside the integration of personal and professional selves. This development is supported by engaging in personal therapy, seeking peer support and mentorship, and maintaining a commitment to linking theory with practice. It also calls for a consistent sensitivity to issues of diversity and inclusion, and a willingness to engage with the evolving challenges of contemporary practice. Through these efforts, as practitioners we can hope to cultivate a resilient, authentic and effective professional identity – one that not only strengthens therapeutic work but also provides a sense of purpose and fulfilment, and supports us in navigating the complexities of the field with integrity and ethical awareness.

Exercise: Personal reflection task

Take a moment to consider the values and beliefs that you hold close. How do these shape your perspective on what it means to be a therapeutic practitioner? Reflecting on your core values – such as empathy, integrity, respect, or justice – can provide insight into your unique therapeutic stance.

- **Task:** Write down your top three core values. Think about how each value manifests in your approach to therapy. For example, if integrity is a core value, how does this show up in your commitment to honest and transparent communication with clients?
- **Reflection:** Consider any potential conflicts between your personal values and professional ethical guidelines. How might you navigate these if they arise in your practice?

Top takeaways

- **Ethical standards as a foundation**: Adhering to ethical standards provides a framework that supports both client welfare and the integrity of the therapeutic profession.
- **Continuous skill enhancement through CPD**: Lifelong learning through CPD keeps practitioners informed and competent, ensuring that therapeutic skills and knowledge remain relevant and effective.
- **Cultural sensitivity and intersectionality**: Recognising and respecting the diversity of client experiences enhances therapeutic rapport and allows for a more inclusive practice.
- **Value of supervision and self-care**: Regular supervision and prioritising self-care are essential for sustaining wellbeing and resilience in the profession, especially when dealing with complex or emotionally demanding cases.
- **Commitment to advocacy and social justice**: Practitioners are encouraged to integrate social justice into their work, advocating for equitable and accessible mental health services that respect and empower all clients.

Questions for reflection

1. What helps you navigate ethical dilemmas in your practice?
2. How do you incorporate cultural humility and sensitivity in your work?
3. In what ways do supervision and CPD contribute to your professional development?
4. How does your personal identity affect your professional identity?
5. How do you balance self-care with professional responsibilities?

Recommended reading and key resources

- Douglas, B., Woolfe, R., Strawbridge, S., Kasket, E. & Galbraith, V. (Eds.). (2016). *The handbook of counselling psychology* (4th ed.). Sage.

A comprehensive and scholarly overview of the field of counselling psychology, this handbook provides critical insights into theory, practice and research, helping practitioners situate their work within wider psychological and social contexts.

- Murphy, D. (Ed.). (2017). *Counselling psychology: A textbook for study and practice*. Wiley-Blackwell.

A clear and accessible core text that introduces key concepts, debates and contemporary issues in counselling psychology, making it highly useful for both trainee and experienced practitioners seeking to reflect on their professional identity and practice.

- British Association for Counselling and Psychotherapy. (2018). *Ethical framework for the counselling professions*. https://www.bacp.co.uk/events-and-resources/ethics-and-standards/ethical-framework-for-the-counselling-professions/
- British Psychoanalytic Council. (2024). Standards of conduct, practice and ethics. https://www.bpc.org.uk/download/12595/Standards-of-Conduct-Practice-and-Ethics-2024-FINAL.pdf
- British Psychological Society. (2021). *Code of ethics and conduct*. https://explore.bps.org.uk/content/report-guideline/bpsrep.2021.inf94
- Health and Care Professions Council. (2023). *Standards of proficiency: Practitioner psychologists*. https://www.hcpc-uk.org/globalassets/resources/standards/standards-of-proficiency---practitioner-psychologists.pdf
- Health and Care Professions Council. (2024). *Standards of conduct, performance and ethics*. https://www.hcpc-uk.org/globalassets/resources/standards/standards-of-conduct-performance-and-ethics-2024.pdf
- UK Council for Psychotherapy. (2019). *UKCP code of ethics and professional practice*. https://www.psychotherapy.org.uk/media/bkjdm33f/ukcp-code-of-ethics-and-professional-practice-2019.pdf

References

Khan, M. (2023). *Working within diversity: A reflective guide to anti-oppressive practice in counselling and therapy*. Jessica Kingsley Publishers.

Winter, L.A. & Charura, D. (Eds.). (2023). *The handbook of social justice in psychological therapies: Power, politics, change*. SAGE Publications.

14.

Career pathways and working in different contexts and systems

Emma Bradshaw

Introduction

When nearing the end of professional training, attention will turn to finding a suitable environment within which to work. This chapter considers the career pathways that may be chosen, before focusing on working in different contexts and systems. It explores working with different client groups and work environments, including matters relevant to working in each. Specialist services in which to work will also be outlined. Then, I will share my career pathway as a case study of working in different contexts and systems. It will demonstrate how working with different clinical models, work environments and client groups can be integrated.

Before the job search begins, reflect on what was enjoyable during training placements to identify personal skills, experience, aspirations and preferences. Consideration of preferred client groups, clinical settings and ways of working will support ethical working that meets personal values. Awareness of race, culture, diversity, ethics, politics and religion will inform decisions on whether to work with a specific group of people; for example, refugees and asylum seekers, those living with disability, or those practising a particular faith.

While traditionally therapy has been face-to-face, many practitioners moved online during the Covid-19 pandemic, and this is now an accepted way of working. While therapists have cited difficulties including reduced interpersonal cues, feelings of isolation and fatigue, and technical issues, online working is effective and many choose to work wholly or partially in this way (McBeath et al., 2020).

Also important is reflection on working as an individual clinician, within a team of therapists or within a multi-disciplinary team (MDT). It is highly recommended to speak with a potential employer before applying for a job and to visit the service in person if possible. This provides the opportunity to have a prior introduction to potential interviewers and to establish whether the environment aligns with personal preferences.

Scope of the chapter

In this chapter I will cover the following key topics:

- career pathways available to newly qualified clinicians
- working in different contexts and systems.

A case study points to takeaways, and questions for reflection will end this chapter.

Career pathways

Many career pathways are available to those working in the field of counselling, psychotherapy and counselling psychology. Some individuals are clear about their desired way of working at the outset. For others, the path becomes clearer during training placements in environments that feel like a good fit. Many have a career journey that develops over time.

The key skill at the heart of being a counsellor, psychotherapist or counselling psychologist is, of course, conducting psychological therapy. However, several associated decisions need to be made, such as whether to practise using just one treatment model, or to embrace an eclectic approach (using one model for one client and a different model for another client, depending upon their presenting difficulties) or an integrative approach (where aspects of different therapeutic approaches are integrated according to the needs of the client). The decision may be informed by the type of training undertaken, or perhaps the requirements of the employer. Additionally, therapeutic work may focus on one client group, or different groups (e.g. working with both adults and children). Following qualification, further training may be conducted in additional treatment modalities, or clinicians may specialise in a specific area (such as neuropsychology, functional neurological disorders (FND) or eating disorders).

Therapeutic work, however, is not the only pathway that can be chosen. Before starting a new role, it is necessary to establish whether career progression is a possibility, if that is a personal goal. Some may aspire to work in a leadership position, using additional skills in managing and supervising others. The option of developing existing skills beyond therapy may also be important (e.g. by training to become a coach or an expert witness).

Other important options that run alongside therapeutic work are teaching and/or research. Passing therapeutic skills on to others or maintaining an evidence base for therapeutic work may be skills that align with personal values, in addition to adding variety to the workload. Consultancy is another area chosen by some: perhaps working with a team, rather than doing therapeutic work directly with individuals.

Working in different contexts and systems

Here we think about the different contexts and systems within which a counsellor, psychotherapist or counselling psychologist may work. For ease, these have been categorised into client groups, work environments and occupational settings, which will be introduced in turn, alongside the considerations specific to working in that area. Suggestions for further reading have been made to enable deeper understanding of each area.

Client groups

Therapists may choose to work with individuals, couples, families or groups of people. An essential difference is that therapy with individuals focuses on what is going on *inside* people, whereas working with couples, families or groups directs attention to what is going on *between* them (McLeod, 2019). It is important to have received training appropriate to the therapy provided, and to access the support of other professionals if relevant. Working with a combination of different client groups will undoubtably bring greater variety to the job role. Each group is briefly considered below.

Adult mental health

Working with individuals in an adult mental health setting provides opportunities to work with people experiencing a wide range of difficulties including anxiety disorders, depression, trauma, eating disorders, addictions and relationship difficulties. While it is not within the remit of this chapter to cover the complex issues in adult mental health, most therapy training courses will have focused on this area and may align themselves with a related therapeutic approach. A comprehensive understanding of work in this area has been described by John McLeod (2019); see recommended reading.

Considerations specific to working in adult mental health include:

- regardless of the approach used, the therapeutic relationship is key to facilitate change (Charura & Paul, 2014)
- socio-cultural issues such as sexuality, social class and social justice are important and should be taken seriously (McLeod, 2019)
- race, culture and ethnicity are intrinsic to the understanding of adult mental health (Charura & Lago, 2021).

Child and adolescent mental health

Working with children and young people (CYP) is a career choice popular with many therapists. The age range of clients in this category varies according to setting but may include those up to the age of 25 years. Settings within which this work takes place include healthcare settings (outpatient and inpatient), school-based counselling, student counselling services and online or community settings.

Four guiding principles for counselling psychologists working with CYP who are still in statutory education (which are also relevant to counsellors and psychotherapists) have been identified by Hanley et al. (2015): referral source is important to consider, as CYP are usually referred by adults; the need for services to be youth friendly and accessible to ensure that CYP feel comfortable in the setting; navigating the therapeutic relationship may be different from working with adults; and CYP should be at the centre of decision-making. Finally, there is a need to be responsive to the person and presenting issues to ensure sensitivity to power, involvement in decision-making, and desire for an equal relationship. Additionally, professionals are encouraged to remain open to learning from their young clients to develop and enrich their therapeutic practice (Gifford, 2025).

When working with CYP, acknowledging developmental stages is important, as biological and psychological changes occur in the transition from childhood to adulthood. Presenting problems of distress can be internally or externally focused and may be accompanied by formal diagnosis, which should be carefully navigated. As CYP develop, so will their sense of 'self', their social environment and the complex interactions between the two (Hanley et al., 2015). A practical guide to support those working with young people has been written by Helen Gifford (2025); see recommended reading.

Considerations specific to working in CYP mental health include:

- therapeutic approach and modality of working to use (e.g. one-to-one or family/group work)
- adaptations to therapeutic work (e.g. bringing art or technology into the work if language is not a primary way of connecting)
- helping CYP to navigate relationships with others, especially as they are unable to transcend their environment.

Naturally occurring systems (families and couples)

While much therapy is conducted on an individual level, as humans are social beings, it makes sense to work with their wider systems. Therefore, many therapists choose to work with couples and/or families. Recently there has been a growing trend towards working integratively in couples and family work, the advantages of which include greater flexibility of treatment: integrative therapies draw from a broader theoretical base, thereby offering explanations for a wider range of presenting issues and incorporating new understanding as they become available (e.g. evolving definitions and cultural understanding of couples and families). Integrative therapists draw upon the strengths of several individual approaches, directing interventions to suit the specific needs of the couple or family in a way that feels comfortable to them as a therapist (Lebow, 2019). Further understanding of the historical and theoretical aspects of this work are considered by Eddy Street (2003); see recommended reading.

Considerations specific to working in naturally occurring systems (Lebow, 2019) include:

- Many models that are integrated into family therapy are focused on the individual. Therefore, the focus could be on internal processes, diluting the systemic focus of the therapy.
- Therapists are encouraged to practise evidence-based therapies; however, there are more evidence-based individual therapies than couples/family therapies, so it is challenging to keep the systemic nature of the work at the forefront.
- The challenge of deciding *what* should be integrated can be problematic, especially related to issues of gender, culture and other aspects of intersectionality.

Group work

There are many benefits to working with groups of people that are appealing to therapists. Groups can be based on models of therapy – for example, CBT, acceptance and commitment therapy (ACT), compassion-focused therapy (CFT), dialectical behaviour therapy (DBT) and person-centred or psychodynamic approaches, and may therefore differ in approach and content. They may also be integrative in nature, at both a theoretical and an interventions level. Interventions could include confrontation, psycho-education, use of metaphor, accessing emotions and challenging irrational beliefs. They may also focus on a specific theme, experience or human characteristic (Gilbert & Shmukler, 2003), for example, alcohol or drug dependence, assault or disaster, or help with emotion regulation. More can be read about group psychotherapy in the book *The Theory and Practice of Group Psychotherapy* (Yalom & Leszcz, 2020); see recommended reading at the end of the chapter.

Considerations specific to working with groups include:

- Assessment of clients' suitability to join the group is recommended (Gilbert & Shmukler, 2003).
- Training and/or CPD may be necessary prior to setting up a group (Yalom & Leszcz, 2020).
- Contracting needs to be clear and specific and may differ from contracting with individual clients (Yalom & Leszcz, 2020).
- Adequate clinical supervision is vital: this may be in addition to supervision received for individual work.

Work environments

Public sector

The experience of working in public sector organisations such as the NHS can differ greatly. The NHS is divided into trusts, each run separately and providing different working environments according to the focus of the Trust and the allocation of funding. Within each trust are several different departments/teams, which also differ: some focus on physical health and have a mental health practitioner working within the MDT; others focus on mental health, including primary care services such as NHS Talking Therapies for anxiety and depression, and secondary care services such as community mental health teams (CMHT). Working within the NHS can be both demanding and rewarding: standardised pay bands are offered with benefits, including continuing professional development (CPD) and a good pension scheme.

Considerations specific to working in the public sector include:

- Possible tension between the values of the organisation and the psychotherapeutic approach (e.g. between the NHS medical model versus values of relationship/feelings prioritised in psychological therapy) (McLeod, 2019).
- The management of the NHS Trust may be unfamiliar with how therapy works, which is different to medical intervention. Implementation of targets can therefore misalign with therapeutic work.

Private healthcare

Since the first private mental health facility, the Retreat Hospital, York, was established in 1796 (Tuke, 1996), private healthcare providers have continued to offer inpatient and outpatient services. Some operate countrywide, whereas others are smaller, in one region.

Considerations specific to working in private healthcare include:

- the salary offered by private healthcare companies is often higher than the public sector
- smaller companies may benefit from fewer unnecessary rules and regulations
- possibly fewer opportunities for progression
- working with a smaller range of clients, who are either self-funded or paid for by their insurance cover.

Charities

Working for a charity is another option to consider. Some offer paid therapist positions, while others provide volunteering opportunities. Charities such as

MIND or Childline are large, national organisations, whereas others are small, local organisations which specialise, for example, in support for women (e.g. rape or domestic abuse), the LGBTQ+ community, and bereavement (McLeod, 2019).

Considerations specific to working for a charity include:

- advantages involve supporting a social mission that may align with personal values
- clinical supervision and CPD training are often provided to develop and support therapeutic interventions
- difficulties of harmonious integration of paid and voluntary workers can sometimes occur.

Educational environments

Opportunities are available to work as a therapist with CYP in schools, colleges and universities. Working within a school may include one-to-one therapy or sometimes psycho-education when working within a wider teaching team. Therapies such as art therapy are often relevant. The provision of school and community-based counselling services for CYP aged 7–18 in the UK is appreciated by learners, teachers and parents and contributes to improved wellbeing, although services are not necessarily well embedded into the education system (Copeland et al., 2024).

Opportunities are also available to work with young people and adults within a university environment. Provision may vary but can range from occasional contact to monitor mental wellbeing to delivering therapy. Services often operate in liaison with GPs at local health centres, who facilitate access to secondary care services if required. Counselling can support students with a range of issues and can be particularly effective for improving depression, anxiety, wellbeing, hostility, social anxiety and academic distress (Broglia et. al., 2023). More has been written about this specialist area by Dr Katie McArthur (2016); see recommended reading.

Considerations specific to working in an educational environment include:

- Working within a school environment may involve working alongside an educational psychologist as part of the MDT.
- University wellbeing services support students with issues including learning support, housing and funding, in addition to mental health support.

Prisons

Investigations worldwide have shown that mental disorders are higher among prisoners than in the general population, although the extent to which prison contributes to this is uncertain. An increased risk of self-harm, suicidal ideation, violence and victimisation is also present within the prison population (Fazel et al., 2016). Working within a prison environment can be both rewarding and challenging, and therapists can supplement the work of forensic psychologists in both individual and group settings.

CBT and mindfulness-based therapies have been found to be modestly effective when working with prisoners presenting with depression and anxiety, with no difference between the effectiveness of group or individual interventions (Yoon et al., 2017). An overview of the issues related to working within a prison environment has been written by Professor Graham Towl (2002); see recommended reading.

Considerations specific to working in prisons include:

- Delivering therapeutic interventions in prisons can be particularly challenging given that prisons are low-trust environments. Clients often have a history of abuse, which may affect their ability to form trusting relationships. The role of self-care and clinical supervision is particularly pertinent when working in this setting.
- Prisoners may be suspicious about confidentiality, which could impact therapeutic work.
- The work may focus on topics such as reducing the risk of reoffending and addressing domestic violence (Towl, 2002).

Occupational settings

Provision of therapy within an occupational setting is available in organisations including the emergency services (such as the police, fire fighters and paramedics), whose personnel face difficult situations as part of their everyday work. In these settings, therapists may need to balance the needs of the employee with the restraints of the organisation, particularly if it is publicly funded. Therefore, the types of interventions are varied and may include early intervention work as well as trauma therapy programmes (Tehrani, 2015).

Additionally, some commercial organisations offer therapy to support the emotional wellbeing of staff members. This can be offered via employee counselling schemes, often referred to as 'employee assistance programmes' (EAPs), which support employees with mental and physical health problems and aim to maintain performance and attendance at work.

Considerations specific to working in occupational settings include:

- Therapy provision is funded by the organisation, which can lead to mistrust regarding confidentiality.

- An uncomfortable situation could be created if the values of the therapist/therapy conflict with the values of the organisation (McLeod, 2019).

Independent practice

Working in independent practice (sometimes referred to as private practice) is appealing to many therapists, either as an addition to working as an employee or as a sole way of working. Working in independent practice can be in a self-employed capacity alone or as an associate for an established organisation. Some therapists work as sole traders, whereas others set up a limited company; it is advisable to seek guidance from an experienced accountant familiar with the field to establish the best route.

Several advantages and disadvantages of working in independent practice were identified by Robert Bor and Anne Stokes (2011):

Advantages

- the ability to supplement a part-time role if full-time work is difficult to find
- freedom to work without the restrictions of an organisation, including choosing which clients to work with and where to work with them
- choices in diary management according to individual commitments and lifestyle
- options of specialising in a specific area and of using additional skills (such as coaching, supervision or delivering workshops).

Disadvantages

- the absence of security that comes with being an employee (including paid leave)
- additional costs (e.g. CPD, supervision fees, insurances and pension plan)
- working conditions: working in isolation; possible irregular hours; finding appropriate consulting rooms; the lack of legal protection that comes with working for an organisation; and the responsibility of managing personal security.

While it is not within the remit of this chapter to consider these factors in depth, or the actual process of starting your own therapy business, a comprehensive guide aimed to help counsellors, therapists and psychologists to set up in independent practice has been produced by Bor and Stokes (2011); see recommended reading.

Specialist services

Many counsellors, psychotherapists and counselling psychologists choose to work in specialist services, focusing on helping individuals with a particular issue. This work is often conducted within an MDT in liaison with other professionals (e.g. medical doctors, nurses, occupational therapists, physiotherapists and so on), providing a collaborative input with therapy as part of the provision.

Examples of specialist services include those aimed at a specific client group, such as older adults, perinatal services, functional needs and disabilities (including autism and ADHD) and sexual identity (which includes matters relating to gender, sexual, erotic and relational diversity – GSERD). Other services may support individuals to manage specific problematic behaviours, such as addictions or eating disorders. Also, specific services help those who are experiencing or who have experienced difficulties in life, such as physical health issues (including chronic pain, chronic fatigue syndrome, oncology), domestic abuse and psychological trauma, or those who have become a refugee and/or asylum seeker. A helpful guide to working in a range of clinical settings is found in the book *Clinical Psychology in Practice*, edited by Beinart, Kennedy and Llewelyn (2009); see recommended reading.

Considerations specific to working within a specialist service include:

- opportunities to develop expertise in one specific area
- the benefits of networking with therapists from similar specialist services across the country
- the possibility of aligning with one specific evidence-based model relevant to the client group – for example, ACT for chronic pain (McCracken & Vowles, 2014)
- therapists may need to make adaptations to the way they would usually work. For example, those delivering CBT to people who have intellectual disabilities may need to consider neuropsychological processes such as memory and executive functioning – for example, ability to manage planning, problem-solving and self-regulation (Dagnan et al., 2023)
- therapists may need to accommodate additional guidelines specific to working with a particular group.

Case study

To demonstrate working in different contexts and systems, I will share my own career pathway as an example. I began by studying for a psychology degree part time while looking after my two young children, simultaneously working as a support worker in a brain injury hospital, witnessing applied psychology in action. I also volunteered with the Samaritans, receiving training in person-centred listening. These experiences led to my decision to train as a counselling psychologist. I completed a Certificate in Counselling Skills and applied for the Doctorate of Counselling Psychology course at Teesside University.

During the three-year, full-time training programme, I had three placements. The first was in a private therapy practice, working with self-funding adults. My supervisor (an experienced counsellor and Jungian analytic psychotherapist) was kind, supportive and often helpfully challenging. My second placement was in an alcohol addiction service. Not initially my first choice, but I was glad that I pushed myself outside of my comfort zone. Both the individual and group work were rewarding, giving me a deeper understanding of the ways that people cope with adverse life experiences. My third training placement was in an NHS psychoanalytic service. The intensely supervised work was with one client for 40 sessions, teaching me to work and think psychodynamically.

Once qualified, I gained a temporary contract with a supportive team of psychologists in a large hospital, working with chronic pain, cystic fibrosis and neurotology. This taught me about the close links between physical and mental health. I then joined an NHS chronic pain service on a permanent contract. I worked in an MDT using the ACT model (for which I received additional training) with individuals and groups. I also trained in eye movement desensitisation and reprocessing (EMDR) therapy and was amazed to see how this helped those suffering with chronic pain. Additionally, I trained in clinical supervision and supervised a trainee clinical psychologist from the local doctorate course.

After two years I moved jobs to work closer to home and develop my skills in adult mental health. I returned to the setting of my first ever placement, now feeling more confident to work with different client presentations. I trained in CFT and DBT, and became accredited in EMDR, all of which added more skills to my 'toolbox'. I worked with outpatients, but also facilitated groups and individual therapy for inpatients experiencing trauma-related dissociation. I became line manager to a newly qualified psychologist and an assistant psychologist.

After three years, the service partially closed, so I started working part time as a senior lecturer on a new Doctorate in Counselling Psychology course at York St John University, enabling me to develop teaching and research skills. I wrote and taught one of the course modules, and supervised trainee research.

I now felt ready to start an independent practice alongside my university role, setting up as a sole trader. In 2020, the Covid-19 pandemic enforced sudden changes and both my teaching and therapeutic work moved online: an option I had not considered before. While I had always rejected online therapy prior to the pandemic, I briefly worked part time online for an NHS IAPT service in a different part of the country and enjoyed working this way. Importantly, clients reported the benefits of attending online, so I felt that the quality of my therapeutic work was not compromised.

In line with my values as a counselling psychologist, I have supervised clinicians who work with refugees and asylum seekers, with women who have experienced domestic abuse, and with men recovering from trauma.

After three years in independent practice, the work was going well, so, in the interests of work/life balance, I concentrated on that full-time. I now have a therapy room in my garden and do a mixture of online and face-to-face therapeutic work. I collaborated with two colleagues on a book project, which added a further dimension to my work. I am not sure what the future holds, although I understand there is a group of psychologists who are 'digital nomads', travelling the world while continuing to work, which is rather tempting!

Top takeaways

Top tip: when applying for a job, I recommend meeting the interviewer/team first: both to stand out as an applicant and to ensure that the job is right for you.

- Think carefully about the type of work that you want… don't accept a job just because it is offered if it is not right for you.
- Be open to considering client work that might be outside your comfort zone.

Questions for reflection

- What client group would you like to work with and why? Would you consider working with a client group/service outside your comfort zone?
- What type of organisation would suit you best? Why? What type of organisation would you definitely not consider working for and why?
- Do you want to work with individuals, couples or groups? Why is this your preference?
- Would you like to work on your own or within a team? What is your reason for this?
- What further training would you be interested in pursuing after qualification?
- Have you considered the pros and cons of online working?

Recommended reading and key resources

Specialist services

- Beinart, H., Kennedy, P. & Llewelyn, S. (Eds.). (2009). *Clinical psychology in practice*. John Wiley & Sons.

Although aimed at the practice of clinical psychology, this book nonetheless offers a helpful guide to working in a range of clinical settings, with a variety of client groups, across the lifespan. Chapters include helping those with different physical and mental health conditions, as well as working with specific groups.

Independent practice

- Bor, R. & Stokes, A. (2011). *Setting up in independent practice: A handbook for counsellors, therapists and psychologists*. Macmillan International Higher Education.

This comprehensive guide acts as a handbook to have alongside you as you set up and work in independent practice.

Work environments

- Douglas, B., Kasket, E., Strawbridge, S. & Woolfe, R. (2016). *The handbook of counselling psychology* (4th ed.). Sage.

This core text of counselling psychology is now in its fourth edition. It covers a comprehensive range of topics, including working with clients across the lifespan, groupwork, different workplace settings, diversity and ethical issues.

Child and adolescent mental health

- Gifford, H. (2025). *A practical guide for working therapeutically with teenagers and young adults*. PCCS Books.

An engaging and practical guide to support professionals working with CYP.

Occupational settings

- https://www.bacp.co.uk/bacp-journals/bacp-workplace/

BACP has a division and dedicated journal called *BACP Workplace*, which focuses on counselling in the workplace and the wider emotional and psychological aspects of health at work.

School-based counselling

- McArthur, K. (2016). *The school-based counselling primer: A concise, accessible introduction*. PCCS Books.

This introductory text provides an overview of working in a school setting.

Adult mental health

- McLeod, J. (2019). *An introduction to counselling and psychotherapy: Theory, research and practice* (6th ed.). McGraw Hill Education.

This best-selling book provides a comprehensive overview of the theory and practice of counselling and psychotherapy. It includes different ways of working with various client groups, adding depth to the points raised in this chapter.

Couples and families

- Street, E. (2003). Counselling psychology and naturally occurring systems. In B. Woolfe, W. Dryden & S. Strawbridge (Eds.), *Handbook of counselling psychology* (pp. 419–441). Sage Publications.

Street's chapter explores the development of working with couples and families as a counselling psychologist. It considers the theoretical aspects of the interactional/ systemic approach and empirical evaluation of the field.

Prisons

- Towl, G.J. (2002). Working with offenders: The ins and outs. *The Psychologist, 15*(5), 236–239.
- Tuke, S. (1813/1996). *Description of the Retreat: An institution near York for insane persons of the Society of Friends: Containing an account of its origin and progress, the modes of treatment, and a statement of cases.* W. Alexander. (First published 1813, Process Press.)

These two resources consider therapeutic work in forensic settings.

Group work

- Yalom, I.D. & Leszcz, M. (2020). *The theory and practice of group psychotherapy.* Hachette.

A popular and comprehensive text on group psychotherapy, which covers groupwork from different theoretical orientations, and working with different client groups.

References

Beinart, H., Kennedy, P. & Llewelyn, S. (Eds.). (2009). *Clinical psychology in practice.* John Wiley & Sons.

Bor, R. & Stokes, A. (2011). *Setting up in independent practice: A handbook for counsellors, therapists and psychologists.* Macmillan International Higher Education.

Broglia, E., Ryan, G., Williams, C., Fudge, M., Knowles, L., Turner, A., Dufour, G., Percy, A., Barkham, M. & on behalf of the SCORE Consortium. (2023). Profiling student mental health and counselling effectiveness: Lessons from four UK services using complete data and different outcome measures. *British Journal of Guidance & Counselling, 51*(2), 204–222. https://doi.org/10.1080/03069885.2020.1860191

Charura, D. & Lago, C. (2021). *Black identities + white therapies: Race, respect and diversity.* PCCS Books.

Charura, D. & Paul, S. (2014). *The therapeutic relationship handbook: Theory & practice*. McGraw Hill Education.

Copeland, L., Willis, S., Hewitt, G., Edwards, A., Jones, S., Page, N., Murphy, S. & Evans, R. (2024). School- and community-based counselling services for children and young people aged 7–18 in the UK: A rapid review of effectiveness, implementation and acceptability. *Counselling and Psychotherapy Research*, *24*(2), 419–458.

Dagnan, D., Taylor, L. & Burke, C.K. (2023). Adapting cognitive behaviour therapy for people with intellectual disabilities: An overview for therapist working in mainstream or specialist services. *The Cognitive Behaviour Therapist*, *16*, e3. https://doi/10.1017/S1754470X22000587

Fazel, S., Hayes, A.J., Bartellas, K., Clerici, M. & Trestman, R. (2016). Mental health of prisoners: Prevalence, adverse outcomes, and interventions. *The Lancet Psychiatry*, *3*(9), 871–881.

Gifford, H. (2025). *A practical guide for working therapeutically with teenagers and young adults.* PCCS Books.

Gilbert, M. & Shmukler, D. (2003). Psychological therapy in groups. In B. Douglas, R. Woolfe, S. Strawbridge, E. Kasket & V. Galbraith (Eds.), *Handbook of counselling psychology* (pp. 442–460). SAGE.

Hanley, T., Frzina, J. & Nizami, N. (2015). Counselling psychology for children and young people. In D. Murphy (Ed.), *Counselling psychology: A textbook for study and practice* (pp. 171–184). John Wiley & Sons Ltd.

Lebow, J. L. (2019). Current issues in the practice of integrative couple and family therapy. *Family Process*, *58*(3), 610–628.

McArthur, K. (2016). *The school-based counselling primer: A concise, accessible introduction.* PCCS Books.

McBeath, A.G., Du Plock, S. & Bager-Charleson, S. (2020). The challenges and experiences of psychotherapists working remotely during the coronavirus pandemic. *Counselling and Psychotherapy Research*, *20*(3), 394–405.

McCracken, L.M. & Vowles, K.E. (2014). Acceptance and commitment therapy and mindfulness for chronic pain: Model, process, and progress. *American Psychologist*, *69*(2), 178.

McLeod, J. (2019). *An introduction to counselling and psychotherapy: Theory, research and practice.* McGraw Hill Education.

Street, E. (2003). Counselling psychology and naturally occurring systems. In B. Douglas, R. Woolfe, S. Strawbridge, E. Kasket & V. Galbraith (Eds.), *Handbook of counselling psychology* (p. 419). SAGE.

Tehrani, N. (2015). Counselling psychology for trauma in emergency services occupations. In D. Murphy (Ed.), *Counselling psychology: A textbook for study and practice* (pp. 214–227). John Wiley & Son.

Towl, G.J. (2002). Working with offenders: The ins and outs. *The Psychologist*, *(15)*5, 236–239.

Tuke, S. (1813/1996). *Description of the retreat: An institution near York for insane persons of the Society of Friends: Containing an account of its origin and progress, the modes of treatment, and a statement of cases.* W. Alexander. (First published 1813, Process Press).

Yalom, I.D. & Leszcz, M. (2020). *The theory and practice of group psychotherapy.* Hachette.

Yoon, I.A., Slade, K. & Fazel, S. (2017). Outcomes of psychological therapies for prisoners with mental health problems: A systematic review and meta-analysis. *Journal of Consulting and Clinical Psychology*, *85*(8), 783.

15.

Navigating accreditation and governance in psychological therapies

Sarah Niblock

Introduction

At a time when mental health challenges are on the rise and waiting lists for services are growing longer (BMA, 2024), understanding how the psychological professions are governed is vital – for students and trainees entering the field, as well as for those who teach and support them. While registration and accreditation are crucial for upholding the standards and integrity of psychological therapy professions, the UK's professional landscape remains complex and, in many ways, opaque. Navigating registration, accreditation and professional recognition can be a confusing and overwhelming experience, not only for new practitioners but also for the public and employers.

This chapter aims to offer a clear and accessible overview of how the system currently operates, while also highlighting opportunities for positive reform. It begins by setting out the different forms of registration and governance currently in place – focusing on the shared landscape of counselling and psychotherapy (which are often treated interchangeably in practice), and the distinct statutory framework for counselling psychology. This approach reflects the real-world overlap and tensions between counselling and psychotherapy in terms of training, membership bodies and professional identity, and responds to ongoing challenges around the lack of title protection and public understanding.

The second half of the chapter then explores the wide challenges and frictions in the current system – from inconsistent standards and public confusion, to barriers to access, issues of diversity, and debates around professional autonomy. It concludes by outlining a vision for a more collaborative and coherent ecosystem, where governing bodies work together to support both practitioners and clients through shared ethical principles, clearer standards and inclusive innovation.

A case study, practical takeaways and reflective questions are included to encourage deeper engagement with both the structural realities of the profession and the values that underpin meaningful practice. Readers are invited to reflect not just on how the system operates now, but, as future leaders, on how it might evolve to better serve society's growing mental and emotional health needs.

Scope of the chapter

This chapter explores the following key topics:

- the current landscape and exploration of benefits of registration with governing bodies
- the protection of titles
- the importance of balancing regulatory roles, finding a shared vocabulary and engaging in collaborative innovation
- accessibility for practitioners and members of the public from diverse populations.

I also provide a case study and pose questions for reflection at the end of the chapter.

Understanding the current system

The registration and accreditation system for psychological professions in the UK is complex, reflecting both the rich diversity of therapeutic approaches and the fragmented nature of professional governance. Unlike many healthcare fields, counselling and psychotherapy (with the notable exception of arts therapies) are not statutorily regulated and do not benefit from protected professional titles, which has led to a plethora of voluntary registers and a patchwork of standards. Counselling psychology, by contrast, operates within a clearly defined statutory framework regulated by the HCPC, with legally protected titles and a uniform doctoral training pathway.

This section offers an overview of the current system as it applies to:

- counsellors and psychotherapists – a shared landscape for the most part, governed by a variety of associations and voluntary registers
- counselling psychologists – a distinct profession regulated by statute, with specific training and protected status.

By outlining clearly how these systems operate, this section aims to equip trainees and trainers with the knowledge they need to navigate this landscape with confidence, while also highlighting the structural challenges that shape professional identity, accessibility and accountability.

Counsellors and psychotherapists

In the UK, the titles 'counsellor' and 'psychotherapist' are not legally protected, apart from arts therapists. There is no single regulatory body overseeing these roles. Instead, practitioners typically register with one or more professional membership organisations – often referred to as governing bodies – which uphold codes of ethics and professional standards, offer accreditation and support ongoing professional development. These include well-established bodies such as the British Association for Counselling and Psychotherapy (BACP), the UK Council for Psychotherapy (UKCP), the British Psychoanalytic Council (BPC), the College of Sexual and Relationship Therapists (COSRT) and the National Counselling and Psychotherapy Society (NCPS).

These bodies sit within a voluntary regulatory framework accredited by the Professional Standards Authority for Health and Social Care (PSA). The PSA does not set the standards itself but accredits registers that meet its quality assurance criteria. This means that although these bodies enforce professional standards internally, including complaints processes and sanctions, they do not have powers to prevent someone from practising, even if they are removed from a register.

Training for counselling and psychotherapy varies widely. Courses may be delivered at certificate, diploma, undergraduate or postgraduate level with no single mandatory route into practice. Requirements often include a combination of academic study, personal therapy, supervised clinical hours and adherence to ethical frameworks. Because each body has its own criteria for accreditation, practitioners frequently undertake further qualifications or register with multiple bodies to strengthen their professional standing and employability.

In the absence of statutory regulation for counselling and psychotherapy, professional registration serves as a critical safeguard for the public, signalling that practitioners meet established standards and protecting clients from unqualified or unethical providers. However, the overlap in terminology, particularly around terms like 'registered', 'accredited' or 'trainee' can be a source of significant confusion. For example, being registered with a PSA-accredited body may indicate very different levels of training and experience depending on the membership tier. This lack of shared vocabulary presents risks for both clients and employers, who may assume certain standards are met, and for practitioners, who must navigate a system with uneven public understanding.

The SCoPEd framework, which was initiated by BACP, BPC and UKCP, was intended to bring greater clarity and consistency to these distinctions. However, it has sparked debate for appearing to introduce hierarchy, threaten flexibility and centralise power within a few major bodies (Albertsen & Shennan, 2020; Cotton, 2024). At the time of writing, the sector remains diverse, decentralised and often difficult to navigate.

Despite this complexity, many governing bodies provide valuable benefits: access to CPD, peer networks, research funding, and a sense of professional identity that is important for early-career practitioners seeking credibility and community, even as they contend with both the practical and financial demands of maintaining multiple memberships and meeting accreditation standards.

Counselling psychologists

In contrast to counselling and psychotherapy, the profession of counselling psychology is statutorily regulated under UK law. Counselling psychologists must be registered with the HCPC, the statutory body that oversees standards of training, conduct and performance for a range of health and care professions. The HCPC protects titles such as 'counselling psychologist', 'clinical psychologist' and 'educational psychologist', meaning that only those who have completed approved training and met the HCPC's rigorous registration standards may legally use these professional titles.

Training to become a counselling psychologist typically involves completing a doctoral-level qualification, such as a doctorate in counselling psychology (PsychD or DPsych), which integrates clinical practice, personal therapy and research. These programmes are accredited by the BPS and approved by the HCPC, ensuring that graduates meet the standards required for safe and effective practice. Registration is mandatory and requires successful completion of both academic and clinical components, alongside evidence of CPD, throughout a practitioner's career.

Unlike the voluntary registration system for counsellors and psychotherapists, the statutory regulation of counselling psychology provides legal protection for the title and enforces compliance through the HCPC's fitness-to-practise processes. Practitioners who fail to meet professional standards can be struck off the HCPC register and legally prevented from practising under the protected title.

The title 'psychologist' is not protected by law on its own, but there are nine protected titles for practitioner psychologists, including 'counselling psychologist'. The disparity between the protection of this title and the lack of protection for 'counsellor' and 'psychotherapist' stems from historical, regulatory and professional factors. Psychology has a longer history of formal regulation, evolving as a scientific field with established academic and professional pathways (Jackson, 2019).

This regulatory clarity provides significant benefits for public trust, client safety and professional status. It also allows counselling psychologists to work more easily within statutory services such as the NHS, education and forensic settings, where a protected title and clear regulatory oversight are often prerequisites for employment. While the protected title offers legal recognition, counselling psychologists must still engage with broader debates around professional identity and scope of practice, especially as the boundaries between counselling, psychotherapy and psychology continue to evolve.

While both systems – the voluntary registration of counsellors and psychotherapists, and the statutory regulation of counselling psychologists – offer paths to professional regulation, they also highlight significant structural challenges within the broader field. Variability in standards, the lack of protected titles for some professions, and public confusion about qualifications and competence all contribute to a fragmented professional landscape. These issues not only affect practitioners but also have profound implications for client safety, accessibility and the profession's ability to respond to evolving societal needs.

In the next section, we will explore these cross-cutting challenges in greater detail and consider how a more coherent and collaborative ecosystem might strengthen the future of psychological therapies in the UK.

Cross-cutting challenges in the psychotherapeutic ecosystem

The current structure of psychological therapies in the UK reflects a rich diversity of approaches, but it also exposes significant systemic challenges. The co-existence of voluntary and statutory regulatory systems, the absence of legal protection for key professional titles, and inconsistencies in training and accreditation pathways all contribute to a landscape that can be difficult for clients, trainees and even experienced practitioners to navigate. These challenges are not merely administrative, they have deep implications for public trust, professional identity and equitable access to services. Without a consistent and accessible system, there is a risk that clients may be confused about what qualifications to look for, that aspiring practitioners from diverse backgrounds may face insurmountable barriers to entry, and that the profession as a whole may struggle to advocate effectively for its role in addressing the nation's mental health needs.

This section examines the core challenges in greater depth, including:

- the lack of a shared vocabulary across professional bodies
- fragmentation and competition between modalities
- barriers to access and diversity within the profession
- tensions around title protection and professional autonomy.

By understanding these systemic issues, students, trainees and trainers can better appreciate the complexity of the current landscape, and understand why a more unified, inclusive and collaborative ecosystem is urgently needed.

Fragmentation and the need for a shared vocabulary

One of the most persistent challenges within the current system is the lack of a shared vocabulary between the different governing bodies and registers. Terms such as 'registered', 'accredited' and 'trainee' can have different meanings depending on the organisation or modality, creating confusion for clients, employers and even fellow professionals.

For example, 'registered' practitioner with one organisation may be a student or trainee, while with another the same term signifies full professional membership. Similarly, accreditation can reflect very different levels of training and clinical experience, with some bodies requiring extensive post-qualification practice and others offering accreditation earlier in a practitioner's career. This inconsistency makes it difficult for clients to make informed choices about their care, particularly when in need of timely support. Clients may understandably assume that registration implies a minimum standard of competence and accountability; however, the assurance this provides varies widely. The issue is compounded in contexts such as online therapy platforms, where clients are often left to interpret practitioner credentials without clear guidance.

For practitioners, the lack of shared definitions can create barriers to professional mobility and mutual recognition between different bodies. It can also lead to frustration and feelings of competition rather than collaboration within the profession, as different groups struggle to establish their legitimacy in a crowded and often opaque marketplace. Efforts such as the SCoPEd framework represent attempts to address these issues by creating a common set of standards and competencies across counselling and psychotherapy. However, as critics have pointed out, such initiatives can risk further entrenching divisions rather than genuinely unifying the profession. Developing a more consistent and transparent language across governing bodies would be a key step towards improving both public trust and professional cohesion.

Barriers to access and diversity

Another significant challenge within the current ecosystem is the persistent lack of diversity and accessibility across the psychological professions. The pathway to becoming a registered counsellor, psychotherapist or counselling psychologist is often prohibitively expensive and time-consuming, creating barriers that disproportionately affect individuals from under-represented and less affluent backgrounds (McEvoy et. al., 2021). Training typically demands significant investment in tuition fees, personal therapy, supervised clinical placements (often unpaid) and ongoing CPD. While these requirements are grounded in the need for safe and competent practice, they also risk excluding those without the financial resources or flexibility to undertake several years of intensive study and practice.

Moreover, the profession's demographic profile reflects this inaccessibility. Data from the 2023 NHS *Psychological Professions Workforce Census* show that 75% of practitioners are white and 82% are female, with nearly half over the age of 40 (NHS, 2023). Although this may partially reflect broader societal factors, it underscores the reality that the profession has struggled to widen participation and fully reflect the communities it serves. Some innovative pathways have also demonstrated alternative models offering training routes and greater financial support to reduce these barriers (NHS England, 2022). However, such models remain the exception rather than the rule and are not yet widely integrated across the sector.

The financial demands continue post-qualification, with costs for supervision, insurance, ongoing CPD and membership fees adding to the burden, particularly for those establishing themselves in private practice. While some governing bodies offer bursaries or reduced fees for under-represented groups, systemic change would require a broader rethinking of how the profession recruits, supports and retains practitioners from diverse backgrounds.

Addressing these barriers is not just a matter of fairness, it is essential for ensuring that psychological therapies are relatable, accessible and culturally competent for a changing society. Without a more diverse practitioner base, there is a risk that therapy will remain perceived as inaccessible or irrelevant to many.

Tensions around title protection and professional autonomy

The lack of statutory protection for the titles counsellor and psychotherapist continues to be a source of tension and concern within the psychological professions and undermines public trust. The disparity between protected and unprotected titles stems from historical and political factors. Attempts to regulate counselling and psychotherapy under statutory frameworks date back to the 1971 Foster Review and the Department of Health's 2007 Trust, Assurance and Safety report (UK Government, 2007). However, these efforts stalled due to substantial resistance within the profession, driven by fears that statutory regulation would impose uniform standards and diminish the diversity of theoretical approaches that enrich the field (Arbours Association et al., 2009).

For many practitioners, maintaining the distinctiveness of their therapeutic approach and the freedom to practise according to their training and theoretical orientation is non-negotiable. Yet without title protection and shared standards, the field remains vulnerable to reputational damage, inconsistencies and the potential for harm. Navigating this tension between the desire for professional autonomy and the need for public protection remains one of the most pressing challenges facing the sector. Without progress, there is a risk that the current fragmented system will continue to erode public trust and limit the profession's capacity to advocate effectively for its role in a rapidly changing mental health landscape.

A vision for a joined-up future

The challenges outlined in the previous section may seem formidable, but they also highlight opportunities for meaningful reform. If the profession is to meet the evolving mental health needs of society and retain public trust, a more joined-up, collaborative and accessible ecosystem is essential. Rather than aiming for complete uniformity, which risks flattening the rich diversity of therapeutic approaches, the goal should be to foster greater coherence and collaboration across the sector. Professional bodies, statutory regulators and voluntary registers must work more closely together, aligning their standards where possible, developing a shared ethical foundation and advocating collectively for the profession's future.

This section proposes a vision for a more connected and inclusive professional ecosystem, focused on:

- developing a shared ethical and professional framework
- encouraging cross-modality and interdisciplinary collaboration
- creating more accessible and diverse pathways into the profession
- strengthening public understanding and trust through clearer standards and communication.

By imagining what a collaborative future could look like, students and trainees can not only navigate the current system but also position themselves as part of the next generation of leaders and change-makers in the psychological professions.

Developing a shared ethical and professional framework

A key step towards a more unified ecosystem lies in developing a shared ethical and professional framework, one that preserves the diversity of therapeutic approaches while offering a consistent foundation for practice.

Currently, each professional body maintains its own code of ethics and professional practice, often with subtle but significant differences in standards and expectations. While these frameworks are vital for reflecting the nuances of different modalities, the absence of a shared baseline contributes to fragmentation and confusion, particularly for clients trying to understand what professional standards they can expect.

By agreeing on core ethical principles, such as confidentiality, informed consent, competence, cultural humility and client welfare, governing bodies could establish a consistent ethical bedrock across the profession. This would not replace the unique ethical nuances of individual modalities but would offer a common language and set of expectations that clients, employers and the public could more easily recognise and trust.

In an ideal scenario, governing bodies would unite to develop a shared ethical framework applicable to all practitioners, regardless of their therapeutic orientation. Such a framework could also simplify complaints procedures, foster greater mutual recognition across bodies and reduce the risk of practitioners facing conflicting standards when holding memberships in multiple organisations. Importantly, it would respect the autonomy and integrity of the different therapeutic approaches while creating a clearer, more accessible landscape for those outside the profession. It would also strengthen the profession's ability to advocate collectively for its role within the wider health and social care system.

Encouraging cross-modality and interdisciplinary collaboration

Another critical aspect of a more unified and effective future lies in encouraging cross-modality and interdisciplinary collaboration. Although different therapeutic traditions have distinct theoretical underpinnings and methods, they often share common goals: to alleviate psychological distress, foster wellbeing, and empower clients to live more fulfilling lives.

At present, however, the profession is often characterised by silos, with different modalities working in parallel rather than in partnership. This fragmentation limits opportunities for shared learning, stifles innovation and can lead to unnecessary competition for resources, recognition and influence.

Collaboration between modalities, such as psychodynamic, cognitive behavioural, humanistic and integrative approaches, could open the door to more flexible, client-centred care pathways. Imagine, for example, a model where a client struggling with anxiety could receive targeted cognitive behavioural interventions while also engaging in psychodynamic work to explore deeper relational patterns, all through coordinated and collaborative practitioner networks. Such an approach would honour the complexity of human experience and avoid the pitfalls of a one-size-fits-all model.

Beyond collaboration within the field, there are also rich opportunities for interdisciplinary partnerships. Professionals from neuroscience, psychiatry, education, social work and community health working alongside each other could foster more integrated care models that recognise the interplay between psychological, social and biological factors. By working together, professional bodies are well positioned to facilitate interdisciplinary partnerships.

Encouraging a culture of curiosity, respect and openness between different approaches would not only enhance the quality and responsiveness of care but would also strengthen the profession's collective voice in policy and funding discussions – areas where a fragmented field is often at a disadvantage. Ultimately, fostering collaboration, both within and beyond the psychological therapies, would help create a more resilient, innovative and future-ready profession. One recent development is the creation of the Partnership of Counselling and Psychotherapy Bodies (pcpb.org.uk), formed by the six SCoPEd organisations to monitor progress on the framework and raise public awareness. While its membership is currently narrow, it illustrates how collective structures may begin to evolve.

Creating more accessible and diverse pathways

For the psychological professions to thrive and remain relevant, they must reflect the diversity of the society they serve. Yet, as noted earlier, the current pathways into the profession can be inaccessible to many, particularly those from under-represented or economically disadvantaged backgrounds. Tuition fees, unpaid clinical placements and the expectation of personal therapy throughout training present substantial financial and time barriers. These factors not only limit who can afford to enter the profession, but also shape the demographics of those who remain within it, often excluding voices and perspectives that are crucial for effective, culturally competent care.

Addressing this challenge will require a reimagining of how training is structured and supported. Initiatives such as the HEE programme show that alternative models are possible. These programmes, which reduce financial barriers and offer paid supervised clinical experience, have potential to widen access and make the profession more representative. Building on these examples, a more unified profession could advocate for:

- increased availability of funded training routes and placements
- bursaries and scholarships targeted at under-represented groups
- flexible training pathways that accommodate individuals with caring responsibilities or who are working alongside study
- recognition of prior learning and experience for those entering the profession from other careers.

These measures would not only improve access but enrich the profession by bringing in a broader range of life experiences, perspectives and cultural understanding – key ingredients for offering responsive, empathic care to diverse populations. A more diverse and accessible profession is not merely an aspiration; it is essential for ensuring that psychological therapies remain relevant, effective and trusted by all members of society.

Strengthening public understanding and trust

At the heart of the many challenges facing the psychological professions is a gap in public understanding. Without clear, consistent information about what different titles mean, what standards practitioners are held to, and what clients can expect from therapy, public trust is easily undermined.

Currently, the complexity and inconsistency across registration and accreditation systems make it difficult for clients to make informed choices. The unprotected status of titles like counsellor and psychotherapist further complicates matters, leaving the public vulnerable to unqualified or unethical practitioners. A more collaborative, unified profession could work together to develop clearer public-facing standards and messaging. This could involve:

- joint public education campaigns explaining the differences between types of practitioners, and what to look for and expect when seeking therapy
- standardised, transparent descriptions of registration and accreditation across professional body websites and directories

- greater emphasis on core ethical commitments and competencies that are shared across modalities
- stronger advocacy for statutory protection of key professional titles to ensure client safety.

These developments would not only protect clients but also enhance the standing and credibility of the profession at large.

In an era where mental health is increasingly recognised as critical to overall wellbeing, the psychological therapies must present a unified, trustworthy and accessible face to the public. Only by doing so can the profession fully realise its potential to meet the complex and growing needs of society. This vision will not come about overnight. It requires sustained effort, collective will and a commitment to balancing professional diversity with shared values and standards. Yet the potential benefits for clients, practitioners and society at large are profound.

In the next section, we turn to a real-world example that illustrates some of these challenges in practice: the rise of online therapy platforms and the complexities they reveal about registration, qualification and public understanding. This case study invites reflection on how the principles outlined in this chapter might be applied to strengthen both client trust and professional integrity in an evolving therapeutic landscape.

Case study: The challenge of online therapy platforms

The rapid expansion of online therapy platforms has offered clients new ways to access psychological support, especially at a time when traditional mental health services are under strain. Through video calls, messaging and live chat, these platforms promise convenience and accessibility. However, they also reveal some of the weaknesses and inconsistencies in the current system of regulation and accreditation.

Some prominent online providers require only that their practitioners are 'registered' with a professional body in the UK. While this might sound reassuring, registration can mean very different things depending on the body and membership level. For example, some registers accept student, trainee or associate members who have not yet completed their training or gained substantial clinical experience. Clients – often seeking therapy at a time of vulnerability – may not understand these distinctions and may reasonably assume that any 'registered' therapist is fully qualified and experienced.

This creates serious risks. Practitioners still in training may not be equipped to handle complex cases or work independently without supervision, particularly in an online environment where the nuances of in-person support are missing.

Additionally, some platforms may not verify the level of registration or require additional safeguards, such as supervision checks or mandatory professional indemnity insurance.

Without a standardised level of full qualification and registration, online therapy platforms face challenges in maintaining consistent service quality, which can negatively affect client outcomes. The lack of a shared vocabulary and standardisation across the profession exacerbates these risks. Clients often have no easy way to distinguish between levels of practitioner qualification, leaving them to navigate a confusing landscape alone.

This case highlights why a shared ethical and professional framework, clear public communications and stronger collaborative standards are essential. Without them, even well-intentioned efforts to expand access to therapy may unintentionally expose clients to inconsistent, and sometimes unsafe, care.

As the profession continues to adapt to technological and societal changes, ensuring clarity, consistency and client safety must remain at the forefront of efforts to build a more unified and resilient ecosystem.

Top takeaways

- **Understand the landscape**: familiarise yourself with the difference between statutory and voluntary regulation, and the various routes into counselling, psychotherapy and counselling psychology in the UK.
- **Support informed choice**: be clear with clients about your own professional status and qualifications, and help demystify the system where possible to empower client autonomy and safety.
- **Value shared ethics**: recognise the importance of a common ethical foundation across modalities, even as you preserve the uniqueness of your own approach.
- **Embrace collaboration**: engage with practitioners from different modalities and disciplines to enrich your practice and contribute to a more joined-up profession.
- **Challenge inaccessibility**: reflect on how training routes and professional standards may inadvertently exclude some people and consider how your own practice or teaching might support greater inclusion.
- **Be a change agent**: whether as a trainee, practitioner or trainer, see yourself as part of the profession's future – able to advocate for clarity, diversity, integrity and innovation.

Questions for reflection

1. Which aspects of the current regulatory system do you find most confusing or difficult to explain? How might you approach discussing this with a client or peer?
2. What responsibilities do you consider governing bodies have in ensuring diversity, accessibility and cultural competence within the profession?
3. In what ways might your route into the profession shape your perspective on inclusion and equity? What changes would you like to see for future trainees?
4. How can different therapeutic modalities retain their unique values while contributing to a shared ethical and professional ecosystem?
5. What does professional autonomy mean to you – and how might it be maintained within a more unified system of regulation and training?
6. How well does the public understand what psychological professionals do? What small actions could you take to contribute to greater clarity and trust?

Recommended reading and key resources

The following resources offer further insight into the issues of regulation, diversity, ethics and collaboration in the psychological therapies, supporting deeper reflection and critical engagement for students, trainees and educators.

- ACC, BACP, BPC, NCPS, HGI and UKCP (2022, amended 2025) *SCoPEd framework: A shared framework for the scope of practice and education for counselling and psychotherapy with adults*: https://www.pcpb.org.uk/wp-content/uploads/2025/08/SCoPEd-Framework-January-2022-amended-2025.pdf

Essential reading to understand one of the most high-profile efforts to standardise counselling and psychotherapy roles, and the debates surrounding it. Please refer to respective professional bodies' websites for how they are each implementing the framework.

- Cooper, M. & Dryden, W. (2015). *Handbook of pluralistic counselling and psychotherapy*. Sage Publications.

This handbook explores pluralism in therapeutic practice, supporting the idea that collaboration and shared standards need not come at the expense of diversity or client choice.

- Health and Care Professions Council. (HCPC): https://www.hcpc-uk.org

The statutory regulator for practitioner psychologists and other health professions. Visit for standards, registration requirements and public protection information.

- NHS Psychological Professions Network. (2023). *Psychological Professions Workforce Census Report*: https://s3.eu-west-2.amazonaws.com/nhsbn-static/Psychological%20Professions/2023/Psychological%20Professions%20Workforce%20Census%20Report%20-%202023.pdf

Offers data on demographics and workforce makeup, highlighting challenges around diversity and inclusion in the field.

- Norcross, J.C. & Wampold, B.E. (2018). A new therapy for each patient: Evidence-based relationships and responsiveness. *Journal of Clinical Psychology*, *74*(11), 1889–1906.

A foundational paper emphasising the role of the therapeutic relationship and the need for responsiveness to individual client needs – central to any discussion of regulation and flexibility.

- Professional Standards Authority for Health and Social Care: https://www.professionalstandards.org.uk

A useful starting point for understanding the difference between statutory regulation and voluntary registration, and for accessing accredited registers.

References

Albertsen, M. & Shennan, T. (2020). *A critical evaluation of the revised SCoPEd framework.* https://d1wqtxts1xzle7.cloudfront.net/64425830/CritEvalSCoPEdCTUK-libre.pdf?1600045170=&response-content-disposition=inline%3B+filename%3DA_critical_evaluation_of_the_revised_SCo.pdf&Expires=1763755169&Signature=LHDMW7uGes5u5rLGw0~8gv1ejgotR-roMofnBmDDdi

Arbours Association, Association for Group and Individual Psychotherapy, Association of Independent Psychotherapists. (2009). *The Maresfield report on the regulation of psychotherapy and counselling in the UK.* https://psychoanalysis-cpuk.org/cpuk/wp-content/uploads/2019/06/MaresfieldReport.pdf

British Medical Association [BMA]. (2024). *Record waiting lists are predictable but not an inevitability.* BMA Media Team. https://www.bma.org.uk/bma-media-centre/record-waiting-lists-are-predictable-but-not-an-inevitability-says-bma#:~:text=Responding%20to%20new%20NHS%20England,began%20taking%20industrial%20action1

Cotton, E. (2024). *Professional cannibalism and SCoPEd.* https://www.survivingwork.org/surviving-work-blog/psascoped

Department of Health (2007). *Trust, assurance and safety: The regulation of health professionals in the 21st century.* https://www.gov.uk/government/publications/trust-assurance-and-safety-the-regulation-of-health-professionals-in-the-21st-century

Foster, J. (1971). *Enquiry into the effects and practice of scientology. Her Majesty's Stationery Office.* https://ia803209.us.archive.org/1/items/FosterReportEnquiryIntoThePracticeAndEffectsOfScientology/Foster%20Report%20-%20Enquiry%20into%20the%20Practice%20and%20Effects%20of%20Scientology.pdf

Jackson, C. (2019). A history of psychology in the United Kingdom: Meeting of minds – the road to professional practice. *British Journal of Psychology*. https://cms.bps.org.uk/sites/default/files/2022-06/A%20History%20of%20Psychology%20in%20the%20United%20Kingdom%20-%20Claire%20Jackson.pdf

McEvoy, C., Clarke, V. & Thomas, Z. (2021). 'Rarely discussed but always present': Exploring therapists' accounts of the relationship between social class, mental health and therapy. *Counselling and Psychotherapy Research, 21*(2), 324–334.

NHS. (2023). *Psychological professions workforce census.* https://s3.eu-west-2.amazonaws.com/nhsbn-static/Psychological%20Professions/2023/Psychological%20Professions%20Workforce%20Census%20Report%20-%202023.pdf

NHS England. (2022). *Workforce, training and education.* https://www.hee.nhs.uk/

UK Government. (2007). *Trust, assurance and safety: The regulation of health professionals in the 21st century.* https://www.gov.uk/government/publications/trust-assurance-and-safety-the-regulation-of-health-professionals-in-the-21st-century

16.
Personal and professional reflective journeys
Robin Shohet and John Wilson

Introduction

This chapter aims to explore the journey to becoming a reflective practitioner in the counselling psychology and psychotherapy professions, emphasising the significance of ongoing personal reflection for both trainees and seasoned professionals.

We have adopted a duoethnographical approach (Sawyer & Norris, 2012), which allows us to reflect together on our process, key topics and learning experiences. We carried out this dialogue by email over a two-month period, allowing time for reflection between exchanges. We chose this approach because it provides a collaborative and dynamic way to explore the nuances of reflective practice, helping us and the readers to engage more deeply with the content.

Scope of the chapter

This chapter addresses several key topics integral to supporting practitioners in developing as reflective professionals in counselling psychology and psychotherapy.

- **Early influences and countertransference:** We delve into the impact of early experiences on our professional lives and how they shaped our approach to training and supervision. This section also addresses the concept of countertransference and the importance of understanding how our past influences our present work.
- **Training and organisational context:** We explore the role of both the trainer and the organisational context in fostering an environment conducive to reflection. We discuss how a supportive container, created by leadership, is essential for students to expand their reflective capacity. We recognise that training takes place in a wide range of settings, and may be facilitated by teachers, lecturers, tutors or trainers, and we use the term 'trainer' throughout this chapter as a broad reference to

these roles. We discuss different philosophical approaches to training, emphasising the importance of creating safety, love and challenge.

- **Reflective practice in action:** We examine the practical aspects of reflective practice, including the challenges of maintaining an open and fluid state of awareness. This involves understanding Rogers' (1961) stages of process theory and how they relate to becoming a reflective practitioner.

At various points, invitations for reflection and methods are presented throughout our dialogue to help students and practitioners engage in the chapter. These include points of reflection to uncover core beliefs, deconstruct personal work, and address fears and vulnerabilities within the training context.

A bit about us: Autobiography and countertransference to the work

Robin: I wondered about starting by telling the readers a little about ourselves, our backgrounds, philosophies and approaches as we imagine them to be, and then thought, 'that could be two books'. So, instead, I will ask you, in relation to this chapter, in two or three sentences, what would you most like the reader to know about you?

John: I am from a working-class background where doing a hard job well is really valued; the capacity to go to tough places and be competent is still with me as a practitioner and a trainer. The job that we do as practitioners is a serious one; we can be with people on the precipice of life and death. I believe that the training and ongoing development we undergo needs to be both high challenge and high support so that we can offer this to the people we work with.

And you, Robin?

Robin: So many things. I guess that I believe love is who we are, and it is obscured by the dark clouds of fear. And my job as a trainer is to help to bring the best out of the students, which will never happen if there is too much fear – or to put it positively, they flourish when they feel safe. Our work is a mixture of appreciative inquiry, and spiritually influenced by The Work of Byron Katie (Katie, 2002), the Sufi poet Hafiz (Hafiz, 2006), Indian non-dual philosophy, and *A Course in Miracles* (Foundation for Inner Peace, 1996).

There is no doubt we are influenced by early experiences and they will have informed how we practice. Would you say a bit about yours?

John: I grew up in a cult environment that preached love, community commitment and spiritual openness. However, the deep-rooted fears instilled in me and other children, through ideas of global genocide and mistrust of others promoted by the leadership, led to a suppression of any experiences that contradicted the community's beliefs, hindering our ability to genuinely explore different perspectives.

I hoped that leaving and being excommunicated from this community, and joining the therapeutic community, would offer a new way to connect with others. While I've experienced wonderful moments of openness, I've also seen how clinging to therapeutic doctrines and excluding those with differing views can close us off from genuine reflection and diminish our capacity to engage with others' experiences.

I know these early experiences remain deep within me, as they do for all of us. This makes reflection essential – to understand how these experiences shape us, limit us and create boundaries within our organisations that restrict growth for ourselves and our students.

Would you like to say something of how your experience has influenced your philosophy and the way you train supervisors?

Robin: Yes. I have wondered why I have chosen supervisor as my form of being a reflective practitioner. I think the way I tried to create safety in my family was sort of supervising my parents. It seems that neither of us felt safe in our families, so we are trying to create the safe environment neither of us felt we had. The role of supervisor gives me an outsider perspective – to be involved directly is too dangerous. So, first being a reflective practitioner/supervisor fits my temperament, a wish to stand outside, as the family system was too threatening. With regard to our training, what gives me most pleasure is the peer groups that have evolved after the training. It is easy to deliver training, and we can talk more about this, but what happens after that is for me the crux. I so wanted to see people flourish, and I went behind that and saw that when I can help do that, I contradict a core belief that I am a bad person. I have an 'alternative' bio where I include as part of my qualifications a psychotic experience in my 20s and mention the tyrant within and such like.

It is stuff like this that I believe should go into our training manuals. Not our external qualifications.

John: We both bring our early life experiences into the training we offer – often attempting, whether consciously or not, to create the kind of holding environments we ourselves may have needed. This shared understanding formed the basis for writing this chapter together and underpins our commitment to reflection as a core part of professional development.

John: We both mentioned training, so should we go there?

Robin: Yes.

The role of training organisations and professional bodies

We believe that training organisations and professional bodies play a vital role in creating an environment conducive to developing as a reflective practitioner. The 'container' in which training takes place has a profound impact on the student's ability to reflect and grow. When training organisations and professional bodies are intentional about how they use their power, they create environments that are safe and supportive. This is crucial because the process of reflective practice often requires individuals to explore challenging, vulnerable and deeply personal areas of their experience.

Training organisations and professional bodies must be committed to fostering safety, transparency and openness within their leadership and training structures. When these organisations model reflective practice themselves, it creates a ripple effect that encourages trainers and students alike to engage in deep, meaningful reflection. Conversely, when power dynamics are left unchecked, or when organisational leadership fails to embody reflective practices, it can create an environment that stifles growth, discourages vulnerability and ultimately hampers the development of reflective practitioners.

Understanding the relationship between organisational context and reflective capacity helps trainees appreciate why the support structures around them are so important. A well-held training environment makes it possible for students to navigate the difficulties inherent in personal and professional growth, expanding their ability to be reflective, and ultimately enhancing the quality of their work with clients.

John: Often, the demand to become a reflective practitioner is placed squarely on the student. Of course, as a student one needs to expand this capacity. However, I think we first need to focus on the role of the trainer and the organisational context in which the training occurs, so that the container in which the student is developing can support this incredibly challenging journey.

Robin: I am glad you have brought in the trainer and the organisational context. At some level I believe the students will act out the unconscious of the trainer. Would you like to say more about that? Do you agree, and if so, what is your experience in your training and others you might know about?

John: This is very much my experience. A wise practitioner once said that the group always reflects the container, which resonated deeply with my experience in community and groups. In the contexts I steward, I often react outwardly, sometimes with blame. However, what happens within the tutor, tutor team and organisational leadership is often mirrored in the group and the student.

Carl Rogers' (1951, 1957, 1959) approach described an environment where experiences excluded from our awareness could be brought into awareness for reflection and integration. The six conditions (Rogers, 1957) outline an environment with high levels of both safety and challenge. For students to expand their reflective capacity, I believe the organisation must foster this within its leadership, allowing it to flow to the tutor team and then to the students. Expecting students to grow as reflective practitioners without the organisation doing this work is potentially harmful and may negatively affect their current and future client work.

Rogers (1957) described six facilitative conditions for therapeutic personality change:

1. **psychological contact** between client and practitioner
2. **incongruence** experienced by the client, who presents as vulnerable or anxious
3. **congruence**, or relational integration, is experienced by the practitioner
4. **unconditional positive regard** for the client from the practitioner
5. **empathic understanding** of the client's internal frame of reference and an endeavour to communicate this experience to the client
6. **communication to the client** of the practitioner's empathic understanding and unconditional positive regard needs to be achieved to a minimal degree.

Rather than functioning as a prescriptive model, these conditions describe an optimal environment in which excluded experiences can come into awareness for reflection and integration – a process that is equally vital within training organisations.

Robin: I think we could quote examples where we feel that the training body has not done its reflective practice and there are power dynamics – we hold the pass/fail dynamic and students will try and second-guess our currency and adapt. I will talk a little about what we do and our philosophy in training supervisors. You have mentioned Rogers (1951, 1957, 1959) and how his philosophy holds you. I am held by believing that love is who we are, as already mentioned. I remember, also, a former colleague, Keemar Keemar, saying we are just acting out our autobiographies, that is, the positions we take are a result of early experiences. How might you be acting out yours? And of course, I will share how I am doing mine. I have a hunch that your early experience of community did not hold you and was not honest and you have tried to be a better container. That is certainly true for me and I will come on to that in a minute.

John: As I was waiting for your reply [A reminder that we are doing this as a backwards and forwards email] I was thinking about Rogers'(1961) seven stages of process theory where he describes a move from the rigidity of excluding from our awareness our experience through to the fluidity of being able to experience, symbolise and integrate our experience.

Robin: I don't know about these seven stages. Could you say a bit more about them?

John: Rogers' (1961) seven stages theory describes the movement from a fixed, externalising state – where everything is seen as someone else's fault – to the 7th stage, where we recognise external influences while also understanding our own internal motivations. This involves taking responsibility for our thoughts, feelings and actions. At this stage, there is a capacity for fluidity, allowing us to receive, symbolise and adjust to new experiences. This is precisely the capacity we explore in this chapter: to hear others deeply, understand the impact on us, and grow through meaningful dialogue for the benefit of both our clients and ourselves. See Table 16.1 for details of the seven stages of process.

Table 16.1 Carl Rogers' seven stages of process

Stage	Description
Stage 1: Unwillingness to communicate about self	The person is rigid and closed. Problems are seen as external; there is no desire to explore inner experience.
Stage 2: External description of feelings	Feelings may be mentioned but are viewed as external or caused by others. Communication is impersonal and guarded.
Stage 3: Recognition of personal involvement and responsibility for self	The person begins to acknowledge involvement in their difficulties, though may still avoid deep ownership of feelings.
Stage 4: Expression of current feelings	Emotions are expressed in the present tense. The person begins to take more ownership of their internal experience.
Stage 5: Acceptance of feelings and a desire to be real	Feelings are accepted. There is a growing wish to be authentic and congruent in relationships.
Stage 6: Experience is fully in awareness and owned	Emotions are fully felt, owned and clearly symbolised. Defensiveness is minimal.
Stage 7: Fluidity, trust in self, and openness to experience	The person is open to experience, trusts their inner process, and demonstrates a consistent capacity for self-reflection and integration.

Robin: Thank you, John. Really interesting. Taking responsibility for our responses to external events – moving from victim consciousness. I think therapy can collude with victim consciousness if we over-focus on childhood from a victim place. I remember the moment when I felt viscerally that my parents had done the best they could, and it was a release.

John: Here we are reflecting on how our early experiences not only influence but are recreated in the training we offer, which is why we both agreed to write this chapter. We are both trying to address what was missing for us as children. Reflecting on these experiences allows us to channel our energy into creating what was missing for us, using it to serve those we work with. Without this reflection, our training practice could easily become a rigid doctrine, claiming to lead others to an ultimate 'truth'. In reality, we are both trying to heal ourselves and, hopefully, others as well (Jung , 1993).

This is precisely what we want for students, tutors and organisations reading this chapter: to reflect on what we are trying to heal within ourselves. Understanding this deeply, in all its nuances, will help us channel our energy in service of others. Rather than creating restrictive 'truths', we aim to construct environments where we can all grow and thrive, even if, in the end, I am simply advocating for what I want for myself.

Having written a little of our countertransference, could we perhaps look at what we do and why. It is probably time to say something about how we construct the training experience to help develop the trainee's capacity as a reflective practitioner.

Constructing the training experience

John: In Temenos (a counselling and psychotherapy training institute based in Sheffield, UK, and online), we train counsellors and psychotherapists without a fixed curriculum, although we provide a handbook with criteria and learning outcomes for practice and academic writing. We believe that fluidity and health come from being open to more of our experience. To operationalise this, we create a group environment where students' excluded experiences are welcomed. Without a structured curriculum, weekends allow space for silence, conflict and deep contact. Structure often helps us avoid our true experiences by keeping us busy; without it, what we have denied gets closer and harder to ignore.

In this context, we often react in ways we find embarrassing or shameful – hiding, attacking or shaming others. These are human tendencies, present in all of us, yet hard to accept in others and even harder in ourselves. No wonder we exclude them from awareness; we often avoid reflecting on how we treat ourselves and others. Yet, in this training environment, these suppressed ways of interacting emerge, offering a chance to know and reflect on our experiences.

I think you're doing something similar, perhaps by a different route?

Robin: Yes, I think we agree on bringing to awareness the parts of ourselves that for whatever reason (usually fear and shame) we have kept hidden from others, but most of all ourselves.

So, in different ways, we are asking people to go beyond their expectations. To be explicit about these different ways. We run a Diploma in Supervision as Spiritual Practice, and we believe that at core everyone is love, but we have been subject to many levels of conditioning. Our work is to help people examine their core beliefs (e.g. I must be useful; I am not good enough) in order to go beyond them. And paradoxically, for this not to be abusive, there has to be an incredibly strong container – the easy option would be to have a syllabus and fall back on that. So we have to use ourselves as the strong container and constantly challenge ourselves to go deeper. I think this is important. Incidentally, we do not have written work for our Certificate in Supervision; I have seen my nephew spend weeks to get his essays in, to fit the criteria, to adapt, and this has nothing to do with his ability as a practitioner.

We tell students that we do not fail people; that in fact they are A students – quoting Ben Zander (Zander & Zander, 2000). Our job is to release their 'A ness' (pun not intended when I first said it), and it is we who fail if we do not find the best in them. I don't like to compare (well that can't be true because I am), but I supervised someone who was on another training course and almost everyone failed. That has to be about the course and not them. But the power structures make it difficult to challenge.

[Authors' note: We had a break of a couple of weeks before resuming writing.]

John: Thinking about what you said about the facade melting and students truly being themselves in the training environment, and then in their work and life: the ability to mediate their presence – to avoid both 'diarrhoea of congruence' and hiding – is key. Showing up appropriately for themselves and others, while having an environment in which to play, experiment and reflect, both internally and with peers and tutors, is crucial.

Wondering whether you have any reflections that may help with this? I know at Temenos we use the extreme group experience as a way of highlighting some of the issues we have been talking about.

Dialogue on ways of seeing

Robin: I go into this in *Supervision as Spiritual Practice* (Shohet, 2024) when I describe looking through different lenses – fear, judgement, curiosity or love. The same incident is viewed so differently.

John: For me, this is where love comes in. We only take students on if we believe we can love them enough to support them through a journey of at least four years. Being loved deeply enables people to stretch into the capacity to reflect on themselves, allowing the shadow to emerge, and critique themselves, colleagues and the systems around them.

Most importantly, it helps them truly love the people they work with, creating space for clients to transform and grow beyond previous limitations.

Loving deeply so that others can love deeply…

Would it be helpful to consider reflecting on core beliefs?

Robin: I guess there is a difference – you are training students for four years, from scratch, so to speak. We only have 12 days for people who are already working in the field. So can I look at some of my core beliefs before engaging with this point of reflection? Just for starters:

1. Love is at the core of our being.
2. Unrecognised fear distorts that love.
3. If you don't know about and won't look at shadow it will get acted out on clients/supervisees.
4. We are not immune from ignoring our own shadow as trainers, therapists and supervisors.
5. The core belief I have about core beliefs is that any difficulty can be traced back to a core belief.

This reflection around accessing core beliefs is simply a sentence completion: People should never… People should always… I must never… I must always…

'People should never lie' and 'I must always tell the truth' are examples. So interesting, because we all lie in subtle ways. When people begin to understand how dominated we all are by our belief systems, there is relief. We see how many rules we have introjected from society, school, our parents, from training bodies (including ours). These rules, core beliefs if you like, present as self-evident truths. I remember saying in a lecture that we are all far more conditioned than we think and one woman said, 'I'm not', and I replied, 'So you think'. She came back with, 'I don't need a man to tell me how to think'. Half the audience cheered her and the other half got that she was proving my point – this was not a man telling her what to think, but a recognition that even gender roles are conditioned, and we are all victims of that.

So we look at core beliefs. Drawing on Byron Katie's teachings, those we see as 'enemies' can act as mirrors for our own thinking. They reveal where we are attached to being right, seeing the world in a certain way, and expecting others to see it the same way (Katie, 2002).

Another reflection that can highlight about our instinctive need to hide is we ask people to finish this sentence:

What I would least like my supervisor to know about my work is…

We stress that we don't want them to share it and it is just for them. The next sentence to complete is:

I don't want them to know because…

And this we ask them to share. It boils down to a fear of being judged, of not being good enough. We ask everyone to participate and share their 'I don't want them to know' reason because these experiences are universal. And then we can see ourselves in each other, join in recognising our human vulnerability and frailty.

So those are two points of reflection – the first sentence completion to access core beliefs and the second sentence completion to show how and why we are hiding – and for the trainer to help students to recognise how fear and shame can inhibit our learning. John, do you have any favourite reflective practices?

John: I'm not sure if this qualifies, but one of my favourite group activities is to deconstruct personal work, especially a rupture and repair. Together, we explore what transpired in me, how I responded, and whether my responses were helpful. We avoid blame and focus instead on what surprised us about our reactions, and what others found helpful or unhelpful. This is a powerful way to reflect on ourselves and uncover thoughts, feelings and expressions not yet in our awareness.

Top takeaways

Robin: I am thinking here of a book called *Finite and Infinite Games* (1986) where the author James Carse describes a finite game as one that is played for a result, and an infinite game is played for the love of it. So when we play a finite game, we want an outcome that involves success and failure, whereas in the infinite game there can be no failure because everything is part of the game. So a takeaway for me might be that you don't define the takeaways but simply enjoy the chapter and our dialogue. However, I will contradict myself and try to offer some.

- Training organisations will carry a lot of shadow. We almost inevitably have blind spots around our power – underestimating it. So, we as trainers need to be constantly challenged and welcome challenges.
- Creating safety as trainers is vital – and this begins with us. We ourselves need to feel safe in order to offer the kind of holding that supports genuine reflection and growth.

- I see a lot of training now where training bodies are under pressure to conform – to regulatory frameworks, assessment criteria or institutional expectations. This pressure is often unconsciously passed on to students, who then feel the need to adapt or comply, rather than find the freedom to reflect in the way we've described earlier in this chapter. When conformity replaces inquiry, the safety needed for authentic exploration is compromised.
- People will flourish when the conditions are right, and if our students are not flourishing it is our responsibility. How is that for starters?

John: Sounds good to me. Here are a few more points:

- Reflective practice necessitates the transition of experiences that have previously been excluded because they are too painful or threatening, into awareness.
- This process of bringing painful and threatening experiences into awareness requires both the tutor and the student to be motivated to remain in challenging relational processes.
- Being able to respond while maintaining as much of our experience as we can in our awareness is what renders us reflective practitioners and as helpful as possible to the people we work with.

Robin: I like these. Shall we move on to questions? We have talked a lot about shadow and bringing things into awareness.

Questions for reflection

1. How has being a reflective practitioner/trainee enriched your life?
2. What key moments in your life have contributed to your being a reflective person?
3. If you see your work as a love affair, how would you describe that relationship?
4. What environments support you – for example, in nature (by mountains, alongside a river) – and open up space for reflection?
5. Who are the people you might be with that can help support the movement into reflection?
6. Do you have favourite forms of media that can move you into a reflective state (e.g. literature, music, movies)?

In conclusion

Robin: I think of the Socrates quote, 'The unexamined life is not worth living'. I see the work we do as not just being a reflective practitioner but a way of *being* in all our lives. I have often said that I wish I could live all my life like how I work, where I see everything that happens as an opportunity to grow, learn, combine and of course reflect. Your thoughts?

John: I think this is so true about wanting to live and work reflectively. It creates safety for us and those around us, as we can access our deepest intentions and choose responses that are helpful and growthful. We can be truly present with ourselves and each other. Our time with clients and loved ones is transient. Being a reflective practitioner enables us to savour every moment.

Recommended reading and key resources

- Gibbs, G. (1988). *Learning by doing: A guide to teaching and learning methods.* Oxford Polytechnic. Available at: https://shop.brookes.ac.uk/product-catalogue/oxford-centre-for-staff-learning-development/books-publications/ebooks/learning-by-doing-a-guide-to-teaching-and-learning-methods-by-graham-gibbs-ebook

This book introduces Gibbs's reflective cycle, a structured model that supports reflective learning through lived experience. It offers practical tools that align well with the kinds of reflective practices and training methods we have explored in this chapter.

- Kolb, D.A. (2015). *Experiential learning: Experience as the source of learning and development* (2nd ed.). Pearson FT Press.

Kolb's experiential learning theory emphasises the transformation of experience into learning – a core idea underpinning the reflective practices we discuss. His work provides a conceptual foundation for trainers and students seeking to understand how reflection deepens personal and professional development.

- Schön, D.A. (1992). *The reflective practitioner: How professionals think in action.* Taylor & Francis.

Schön's exploration of 'reflection-in-action' resonates with our focus on presence, responsiveness and the inner process of practitioners. His work is particularly relevant for those interested in how reflective capacity is developed in complex, real-time environments like therapy, supervision and training.

References

Carse, J.P. (1986). *Finite and infinite games: A vision of life as play and possibility.* Free Press.

Foundation for Inner Peace. (1996). *A course in miracles.* Viking Penguin.

Hafiz. (2006). *I heard God laughing: Poems of hope and joy.* (D. Ladinsky, Trans.). Penguin Books.

Jung, C.G. (1993). *Psychology of the unconscious: A study of the transformations and symbolisms of the libido.* Routledge.

Katie, B. (2002). *Loving what is: Four questions that can change your life.* Harmony Books.

Rogers, C.R. (1951). *Client-centered therapy: Its current practice, implications, and theory.* Houghton Mifflin.

Rogers, C.R. (1957). The necessary and sufficient conditions of therapeutic personality change. *Journal of Consulting Psychology, 21*(2), 95–103.

Rogers, C.R. (1959). A theory of therapy, personality, and interpersonal relationships, as developed in the client-centered framework. In S. Koch (Ed.), *Psychology: A study of a science* (Vol. 3, pp. 184–256). McGraw Hill.

Rogers, C.R. (1961). *On becoming a person: A therapist's view of psychotherapy*. Houghton Mifflin.

Sawyer, R.D. & Norris, J. (2012). *Duoethnography: Dialogic methods for social, health, and educational research*. Left Coast Press.

Shohet, R. (Ed.). (2024). *Supervision as spiritual practice*. PCCS Books.

Zander, B. & Zander, R. (2000). *The art of possibility: Transforming professional and personal life*. Harvard Business School Press.

17.

Moving beyond decolonisation of the curriculum in research and practice

Amira-Deka Dirie, Roy Moodley and Keisha Greene

Introduction

In the last few decades, the decolonial turn has become a critical movement in academia, research and training. Not least among them are the call for decolonisation of the education curriculum (Zinga & Styres, 2019), sociology (Connell, 2018; Lawrence & Dua, 2005), psychology (Bhatia, 2020; Fanon, 1952/1967) and psychotherapeutic practice (Sharma & Kivell, 2024; Vera & Speight, 2003) to advance equity, social justice, cultural rights and human rights. The project of decolonisation is now being undertaken across the psychological sciences (Adams et al., 2015), with a focus also on teaching decoloniality in community psychology and its allied disciplines (Carolissen & Duckett, 2018). This turn to decolonisation comes on the heels of critical multicultural and diversity counselling and psychotherapy with a focus on addressing social justice issues in clinical settings, particularly relating to the 'big 7' socio-cultural identities (gender, race, sexual orientation, class, religion, disability and age) and beyond – see Moodley (2014) for discussion. Engaging us to think beyond the identity politics of the big 7 ensures the process of decolonisation of psychology and counselling is aligned with the idea that 'decolonizing psychology then pushes the boundaries of our cultural horizons – it is our archway to new confrontations and new knowledges' (Bhatia, 2020, p. 2). Also, as Gone (2021) suggests, 'decolonisation harbors great potential as a profound methodological innovation for advancing social justice in counseling psychology' (p. 268), and as a way to secure the future of counselling and psychotherapy.

However, Frantz Fanon (1961) in *The Wretched of the Earth* makes a less optimistic declaration when he argues that 'decolonisation is a violent phenomenon… which sets out to change the order of the world, [and] is, obviously, a program of complete disorder. But it cannot come as a result of magical practices, nor of natural shock or friendly understanding. Decolonisation is a historical process: that is to say, it cannot be understood or become intelligible nor clear to itself except in the exact measure that we can discern the movements which give it historical form and content' (p. 36). Controversial at the time and even now, Fanon's decolonisation is much more complex than just a violent process against colonial trauma, even if colonialism was forged through a brutal and barbaric engagement of oppression and dehumanisation, particularly of people of the global south. In this chapter, we critique Western psychological frameworks in counselling by exploring the evolution of the 'self' in therapy and unpacking the identity matrix within holistic, body-inclusive practices. Ultimately, this is a call to reimagine psychotherapeutic practice beyond colonial constraints.

Scope of the chapter

In this chapter we will discuss the following:

- **Decolonisation is not a metaphor**
  - → Decolonialism is at its root beyond singular definition. It is a decentring that actively moves away from the linearity of understanding within practice.
- **Beyond the origins of the psychotherapeutic 'self'**
  - → We ask the question, how has the concept of 'self' evolved throughout Western psychotherapeutic history?
- **Beyond the big 7 identities in psychotherapy**
  - → We consider how identity and 'the self' are simultaneously experienced in a pulsating, dynamic, incessantly evolving matrix – shrinking and expanding alongside the world [external and internal] and across timelines.
- **Beyond decolonising and re-constructing identity matrices**
  - → This section explores nuances of decolonial Blackness and Indigeneity identity.
- **Beyond talk therapy: the wisdom of the body**
  - → How do we extend healing beyond cognitive talk therapy? We examine ways in which clients can enhance their mind–body connection by increasing awareness and processing somatic information.
- **Decolonial research methodologies: empowering practitioners**
  - → Repositioning standardised and evidence-based research as the standard, towards embracing nuanced, complex and fluid research for practitioners.

- **Curriculum development and training programmes**
  → Shifting curricula beyond general intersectionality and cultural competency frameworks, into discussions of reimagining personhood outside of colonial bounds of understanding.

This chapter ends with a case study and questions for reflection.

Decolonisation is not a metaphor

The field of counselling and psychotherapy, like other disciplines, is undertaking a concerted effort to critique current Western psychological knowledge, ideologies and paradigms for addressing the trauma of colonialism. If the decolonisation of knowledge entails various forms of transdisciplinarity, although not all forms of transdisciplinarity are decolonial (see Maldonado-Torres, 2019), then dislodging Western knowledge of psychology and psychotherapy, which are based within Western empiricism and Enlightenment ideologies, is a necessary first step. The Manichean interpretation of the symbolic, the dominant medicalisation of the body, with the imaginary as the creative backdrop to individuation and self-actualisation of the subject, are markers of Western dominance of the counselling and psychotherapy field. As Tuck & Yang (2012) state, 'decolonisation is not a metaphor', arguing that 'the metaphorization of decolonisation makes possible a set of evasions or "settler moves to innocence", that problematically attempt to reconcile settler guilt and complicity, and rescue settler futurity' (p. 1), in the projects of decolonisation with their key objectives of human and civil rights based social justice.

Although Western sciences have been presented as emerging from dispassionate inquiry, objective logic and rational thought, contemporary critical scholarship has exposed the idea of objective truth as historically rooted in colonial violence, cultural erasure, scientific racism and white supremacy (Morgan, 2021; Rahmat, 2025; Sheehi & Sheehi, 2024; Thambinathan & Kinsella, 2021). For example, Lazali (2021) explores how historical and colonial oppression shapes psychic life and charts new paths for emancipatory unconscious work. Within this context, psychoanalytic, psychotherapeutic and counselling psychology theories have situated the individual psyche as both a site of colonial inscription and potential decolonial resistance (Beshara, 2021; Rahmat, 2025). In doing so, the fields of psychotherapy, counselling and counselling psychology open a space for examining how psychic life is entangled with structures of power, fantasy and historical trauma. Decolonisation is a process that cannot be plotted linearly. It has been theorised to have five distinct stages: rediscovery and recovery, mourning, dreaming, commitment, and action (Chilisa, 2019; Laenui, 2000). As we mark these five processes of decolonisation, think back to the noted five forces of psychotherapy introduced in Chapter 1 (psychoanalytic, behavioural, existential-humanistic, multicultural and social justice (Ratts et al., 2016) and envision how these stages might align (Chilisa, 2019; Held, 2020; Laenui, 2000). Decolonisation of psychology and psychotherapy and its inevitable consequence, its future corollary – the beyond – beyond decolonisation of psychology, counselling and psychotherapy, becomes possible. Our collective responsibility to unlearn and unwind the tight knots of colonial oppression must begin within ourselves.

Beyond the origins of the psychotherapeutic 'self'

Examining the five forces of psychology reveals a transition from rigid psychoanalytical theories to more nuanced cognitive behavioural frameworks (Fleuridas & Krafcik, 2019; Morgan, 2021). As psychotherapy gained popularity, theorists aimed to move away from earlier models, adopting a holistic, humanistic approach that emphasised empathy and compassionate, person-centred care – marking the emergence of the humanistic-existential model (Portnoy, 1999; Tummala-Narra, 2015). The fourth force hallmarked a segue into diversification, with the integration of multiculturalist psychotherapy during the 1960s (Portnoy, 1999; Tummala-Narra, 2015). Multiculturalism proposed a unilateral understanding of identity, often resulting in a static representation of diverse populations. Despite evolutions of multicultural psychology, practitioners continually struggle to contextualise the complexities of identity within broader social dynamics (Fleuridas & Krafcik, 2019).

Critiques of multicultural frameworks have led to contemporary narratives driven by social justice and integrative holistic practices. This fifth wave of psychotherapy emphasises intersectionality, a concept introduced by Kimberlé Crenshaw in 1989. Intersectionality initiated an analytical enrichment of the discipline by analysing how overlapping identity factors interact with social constructs, shaping individual experiences (Crenshaw, 2017; Keating, 2017). Intersectionality challenges us to analyse how intersecting elements of identity interact with existing social constructs and shape one's subjective experiences (Crenshaw, 2017; Moodley, 2011). These identity elements are in a constant state of dialogue, tension or harmony with one another. Thus, psychotherapists incorporating an intersectional framework within their practice are called to view a client's subjective experiences, of which the client is viewed as being the expert, as well as the intersubjectivities within the cosmos between practitioner and client, as being inundated with an infinite number of tensions and feelings. Understanding this phenomenon allows psychotherapists to view the therapy space as a microcosm of the client's larger life experience, thus expanding our understanding of the client's unique challenges and resources.

It should also be noted that when we reflect on the concept of 'self' across the forces of psychotherapy, we must consider not just identity, but also how we understand the *wellbeing* of 'self'. In past and contemporary psychotherapeutic practice and research, wellbeing was framed and understood – problematically so – from the lens of normal versus abnormal, since 'normality and abnormality play a critical role in understanding health and disease' (Scripcaru et al., 2024, p. 1). This definition of wellbeing is rooted in Eurocentric understanding of positive wellbeing and psychopathology and can be traced back to ethnopsychiatry, or colonial psychiatry – see Buoli & Giannuli (2021) for further discussion. In decolonising practice and research, we need to be aware of the biases that can be held when understanding wellness, so that behavioural differences are not viewed as being representative of flaws in the psyche of the individual (Greene, 2022). Therefore, understanding of wellness cannot be exorcised from our understanding of 'self'. They are inextricably connected; in turn, a decolonised perspective holds variability of 'self' as well as variability in wellness. As we delve further into the self, we must invite ourselves to explore how identity is implicated and nuanced within the scope of psychotherapeutic understanding.

Beyond the big 7 identities in psychotherapy

As mentioned, the big 7 (Kassan & Moodley, 2021; Moodley, 2011) refers to the seven major categories of identity: race, religion, gender, sexual identity, disability, class and age. The big 7 identities provide us with a deeper snapshot into the complexities of self and identity, and how these identities are implicated within past histories and contemporary socio-cultural history, revealing the possibilities of futurities (Kassan & Moodley, 2021). The question that now exists is, how can the discipline of psychotherapy push beyond decolonisation and towards realised and empowered futurities of practice, curriculum and research that are unbound by Western epistemology? Can a discipline still steeped in colonial histories, both past and present, actively work with disenfranchised populations if it does not make room to embrace the Other it has rendered 'other' for decades?

Beyond decolonising and re-constructing identity matrices

Identity matrix: Indigeneity and epistemological violence

Unpacking Indigeneity within an identity matrix is to confront the ways colonial violence has worked to render the spiritual, collectivist and ancestral roots of the Indigenous self as 'Othered' (Dupuis-Rossi, 2021). Western colonial projects of Canada, Britain and the Americas have systematically and historically attempted to silence, stifle and homogenise what is intrinsically rich and individualised spiritual culture and tradition (Dupuis-Rossi, 2021; Held, 2020). Epistemological violence refers to how these powers use empirical 'evidence' and measures to render opposing ideas, data and systems of knowing (and by extension entire cultures) as 'primitive' (Held, 2020). In doing so, these powers could effectively self-appoint their sciences and practices as dominant and position non-Western practices as inferior and problematised – ultimately imposing a disconnect from self and the culture as 'self', what Indigenous scholars would refer to as a 'soul wound' (Dupuis-Rossi, 2021). We must view epistemological violence as an ongoing colonial project, which works in tandem with the sequential acts of disempowerment, dehumanisation and enactments of cultural genocide (Chilisa, 2019; Dupuis-Rossi, 2021; Held, 2020; Laenui, 2000). When mental health practitioners pathologise generations of Indigenous suffering under colonial measurements or ask Indigenous peoples to categorise and singularly define their sense of self through psychological measures or via *DSM-5* diagnostic criteria, both of which are normed using predominantly Eurocentric understanding of wellbeing, this speaks to larger ongoing subjugations of Indigeneity (Gone, 2021).

Whiteness has not only been overrepresented (and hallmarked and equated to represent humanity in its overrepresentation and placement in the 'racial hierarchy') but has worked explicitly to position Blackness as its antithesis, and in turn, Indigeneity and non-whiteness have been pathologised as irregularities to whiteness (Abdulle, 2017; Gone, 2021). Thus, the act of questioning if whiteness is in the room with us is rhetorical. Whiteness is *in* the room; it is also the walls of the room, and consequently, it is the room itself. Even now, trying to decentre whiteness only places it back in the centre of our discussions (Moodley, 2011).

In Western psychotherapy, practitioners must consider, outside the therapy room – who has been granted the ability to express their humanity in all its complexity?

Identity matrix: Critical race theory and Black womanhood

Critical race theory argues that race is a social construct, and that racism is embedded into the systems of the Western world (e.g. laws, policies and institutions) that support the maintenance of narratives of privilege and oppression. When race interacts with other social identities it creates unique experiences of privilege and oppression (Johnson, 2015). Consider the identity matrix of Black women and their sexuality. Black female sexuality and personhood have been positioned as both hyper-visible and invisible within the scope of white society. Some of the most horrific elements of transatlantic Black chattel slavery and white supremacist colonialism were enacted through specific gendered violence, positioning Black women as commodified and exploitable flesh. This has since translated into racist misogynistic tropes that have remained in contemporary circulation (Yancy, 2005). Black womanhood has never been conceptualised through an understanding of personhood – as related to the self in psychological theorisations (affect, cognition, emotion and humanity) – rather this unique experience of womanhood is marked by its historical articulations of subjectivity as alien, primitive and non-human (Brodkin, 1999; Carby, 1987).

How might we as therapists process the inner turmoil that causes psychological impacts due to the clear conflict in the colonial subject's identity of self?

Identity matrix: Spirituality, religion and the metaphysical

Religion as a big 7 identity provides an interesting understanding of personhood and the construction of self evoking the spirit. Religion and spirituality are positioned both in opposition and harmony as interchangeable concepts within psychotherapy (Hodge, 2006; Kassan & Moodley, 2021). In many cases, the connection to the sacred and holy posits it as a driving tool in shaping identity, purpose and value (Parker et al., 2019). As a social construct, religion has indiscriminately enacted violence both societally and throughout history (Exline & Rose, 2005; Fisher & Murtagh, 2016). According to Bernard et al. (2014), every culture has an iteration of religion or spirituality that holds meaning to the individuals within that culture. Immigrants to colonial nations from ethnic minority and religious groups navigate a society that predominantly acknowledges Christianity, while facing a rising wave of secularism that can penalise or stigmatise their personal expressions of faith (Kassan & Moodley, 2021). Therapists are encouraged to engage with clients' spiritual healing practices, as these often shape their worldview and sense of self, fostering resilience for minority and disenfranchised populations (Kassan & Moodley, 2021).

An example of decolonised cultural competence in counselling is the integration of Indigenous epistemologies of spirituality, which articulate a psychological soul and sense of self that challenge Western theories of identity. Indigenous spirituality emphasises cultural and communal healing, offering an anti-pathological framework for understanding mental health (Duran et al., 2008). Additionally, other spiritual frameworks, like Buddhism, Taoism and Confucianism, have been incorporated into Western healing, raising questions about Orientalism's role in exoticising Eastern practices while marginalising others (Moodley, 2011; Said, 1978). Islam and Sikhism, which are prevalent among religious minority communities in the West, have core spiritual frameworks of healing that have yet to be used or integrated within Western scopes of therapy (Rothman & Coyle, 2020; Singh, 2008). There may be an unspoken reluctance to explore and engage with clients as they navigate sites of tension that are a result of their religious identity. It is important to remember to reflect on and locate overt, implicit bias or aversion to exploring these worldviews with clients. The space of reflection can be held on an individual level (a practice of self-reflexivity) or within a space with a supervisor.

Beyond talk therapy: The wisdom of the body

In traditional psychotherapies, there exists an assumption that talking about an emotionally challenging event 'contributes to emotional recovery from an event (recovery effect), which means the alleviation of the emotional impact of the memory of the shared emotional episode' (Zech & Rimé, 2005, p. 271). Viewing talk therapy as the golden standard for healing poses a challenge when clients struggle to articulate their emotional or traumatic experiences. This can stagnate the therapeutic process, trapping both client and clinician in a colonial mindset that prioritises a singular way of knowing.

Connecting to our bodies and the wisdom they hold can deepen our understanding of how information about an experience can be stored in the body. According to Sharratt (2016), 'the body, or what [Merleau-Ponty] terms "the lived body", is our primary medium of experiencing, understanding and "having" a world, built with embodied knowledge and meaning' (p. 80). This integrative mind–body approach to therapy directly contradicts the approach of many traditional therapies that 'downplay or ignore the moment-to-moment shifts in our inner sensory world' (van der Kolk, 2015, p. 275), and the perspective that body-based interventions are only needed when traditional interventions fail (Lake, 2008). Attending to the body introduces interoception into the therapeutic space (Payne et al., 2015), allowing both client and clinician to explore how experiences – such as trauma, anxiety and depression – affect the body. Several of the big 7 identity markers, such as race, gender, age, sexuality and disability are positioned within embodiment and physical ways of knowing (Moodley, 2011; Murken & Shah, 2002). While the Western perspective often views traditional somatic healing practices as an alternative, they are essential to our work with clients (Sointu, 2006). To decolonise our psychotherapeutic practice with diverse clients, we must value somatic knowledge equally, if not more, than narratives, to fully understand a client's full experiences. Further training in body-based therapies (e.g. sensorimotor psychotherapy, somatic experiencing and bodylistening – see Brown, 2025) can be beneficial for those clinicians who are looking to deepen their understanding of how to work with the body. Furthermore, in acknowledging that working with the body to support one's wellbeing is a practice rooted in ancient wisdoms (African, Indigenous, Asian – to name a few) that predates the field of psychotherapy, clinicians may also seek training in traditional practices (e.g. yoga, dance, rituals and ceremony) and integrate it into their psychotherapy practice.

Decolonial research methodologies: Empowering practitioners

Practitioners on the front line of therapeutic work often seek research to gain a theoretical and practical understanding of a client's presenting concern. This reliance on standardised research perpetuates colonial hegemony, by promoting select methods of data collection and analysis, while marginalising alternative approaches through its reliance on a comparative axis of Otherness (Thambinathan & Kinsella, 2021). Standardised research methodologies produce 'a calculative and measurable sense of people's experience' (Talens et al., 2024, p. 5), which takes away from the nuances that relate to a client's presenting concern and generalise it to participants who are 'similar enough'. This positivist approach furthers the erroneous colonial idea that the process of symptom reduction can be standardised across clinical populations and that we can create such a thing as 'universal forms of knowledge' (Levitt et al., 2025, p. 1). This is not to say that there have not been valid research findings in quantitative research (e.g. the Adverse Childhood Experiences Scale) or measurement tools (e.g. the Racial Trauma Scale – see Williams et al., 2022 for further discussion). Rather, we argue that research must close the science-practice gap by moving away from favouring evidence-based practice research and randomised clinical trials (RCTs), to prioritising rich information sustained from and by unique experiences of individuals. In decolonising research methodologies, researchers should focus on the complex, nuanced and multi-layered aspects of a client that influence their presenting concern. Phenomenological and grounded theory research offers avenues that shift towards 'the philosophy of embracing engagement with Otherness in such a way that we meet the other in all its uniqueness, not the perceived or known, but in what emerges in the moment' (Talens et al., 2024, p. 7).

Decolonial research methodologies and scholars who apply a critical and reflexive outlook on data collection are actively working to undo evident power imbalances within research (Thambinathan & Kinsella, 2021). They are concerned with how to steer away from the belief of a method and relying on the Fanonian concept of viewing decolonisation as a 'program of complete disorder' — a non-linear and lifelong commitment to dreaming and challenging (Fanon, 1961; Thambinathan & Kinsella, 2021).

Incorporating body practices in curriculum development and training programmes

Despite recent curricular efforts within counselling, psychotherapy and counselling psychology to incorporate frameworks such as the big 7 identities, intersectionality and cultural competency, these interventions remain insufficient for a truly decolonial transformation of the clinical curriculum. What is required is a paradigmatic shift – one that reimagines personhood beyond Eurocentric constructions of the self, and that confronts the unconscious, embodied and non-cognitive dimensions of coloniality embedded within lived experience. Drawing on Fanon's (1952/1967) *Black Skin, White Masks* insights into the racialised body and the internalisation of colonial violence, psychotherapy must become a site not only of healing, but of ***refusal***, ***resistance***, and ***resilience***. This necessitates moving beyond the confines of Enlightenment rationalism and linguistic determinism, embracing modalities that access what van der Kolk (2015) describes as 'the body keeping the score' of trauma. In this reconfiguration, therapeutic space shifts from being a site of adjustment to colonial norms to a generative space of ontological and epistemological disruption. One such modality is ***body mapping***, an embodied, pre-linguistic method that enables both therapists and clients to access unsymbolised, intergenerational and historical trauma (de Jager et al., 2016; Nummenmaa et al., 2014; O'Brien & Charura, 2024). By attending to what remains repressed or unspoken within the body, body mapping opens therapeutic pathways that extend beyond traditional talk therapy. Incorporating practices such as body mapping, mythopoetic reflection, reverie and daydreaming, Indigenous ceremonies, storytelling and autoethnographies of positionality, psychotherapy begins to cultivate new clinical languages and forms of knowing. These modalities offer a pluralistic reimagining of counselling, psychotherapy and counselling psychology.

Exercise: Body mapping the colonial and decolonial self

This exercise is designed to explore how coloniality has shaped concepts of the self and to open space for decolonial reimagining of identity in clinical practice. For this exercise you will need a large piece of paper (e.g. A3 – or bigger if you feel comfortable working with a partner who will be tracing around your body) and pencil crayons/crayons/markers.

- If you opt to work with a partner, trace or sketch a simple outline of your body on the paper. If you opt to work without a partner (using a smaller piece of paper), sketch an outline of a body – adding any characteristics that make it more representative of your body; you can also use a printout of a body if that is preferred.
- Inside the body outline, draw or write where and how colonialism lives in your body. Use colours, metaphors, cultural symbols, language, spiritual connections and so forth. Where do you carry shame, silence and fear? What identities or stories have been suppressed?
- Around or within the body, add colour, words or symbols that reflect healing, resistance, ancestral wisdom and joy. What does liberation feel like in your body? What ancestral or cultural knowledge returns to you?
- Whether working with a partner or individually, reflect on the following questions. What do you notice about your body? What parts want to be reclaimed or reinhabited? What parts of your identity have been colonised by clinical training? How can you therapeutically support clients in reclaiming their own decolonial self-understanding?

Decolonialism is not a metaphor; it is action and practice – a decentring that moves away from a linearity of understanding. It relies on both the emerging articulations of selfhood within the Black, Indigenous, People of Colour, Two Spirit, plus (BIPOC 2S+) populations and the insights of racialised practitioners in fine-tuning care that uplifts these subjective echoes of self-determination and self-actualisation. In doing so, the discipline can begin to compose a symphony of pluralistic understanding – one that moves beyond a singular narrative and instead weaves together a rich tapestry of diverse voices and experiences. This approach makes meaning within the ambiguous, embraces the unknown and the complex. It acknowledges that the true goal of propelling decolonial psychotherapeutic work arises from engaging with multiple perspectives, recognising the fluidity of identity and the richness of lived experiences. By fostering an environment of continuous dialogue and reflection, decolonial practice allows for a deeper, more inclusive exploration of human psychology and healing.

Top takeaways

- Advancing the field of psychotherapy and counselling as a praxis requires clinicians and researchers to view research participants and clients through a decolonial lens.
- Decolonisation requires clinicians to decentre Western forms of knowledge (which are inherently rooted in colonialism, positivism and racism) towards pluralistic ways of knowing, which allow for diverse voices with lived experience to be centred and amplified.
- Being aware of intersectionality is imperative, as it allows clinicians to understand an individual's unique experiences of oppression and privilege; this is integral to the healing process.
- Traumatic and emotional experiences are held in the body. By shifting away from talk therapy as the 'golden standard' of therapy, we can hold space to explore the wisdom of the body as part of the healing process.

Questions for reflection

Client Grayson is a 21-year-old emerging adult and identifies as non-binary. They use they/them pronouns and are the eldest child of two working-class Korean immigrants; they have three other siblings. They are chiefly seeking counselling to address feelings of shame, guilt and identity and have a current goal of obtaining liberation from their feelings of guilt. They are struggling with anxiety and rumination over their past. They are hoping to work with you to foster self-compassion, forgiveness and acceptance.

Using the big 7 identity dimensions, examine how the intersections within Grayson's identities can give rise to both tensions and areas of coherence. Use the following questions as prompts.

- How can a therapeutic relationship be developed to help Grayson overcome feelings of shame and feel comfortable sharing their experience?
- In what ways can critical reflexivity and decolonial approaches be employed to support Grayson to reach their therapeutic goals by moving beyond Western frameworks and incorporating epistemologies from the global south?
- How do dynamics of race, class, gender, culture, ability, citizenship, or other forms of structural power influence the therapeutic relationship and Grayson's lived experience? In what ways might your own positionality – social location, professional authority, or cultural assumptions – reinforce or challenge these dynamics?

Recommended reading and key resources

- Crenshaw, K.W. (2017). *On intersectionality: Essential writings*. The New Press.

Crenshaw's work critiques the tendency of traditional social justice discourses to address race or gender in isolation. It offers a framework for understanding how multiple identities (big 7 identities: race, gender, class, sexual orientation, disability, religion, age) can intersect in different ways to create experiences of privilege and oppression.

- Fanon, F. (1963). *The wretched of the earth*. Grove Press.

This book explores how colonial domination dehumanises and fractures identity. Frantz Fanon introduces the concept of psychosomatic trauma: how colonial violence lives in the body and mind. He advocates for revolutionary decolonisation as a path towards healing and self-determination.

- Kassan, A. & Moodley, R. (Eds.). (2021). *Diversity and social justice in counseling, psychology, and psychotherapy: A case study approach*. Cognella Academic Publishing.

This edited book offers a critical, intersectional and practice-oriented examination of social justice in mental health fields. It brings together diverse theoretical frameworks – such as decolonial, feminist, critical race, and queer theories – and applies them to real-world clinical cases involving complex identities (e.g. race, gender, sexuality, class, disability, religion). Through case studies and reflective questions, the book illustrates how social, cultural and political factors affect therapy.

- Yancy, G. (2005). *Whiteness and the return of the 'Black body'*. Duquesne University Press.

Yancy's book offers a philosophical and phenomenological interrogation of race, particularly focusing on how Black embodiment is constructed and experienced under the gaze of whiteness. The book offers an in-depth account of how the racialised body is perceived and experienced, especially in therapeutic and clinical settings.

References

Abdulle, A. (2017). An exploratory paper on understanding whiteness. In J. Newton & A. Soltani (Eds.), *New framings on anti-racism and resistance* (pp. 23–34). Brill.

Adams, G., Dobles, I., Gómex, L., Kurtiş, T. & Molina, L. (2015). Decolonizing psychological science: Introduction to the special thematic section. *Journal of Social and Political Psychology, 3*(1), 213–238.

Bernard, W.T., Maddalena, V., Njiwaji, M. & Darrell, D.D. (2014). The role of spirituality at end of life in Nova Scotia's black community. *Journal of Religion & Spirituality in Social Work, 33*, 353–376.

Beshara, R. (2021). Decolonizing everyday Islamophobia through an antiterrorist ethic of resistance. *Journal of Humanistic Psychology, 61*(6), 861–874.

Bhatia, S. (2020). Decolonizing psychology: Power, citizenship and identity. *Psychoanalysis, Self and Context, 15*(3), 257–266.

Brodkin, K. (1999). Studying whiteness: What's the point and where do we go from here? *Queensland Review, 6*(1), 18–34.

Brown, T. (2025). *Bodylistening: A practical approach to body psychotherapy*. PCCS Books.

Buoli, M. & Giannuli, A.S. (2021). Similarities and differences in the management of psychiatric disorders by the colonial empires: An historical overview. *Revista di Psichiatria, 56*(2), 113–119.

Carby, H.V. (1987). *Reconstructing womanhood: The emergence of the Afro-American woman novelist*. Oxford University Press.

Carolissen, R. & Duckett, P. (2018). Teaching toward decoloniality in community psychology and allied disciplines: Editorial introduction. *American Journal of Community Psychology, 62*(3–4), 241–249.

Chilisa, B. (2019). *Indigenous research methodologies*. Sage Publications.

Connell, R. (2018). Decolonizing sociology. *American Sociology Association, 47*(4), 399–407.

Crenshaw, K. (2017). *On intersectionality: Essential writings*. The New Press.

De Jager, A., Tewson, A., Ludlow B. & Boydell, K. (2016). Embodied ways of storying the self: A systematic review of body-mapping. *Forum Qualitative Sozialforschung Forum: Qualitative Social Research, 17*(2). https://doi.org/10.17169/fqs-17.2.2526

Dupuis-Rossi, R. (2021). The violence of colonization and the importance of decolonizing therapeutic relationship: The role of helper in centering indigenous wisdom. *International Journal of Indigenous Health, 16*(1).

Duran, E., Firehammer, J. & Gonzalez, J. (2008). Liberation psychology as the path toward healing cultural soul wounds. *Journal of Counseling & Development, 86*(3), 288–295.

Exline, J.J. & Rose, T. (2005). The impact of spirituality and religion on mental health: A review. *Psychology of Religion and Spirituality, 1*(1), 1–18.

Fanon, F. (1952/1967). *Black skin, white masks*. Grove Press.

Fanon, F. (1961). *The wretched of the earth*. Grove Press.

Fisher, J.W. & Murtagh, N. (2016). Religion, spirituality, and mental health: The role of faith in clinical practice. *Psychology and Health, 31*(10), 1155–1172.

Fleuridas, C. & Krafcik, D. (2019). Beyond four forces: The evolution of psychotherapy. *SAGE Open, 9*(1). https://doi.org/10.1177/2158244018824492

Gone, J.P. (2021). Decolonization as methodological innovation in counseling psychology: Method, power, and process in reclaiming American Indian therapeutic traditions. *Journal of Counseling Psychology, 68*(3), 259–267.

Greene, K. (2022). *'A rough road to the stars': Exploring resilience through overcoming the trauma of anti-black racism* [Doctoral dissertation, University of Toronto]. ProQuest Dissertations Publishing.

Held, B.S. (2020). Epistemic violence in psychological science: Can knowledge of, from, and for the (Othered) people solve the problem? *Theory & Psychology*, *30*(3), 349–370.

Hodge, D. (2006). Do conceptualization of spirituality and religion affect perceptions of compliance with the ethical standards that address religion? An exploratory study. *Journal of Religion and Spirituality in Social Work: Social Thought*, *25*(2), 1–18.

Johnson, L. (2015). The anti-slavery movement to now: (Re)examining the relationship between critical race theory and Black feminist thought. *Race, Gender & Class*, *22*(3–4), 227–243.

Kassan, A. & Moodley, R. (Eds.). (2021). *Diversity and social justice in counseling, psychology, and psychotherapy: A case study approach*. Cognella Academic Publishing.

Keating, A. (2017). *Beyond intersectionality* (Vol. 1). University of Illinois Press.

Laenui, P. (2000). Processes of decolonization. In M. Battiste, *Reclaiming Indigenous voice and vision* (pp. 150–160). UBC Press.

Lake, J. (2008). Integrative mental health care: From theory to practice, part 2. *Alternative Therapies*, *14*(1), 36–42.

Lawrence, B. & Dua, E. (2005). Decolonizing antiracism. *Social Justice*, *32*(4), 120–143.

Lazali, K. (2021). *Colonial trauma*. (M.W. Smith, Trans). Polity Press.

Levitt, H.M., Hamburger, A., Hill, C., McLeod, J., Pascual-Leone, A., Timulak, L., Buchholz, M.B., Frommer, J., Fuertes, J., Iwakabe, S., Martínez, C., Morrill, Z., Knox, S., Langer, P., Muran, J., Weie Oddli, H., Řiháček, T., Tomicic, A. & Tuval-Mashiach, R. (2025). Broadening the evidentiary basis for clinical practice guidelines: Recommendations from qualitative psychotherapy researchers. *American Psychologist*, *80*(3), 389–410. https://doi.org/10.1037/amp0001363

Maldonado-Torres, N. (2019). Ethnic studies are decolonial transdisciplinarity. *Ethnic Studies Review*, *42*(2), 232–244.

Moodley, R. (2011). Critical multiculturalism and diversity in counselling and psychotherapy. In R. Moodley (Ed.), *Outside the sentence: Readings in critical multicultural counselling and psychotherapy* (pp. 3–16). [Essay]. Centre for Diversity in Counselling and Psychotherapy, Ontario Institute for Studies in Education (OISE), University of Toronto.

Morgan, H. (2021). Decolonising psychotherapy: Racism and the psychoanalytic profession. *Psychoanalytic Psychotherapy*, *35*(4), 412–428.

Murken, S. & Shah, A.A. (2002). Invited essay: Naturalistic and Islamic approaches to psychology, psychotherapy, and religion: Metaphysical assumptions and methodology – a discussion. *The International Journal for the Psychology of Religion*, *12*(4), 239–254.

Nummenmaa, L., Glerean, E., Hari, R. & Hietanen, J.K. (2014). Bodily maps of emotions. *Proceedings of the National Academy of Sciences*, *111*(2), 646–651.

O'Brien, C. & Charura, D. (2024). Body mapping Refugees and asylum seekers' perspectives of embodied trauma: An innovative method for psychotraumatology research & practice. *Qualitative Research in Psychology*, *21*(1), 71–106. https://doi.org/10.1080/14780887.2023.2289964

Parker, K.D., Dickens, K.N. & Herlihy, B. (2019). Re-authoring to reconcile religious beliefs with affectional orientation: A narrative study. *Journal of LGBT Issues in Counseling*, *13*(2), 94–113.

Payne, P., Levine, P. & Crane-Godreau, M. (2015). Corrigendum: Somatic experiencing: Using interoception and proprioception as core elements of trauma therapy. *Frontiers in Psychology*, *6*, 1–3.

Portnoy, D. (1999). Relatedness: Where humanistic and psychoanalytic psychotherapy converge. *Journal of Humanistic Psychology, 39*(1), 19–34.

Rahmat, A. (2025). *Decolonization and psychoanalysis: The underside of signification.* Taylor & Francis.

Ratts, M.J., Singh, A.A., Nassar-McMillan, S., Butler, S.K. & McCullough, J.R. (2016). Multicultural and social justice counseling competencies: Guidelines for the counseling profession. *Journal of Multicultural Counseling and Development, 44*(1), 28–48.

Rothman, A. & Coyle, A. (2020). Conceptualizing an Islamic psychotherapy: A grounded theory study. *Spirituality in Clinical Practice, 7*(3), 197–207.

Said, E. (1978). *Orientalism: Western conceptions of the Orient.* Penguin.

Scripcaru, C., Iliescu, D.B., Diac, M., Şpac, S., Iacob, V.T. & Scripcaru, A. (2024). Between normal and abnormal. *Bulletin of Integrative Psychiatry, 2*(97), 85–92.

Sharma, R. & Kivell, N. (2024). A self-heuristic inquiry: Unpacking the used of 'decolonization' in therapy and mental health care with and for racialized communities. *American Journal of Community Psychology, 73*, 170–182.

Sharratt, E. (2016). Group narratives of trauma and healing: Community storytelling as a critique of individual 'talking therapy' amongst survivors of sexual violence. In J. Davidson & Y. Saber (Eds.), *Narrating illness: Prospects and constraints* (pp. 75–82). Inter-Disciplinary Press.

Sheehi, S. & Sheehi, L. (2024). The colonial republic of psychoanalysis: How psychoanalysis polices the psychic sovereignty of 'Others'. *Psychoanalysis, Culture & Society*, 30, 563–582. https://doi.org/10.1057/s41282-024-00490-0

Singh, K. (2008). The Sikh spiritual model of counseling. *Spirituality and Health International, 9*(1), 32–43.

Sointu, E. (2006). Healing bodies, feeling bodies: Embodiment and alternative and complementary health practices. *Social Theory & Health, 4*, 203–220.

Talens, P., Lowenthal, D. & Brooks, O. (2024). Psychotherapeutic research and practice: Do we need to talk about 'efficacy'. *European Journal of Psychotherapy & Counselling, 24*(1–2), 1–15.

Thambinathan, V. & Kinsella, E.A. (2021). Decolonizing methodologies in qualitative research: Creating spaces for transformative praxis. *International Journal of Qualitative Methods, 20*, 1-9. https://doi.org/10.1177/16094069211014766

Tuck, E. & Yang, K. (2012). Decolonization is not a metaphor. *Decolonization: Indigeneity, education & society, 1*(1), 1–40.

Tummala-Narra, P. (2015). Cultural competence as a core emphasis of psychoanalytic psychotherapy. *Psychoanalytic Psychology, 32*(2), 275–292.

van der Kolk. B. (2015). *The body keeps the score: Brain, mind and body in the healing of trauma.* Penguin Books.

Vera, E.M & Speight, S.L. (2003). Multicultural competence, social justice, and counseling psychology: Expanding our roles. *The Counselling Psychologist, 31*(3), 253–272.

Williams, M.T., Osman, M., Gallo, J., Pereira, D.P., Gran-Ruaz, S., Strauss, D., Lester, L., George, J.R., Edelman, J. & Litman, L. (2022). A clinical scale for the assessment of racial trauma. *Practice Innovations, 7*(3), 223–240.

Yancy, G. (2005). *Whiteness and the return of the 'Black body'* [Doctoral dissertation, Duquesne University]. Duquesne Scholarship Collection.

Zech, E. & Rimé, B. (2005). Is talking about an emotional experience helpful? Effects on emotional recovery and perceived benefits. *Clinical Psychology & Psychotherapy: An International Journal of Theory & Practice*, *12*(4), 270–287.

Zinga, D. & Styres. S. (2019). Decolonizing curriculum: Student resistances for anti-oppressive pedagogy. *Power and Education*, *11*(1), 30–50.

Conclusion

In concluding this handbook, our hope is that you have found our collective companionship useful to you throughout your own personal training journey. We also acknowledge that training adventures do not always come to an end, and that you may continue to hold a firm commitment to pursuing continued professional development with anti-oppressive, socially just, decolonised and ethical practice at the heart of it. Rather than writing a chapter that attempts to conclude the book, we wanted to acknowledge that everyone's learning journey is idiosyncratic, and therefore we have chosen to leave you with key themes from the chapters and offer final stimuli for reflection from each.

Section 1: Firm foundations

Chapter 1 – Historical context and development of psychological therapies

Laura Winter and Terry Hanley provided a brief reflection on the historical context in which the psychological therapies were conceived and outlined six major forces of development in this area. They reviewed the psychotherapeutic landscape, including an exploration of the increasing number of therapeutic approaches used in contemporary society. They discussed the way in which narratives on the development of the psychological therapies and the lenses through which we view the professions are often rooted in the colonial frameworks that prioritise Western developments and figures. While the chapter contains core developments in the growth of the psychological therapies, the authors also acknowledged its inevitable incompleteness and wanted to be transparent from the outset that any history is subjective and selective in content and substance. They aimed to illustrate the ways in which we need to think critically about the history and current context of psychological therapies and to acknowledge the social and political factors in which the profession is intertwined. They aimed, in doing so, to present something closer to an anti-oppressive history of psychological therapies than has perhaps come before.

The stimulus for reflection from this chapter is the need to contemplate and critique why the historical context of the psychological therapies is traditionally white, WEIRD and patriarchal. The chapter also invites you to consider how you will challenge or contribute (on your course or CPD journey) to ensure that you apply a more inclusive lens to our collective history, and look forward to decolonising and incorporating anti-discriminatory approaches into your practice and research.

Chapter 2 – The relevance of philosophy to therapy practice and research

In collaboration with Byron Al-Murri and John McLeod, we have demystified often challenging philosophical perspectives, exploring how they relate to research and contemporary practice. We have encouraged you to examine the nature of reality, question what it means to be human, and develop a clear understanding of how your positionality and lens may influence your professional practice and ways of being. Personal reflection exercises have been provided to help you to take stock of your own relationship with philosophy, and to invite you to be open to new philosophical perspectives and ideas. This chapter has also highlighted the possibilities emerging from the use of creative arts to help you to explore unfamiliar ontologies and realities that you may come across in your work. We concluded by asserting that philosophy is a wide-ranging discipline, which has the potential to deepen your insights, practice and writing in a meaningful way that is relevant for you and your clients.

Chapter 3 – Developing theoretical fluency

In this chapter we have aimed, alongside John McLeod, to help you to develop theoretical fluency. Learning about therapeutic theory represents a core aspect of training as a therapeutic practitioner, and thus we have explored with you the nature and structure of therapy theories, and their practical utility in relation to both working with clients and maintaining solidarity within the therapeutic profession as a whole. We invited you to reflect on the personal meaning of theory, and how to use the experience of training to build theoretical skills and awareness to support lifelong learning over the course of your professional career.

The stimulus for this chapter is to reflect on the theories and therapies that you are organically drawn to and to continually devote time to attending to and experimenting with them across your training journey and professional pathways. We encourage you to reflect on how these theories that you are drawn to and integrate into practice iteratively evolve as you immerse yourself further into learning, writing, research and clinical practice.

Chapter 4 – Developing an integrative therapeutic practice

Following on from our exploration of theories and developing theoretical fluency in Chapter 3, we offered a critical discussion of integrative psychotherapy approaches. We invited you to consider the formulation and development of your own integrative process and presented our unique perspectives using the model of 'integration by immersion'. We explored this new integrative approach to psychotherapeutic practice by using a dialogic, duoethnographic process and case study. We also invited you to critique your own approach to integration, identifying its limitations and considering its potential blind spots, opening up opportunities for forward thinking and new ways to integrate practice. Towards the end of this chapter we presented reflective exercises and questions that we hope you will use to grow and explore your own unique approach to integration, which can also be applied to training, supervision and to personal and professional development encounters. We have maintained our assertion that if the integration approaches employed in psychotherapy practice are to be contemporary and fit for our times, then they have to be open to critique, dynamic, anti-oppressive and decolonised, while continuously evolving and transforming with ourselves and the lives of those we work with.

The stimulus for reflection in this chapter is to actively consider your own conceptualisation(s) of love and relationships in your development across the lifespan. We encourage you to reflect on the theories you have learned at this stage in your journey, and reflexively examine where you may want to immerse yourself in your integration, with the clear aim of developing your psychotherapeutic practice further for the best possible care of clients you work with.

Chapter 5 – Developing relational ethics competencies for counselling psychologist and psychotherapist training

Lynne Gabriel and Andrew Reeves showed how a relational ethics approach to practice can be embedded in therapeutic training. In this process, they adopted a relational ontology and associated relational pedagogy informed by pluralistic and pragmatic concepts. They focused on an education and practice context conceived as occurring through dynamic, dialectical, ever-evolving, continually interacting realities and relationships. They stated their commitment to relationship-based and experiential learning, which resonates with their relational ethics stance as a way of being, behaving and relating that espouses care, compassion, co-production and working in anti-oppressive ways. The content in this chapter is applicable across all of the psychological professions. For example, counselling psychologists can align with the BPS; they are statutorily regulated by the HCPC; and they can also be a member of BACP, which holds a voluntary Professional Standards Authority (PSA) register. Associations such as BACP and the British Association of Behavioural and Cognitive Therapy publish ethics codes or ethical frameworks for their members. Practitioners, therefore, need to be aware of the ethical requirements of each of their relevant member associations.

The stimulus for reflection from this chapter is to consider how you begin to embed a relational ethics approach into your own therapeutic work. It also encourages you to reflect on the gaps in your ethical knowledge and to explore these reflexively to support your future research and contribute to the improvement of any training curriculum with which you are involved.

Section 2: The trainee journey

Chapter 6 – Navigating difference, diversity and anti-oppressive practice
In this chapter, Nahid Nasrat and Colin Lago explained the complex psychological, emotional and relational tasks required to explicitly address human difference and diversity. They also explored what these aspects reveal about our personal and interpersonal attitudes and behaviours. Such learning explicitly brings the world outside into the classroom and into trainees' own conscious awareness. While potentially challenging, this vital area of all training programmes has the capacity to sensitise trainees in the therapeutic professions to their ethical and professional responsibilities, and to the diversity of needs of all clients and client groups that we may work with.

The stimulus for reflection from this chapter is to curiously explore your own perceptions, biases, prejudices and aspects of others and self that may surprise, challenge or cause discomfort in you. This can be supported by engaging with personal therapy, personal and professional development groups in your training environment or within the supervisory relationship. Through gaining this understanding, you can become more self-aware and continue to develop your transculturally informed approach to practice, utilising a stance of cultural humility.

Chapter 7 – Assessment, formulation and therapeutic engagement
Sarah Corrie and David Lane helped us to understand that the role of assessment and formulation is an essential part of any therapeutic engagement. These processes help both client and therapist agree a basis for the work that they will do together. Sarah and David articulated the importance of a *holistic assessment* and noted why, as ethical practitioners, we should adopt this approach. They concurred that working on the basis of a shared collaborative journey assists in the maintenance of the working alliance, and provides the compass and the map that can increase the likelihood of better therapeutic outcomes. They also presented and discussed a '4Ps' framework, which incorporates positionality, purpose, perspectives and process in formulation.

The stimulus for reflection in this chapter is to explore your own approach(es) to assessment and formulation and any challenges you may have in relation to the current models. We also encourage you to reflectively engage with your own learning process and any development needs you may have in the areas of assessment and formulation. Supervision is an excellent place to develop these skills, to try out new theoretical approaches and engage with case study examples from your own clinical work.

Chapter 8 – Reading, writing, speaking and finding your voice in therapeutic training

John McLeod helped us to appreciate that the development of skills and competence in professional communication represents a constant thread throughout a psychotherapeutic practitioner's training. This chapter explored the importance of learning to read, write and speak as a therapist, and the issues and opportunities associated with these aspects of the therapist's role. John concluded that a key aspect and outcome of psychotherapeutic training should be to enable trainees to find their own voice as writers and speakers. It is also crucial that we learn how to be critically appreciative and responsive to other writers and speakers in ways that support them to communicate in their own voice and from their own place in the world.

The stimulus for reflection in this chapter is to enable you to find your own authentic voice as a writer and speaker, as well as to learn to offer critique and respond to other writers and speakers in academic, clinical, educational and professional practice.

Chapter 9 – Undertaking impactful psychotherapeutic research

Sofie Bager-Charleson, Alistair McBeath, Mary Atito and Alan McPherson suggested we approach research as a valuable lifelong learning tool, through its capacity to address and potentially improve practice-based problems. They helped us to develop researchable questions in order to produce new knowledge, and encouraged us to critically review the use of methodologies and methods in ongoing research. They advocated for a firm commitment to valuing participants and promoting ethical sensitivity in research, redressing power dynamics, and applying a lens to our research that prizes diversity and social justice.

The stimulus for reflection from this chapter is to value engaging with a diversity of research methods that honour a broad range of ontologies and epistemologies. The authors also encourage you to prize your participants, to enable all voices to be heard, and to treat each individual ethically and humanistically with respect and inclusivity.

Chapter 10 – Clinical placements, supervision and safeguarding

The aim of this chapter was to help you prepare for your placement experiences at the very start of your training journey. Ariana Jordan began by outlining the importance of the placement experience to your learning in clinical practice. Ariana proposed a plan to ensure that you make the most of your placement experience, addressing the types of placement you are interested in, and the client group and/or areas of difficulty you may want to work with. The chapter then considered the value of clinical supervision, including what you can expect from a supervisor, and what to do if you feel uncomfortable in any way. Ariana also explored the place of safeguarding, what it means for your clinical practice, and the importance of knowing the correct procedures at your placement if you have concerns over a client.

The stimulus for reflection from this chapter is to explore your own placement interests, including what client groups and contexts you are interested in working with and why. You might also reflect on what type of CV you would like to have when you leave training to support your career development or further training in a specific area of psychotherapeutic practice. We would also encourage you to reflect upon how you can best use the supervisory relationship and bring matters of safeguarding urgently and openly into it. You may also reflectively engage with the placement process and any development needs you may have regarding it in your personal and professional development groups or with your placement coordinator.

Chapter 11 – Becoming a reflective practitioner

In this chapter Charlie and Divine explored what it means to become a reflective practitioner and why it is necessary both for your own personal and professional development, and to support the broad range of needs of the clients that we serve. We noted the vast array of traditional and contemporary models of reflection that can be utilised on training courses, and emphasised the importance of finding a way of reflecting that supports your own way of being and professional development pathway. We examined ways of reflecting independently, with other peers and in groups, and how we can incorporate technology or creative arts to support our reflective process. We highlighted the importance of engaging with reflection and discussed how to reflexively put our learning back into practice. We also critiqued and challenged the limits of traditionally used models, and considered alternative ways of working that can be adapted to our own physical, cognitive or learning needs.

The stimulus for reflection from this chapter is to try out different models of reflection to see which best supports your own way of learning, personal style or additional needs. We encourage you to use one or two models over a sustained period of time (perhaps over a semester) and consider what you like and do not like about them, and how they help (or do not help) in applying your learning reflexively back into practice. We also encourage you to examine what you have learned about yourself through their use, which you can then apply to your own personal and professional development.

Chapter 12 – Self-care, personal therapy and practical survival tips

Gerrie Hughes helped us to explore our self-concept using the realms of human experiences in the body, mind, emotions, creativity and imagination, and transcendence and spirituality. She also explored what self-care is, recognising its vital significance for personal and professional wellbeing, and acknowledged that it is an important foundation for a career as a therapeutic practitioner. She examined aspects that make up the self, suggesting how readers may increase understanding of their own awareness of their self-care needs and how to fulfil them. Common professional hazards were identified, such as the impact of psychotherapeutic training on the self and on our personal relationships, and suggestions for how their consequences may be minimised were offered. Gerrie also helped us to identify our personal vulnerabilities and responses to stress, and explored how to utilise personal therapy as a form of self-care.

The stimulus for reflection in this chapter is to explore your own methods of self-care, such as engaging with personal journalling, personal therapy, relational support, physical movement or spiritual practices. Consider how you might sustain these practices and incorporate them into your daily routines. You might also gently observe your own responses to stress to increase your self-awareness over time, so that you are able to mitigate their impact and prevent yourself from burning out during your training journey or professional practice.

Section 3: Becoming a practitioner and beyond

Chapter 13 – Professional practice and developing identity as a therapeutic practitioner

Peter Pearce explored the essential elements of developing a professional identity and ethical practice in the field of psychotherapy using a broad array of illustrative case studies to help us to think deeply about each of the topics covered. Key themes included the role of ethical standards as the foundation of professional integrity, the importance of cultural sensitivity and humility in fostering inclusive therapeutic relationships, and the commitment to anti-oppressive practice and advocacy. This chapter also emphasised the significance of CPD and self-care in sustaining effective practice, highlighting how practitioners can integrate personal values and cultural awareness to build a resilient and adaptive professional identity. By combining reflective practice, ethical rigour and ongoing learning, therapists can navigate the complexities of their roles with empathy, integrity and dedication to social justice.

The stimulus for reflection in this chapter is to review your ethical training standards. This might be, for example, the HCPC standards of proficiency for practitioner psychologists or the BACP ethical framework and trainee resources. Consider how these apply to the client's welfare and indeed to your own. Also, highlight any further training or CPD programmes that you might wish to engage with, such as attending a conference, completing an online course, or developing a particular therapeutic skill. Finally, consider how you might develop your own cultural sensitivity. This could be small steps, such as keeping up with the news and current affairs across the globe, or larger steps such as volunteering for a local charity that cares for groups outside of your own cultural context of origin, such as refugees or asylum seekers.

Chapter 14 – Career pathways and working in different contexts and systems
Emma Bradshaw introduced the broad range of career pathways and client group settings that are open to newly qualified clinicians. These include working in public sector organisations, such as the NHS, private healthcare or private practice, charitable organisations, educational environments, the prison service and occupational settings, such as the emergency services. Emma also provided a flavour of what it is like to work with different contexts, systems and client groups by exploring, among others, adult mental health care, working with children and adolescents, families and couples, and group work. Emma also helped us to explore how making these decisions for our career pathways is likely to reflect values and is inherently linked to concepts of social justice, social inclusion and ethical practice. The opportunities available to newly qualified clinicians are vast and can lead to an extremely rewarding career when care is taken to find work that is the right fit. Emma used her own career pathway as an example, so that we may begin to take inspiration from it and find our own path.

The stimulus for reflection in this chapter is to consider what client groups and organisations you would like to work with and why. It also encourages you to begin to reflect on your own ways of working, if you prefer to work as an individual or in a team or group, and what further training you might need to pursue as you develop your career path of interest. You might also consider the pros and cons of working in this field, and the use of supervision, coaching or mentoring to scaffold your continued development and decision-making regarding the career path that you might like to pursue.

Chapter 15 – Navigating accreditation and governance in psychological therapies
Sarah Niblock explored the complexities of the UK's regulatory and registration system for counselling, psychotherapy and psychology, highlighting the challenges that practitioners, governing bodies, and clients face within this fragmented landscape. She emphasised the urgent need for collaboration among governing bodies to address the mental health crisis, streamline training pathways, and work towards shared goals despite philosophical differences. The chapter also critically examined the role of professional bodies in advocating for systemic change and reflects on current debates, such as the SCoPEd project and statutory regulation

that shape the future of the profession. Ultimately, Sarah argued that governing bodies must take urgent and proactive steps towards reform, without waiting for political intervention, to improve access, diversity and care within the field.

The stimulus for reflection in this chapter is to carefully consider which professional body (or bodies) you will choose in your career pathway. Your course may already be approved by a professional body, such as the BPS, but also consider any other professional bodies you may need to be aligned to and why. For example, the NHS may require membership of the HCPC, or accreditation with the UKCP, BPC, or BABCP as a CBT therapist for certain career pathways. This chapter encourages you to think about how you might begin to navigate these often confusing regulatory systems, and who you can ask for guidance and help. It also encourages you to reflect on how we can move the field forward as a change maker and to ensure that our governing bodies are ensuring diversity, accessibility and cultural competence within our professions.

Chapter 16 – Personal and professional reflective journeys

Robin Shohet and John Wilson engaged with us throughout this chapter in a deep, duoethnographical process, which reflected upon their own personal and professional journeys. They showcased how they have developed as reflective practitioners and highlighted the significance of ongoing personal reflection for both trainees and seasoned professionals. They considered the key topics of our early influences in life, psychodynamic concepts of transferences and countertransference, the role of trainers and leadership in organisational contexts, and how to be reflective practitioners in action. By following their duoethnographical process, we learned more about their own personal and professional development as practitioners.

The stimulus for reflection in this chapter is to consider how your own reflective practice can enrich your life, which relationships and environments hold you and encourage your reflective process, and how you can build on your own reflective state by using duoethnographical processes or relationships in your training or professional careers to lead a fully explored and examined life.

Chapter 17 – Moving beyond decolonisation of the curriculum in research and practice

Amira-Deka Dirie, Roy Moodley and Keisha Greene helped us to understand the decolonial turn as a critical movement in academic research and training over the last two decades. Not least among them have been calls for decolonisation of the education, sociology and psychology curricula, and psychotherapeutic practice, to advance equity, social justice and cultural and human rights. They explored the big 7 socio-cultural identities and beyond, thinking about how decolonisation harbours great potential as a profound methodological innovation for advancing social justice in psychological therapies. Finally, they discussed how decolonisation is not a metaphor, how it self-evolved throughout Western psychotherapeutic history, the nuances of decolonial Blackness and Indigeneity identity, and the wisdom of the body.

The stimulus for reflection in this chapter is to explore how we might begin to empower ourselves as future practitioners by using critical reflexivity and decolonial approaches to support clients in reaching their therapeutic goals beyond the WEIRD frameworks that we often use in practice. It also challenges us as future educators to develop our training programmes to include ways of knowing beyond that which is conceptualised by the global north. A good starting point may be to consider your own intersectionality of self, and how you show up in your therapeutic relationships, reflecting on the impact of these dynamics in the therapy room and more broadly in the systems in society in which you work and train.

Key themes

In this training companion we have explored several key themes that we hope you will take with you into your journey ahead. These include the importance of taking a decolonising and anti-discriminating approach to learning and teaching, research and practice. We have encouraged you to immerse yourself fully in the process of learning to read, write and theorise integratively and pluralistically throughout your training journey. It is also essential that you allow yourself to grow and change as you develop across your professional pathways. We have underpinned all that we do as psychotherapeutic practitioners and researchers with firm foundations in philosophical, theoretical and relational ethics, and showcased the need for continued practices of reflection, reflexivity and self-care. As practitioners, we have lit the way for the use of decolonised, anti-discriminatory and transculturally informed assessment and formulation approaches, reconsidered our WEIRD history and roots, and encouraged you to find your own authentic voice as a practitioner. While all these themes can feel at times like a huge task to take on board during your training programmes, your companions are always close at hand. We encourage you to continue to lean into the support and wisdom of your trainers and educators, supervisors and peer groups, your own authentic reflective practice, and indeed to re-engage with the authors in each chapter of this book as you iteratively reflect back on these topics with fresh eyes and new perspectives from your training journey.

As we end this journey together, we would like to wish you the very best on your pathway ahead. We want to encourage you and acknowledge that this is a special period in your training, where you have the opportunity and privilege to become immersed in learning, exploring, metabolising, transforming and challenging yourself, and the concepts and models that you engage with, as you grow into the practitioner that you wish to be. It is also a time to continually reflect on what becoming an ethical, anti-discriminatory practitioner means to you, as you work with clients from diverse communities and learn from each unique person and therapeutic relationship in your own contexts. Always remember to care deeply and compassionately for yourself, as you will inevitably get things wrong, grow and change, and keep on seeking support in our wider communities of practice and from the pages of this book as you continue to bloom. Finally, we hope that you will take with you the knowledge that, as a community of psychotherapeutic practitioners, there is more that unites us than divides us. We urge you to continue to build connections, nourish relationships and learn from each other across the therapeutic professions as we seek how to best serve our clients with a commitment to compassion, cultural humility, respect, deep care and love.

Charlotte O'Brien and Divine Charura, January 2026

Glossary

Actualising tendency Innate propensity in every individual to move towards realising their full potential.

Anti-discriminatory practice Actively challenging systemic discrimination/ oppression and promoting social justice within therapeutic relationships and broader societal contexts.

Assessment An approach to hearing the client's story and to collecting information that will support an understanding of the client's needs.

Authenticity A quality of being true to and living from one's own self, despite external conditions.

Axiology The philosophical study of values. It concerns itself with the research, personal or therapeutic practice values and ethics that are important and pivotal to an individual. It may, for example, help us to understand one's own motivations to conduct research, or deliver therapy, in a particular way and to a particular end.

Behaviourism A modality emerging from the second force of psychology, which is deterministic and assumes that people's behaviour and self-concept are entirely controlled by their environment and their prior learning.

Big 7 identity dimensions This relates to seven identity intersecting markers: race, gender, age, sexuality, disability, class and religion.

Body mapping An approach that uses a body map (outline diagram of the body) as a tool to access unsymbolised, embodied experiences or trauma and to represent these on the body map.

Burnout A state of physical, emotional and psychological exhaustion/fatigue caused by prolonged or excessive stress and lack of support.

Common factors The core factors that research has found to be effective in all forms of therapy, regardless of theoretical model or modality. These include extra-therapeutic change, hope/expectancy, model or technique and the therapeutic relationship. Within counselling and psychotherapy, the therapeutic relationship is agreed to be the most powerful in-therapy factor.

Competencies Specific and focused knowledges, aptitudes, skills and abilities that fall within the umbrella theme. They provide a map or framework through which trainers and trainees can develop skills and knowledge to navigate the complex and evolving terrain of education, development and practice as a therapist.

Conditions of worth As a child develops, they learn that some behaviours attract more positive regard from the primary caregivers than others. When they actively choose or avoid a self-experience because of the need for positive regard, they are said to have acquired a condition of worth.

Congruence The therapist's ability to be present, open, without facade and genuine in relationship with the client.

Containment The therapist's ability to work and maintain the therapeutic frame with whatever experience or way of being the client brings.

Core model The coherent theoretical discipline that the practitioner works from – for example, psychodynamic, cognitive behavioural, person-centred, existential, gestalt and so on.

Co-transference A term commonly used in gestalt therapy to refer to the reciprocal influence and interplay between the therapist's and client's unconscious processes and experiences manifesting within the therapeutic relationship.

Countertransference The process by which the therapist is stimulated by the behaviour or way of being of their client and responds personally from their own material.

Cultural humility The therapist's lifelong commitment to self-evaluation and self-critique of their own cultural inheritance and positioning while taking an anti-oppressive stance and addressing the power imbalances in the therapeutic relationship.

Decolonising psychology/psychotherapy Critically examining and challenging how colonialism has shaped psychological and psychotherapy theories, research and psychotherapeutic practice. Emphasis is placed on being more inclusive and equitable by integrating diverse, non-Western knowledge systems, research methodologies, theories and practices. This includes, for example, African, Indigenous and Asian perspectives on research or healing practices.

Dialogical A process of reaching mutual understanding without necessarily removing or changing points of difference.

Diversity The range and complexity of human identities and experiences present within society and within the therapy room.

Dual relationship This refers to when a practitioner has another significant connection with a client outside the therapeutic context. It risks impairing therapist objectivity and professional judgement.

Duoethnography A collaborative research methodology in which two or more researchers engage in a dialogue over time on their different histories and experiences of a given phenomenon.

Eclectic A mix of theory and practice drawn from a range of models of therapy.

Empathy The ability to enter the perceptual world of the client, and having an accurate understanding of that perceived reality as if it were the therapist's own experience, but without losing themselves in that process.

Epistemic disruption (in psychology) Challenging established frameworks, methodologies, therapeutic approaches, ways of knowing, understanding or validating knowledge within the field of psychology or in society.

Epistemology The philosophical study of what constitutes knowledge, how we know what we know, why, how, and the limits of what can be known.

Eurocentrism Focused on Europe or European/Western people's ideas, concepts and values.

Existential-humanistic A modality of psychotherapeutic approach that combines elements of existentialism and humanistic psychology. It focuses the individual's responsibility, self-determination, and freedom to choose and create meaning in their life as well as acknowledge the inherent human capacity for growth towards their full potential.

Forces of psychology The major perspectives or schools of thought within the field of psychology and how they have/are developing and shifting. We acknowledge that the development of psychological therapies is multifaceted. In this book we have noted these as six major forces: (i) psychoanalysis/psychodynamic; (ii) behaviourism/cognitive; (iii) existential-humanistic; (iv) transpersonal; (v) transcultural; and (vi) social justice.

Formulation A working hypothesis between a therapist and client/s about the client's difficulties, an explanation of their origins and how they are maintained. It helps to clarify areas that need to be prioritised or to identify areas of risk in working with the client.

Frame of reference The perspective an individual has of their reality.

Fully functioning person A state of psychological adjustment when all conditions of worth are dissolved or removed. The individual is aware of and accepting of their feelings, trusts their own judgement, and is spontaneous – able to adapt to their experiences and environment – and thus living fully in the moment.

Guided discovery A process that a therapist uses to help the client reflect on the way that they process information. The therapist asks the client Socratic questions (open-ended questions that stimulate critical thinking and explore ideas), thereby enabling the client to reflect on their thinking processes.

Idiosyncratic Responses or ways of being that are unique to an individual client or therapist.

Incongruence A mismatch between self-concept and experience, which results in a feeling of anxiety, unease or internal conflict.

Integration The way in which we combine psychotherapeutic theories and their associated tools or skills into a coherent therapeutic practice approach, which is authentic to ourselves as practitioners and appropriate for the client(s) we serve.

Interpersonal dynamics The interplay of communication and interaction of psychological forces between people. This can include emotions, attitudes and responses that arise during exchanges.

Interpretation The use of theoretical knowledge to make sense of behaviour. In psychoanalytic or psychodynamic therapy, interpretation is one of the core techniques where the psychoanalyst or therapist helps the patient (or 'client' in other modalities) to gain insight into unconscious or preconscious material by linking it to its potential origins in order to help the patient understand their patterns, thoughts, feelings and behaviours.

Intersubjectivity There is not one reality (the client's) and an objective observer (the therapist) in the therapy room, but two subjective realities.

Introjection The psychological process in which the standards and values of others are unconsciously and symbolically taken within oneself.

Liberation psychology A school of thought that emphasises understanding and addressing the psychological impacts of oppression and social injustice, particularly among marginalised and oppressed communities. It promotes a model for social justice that liberates a client to live and be accepted for their authentic self.

Literature review An overview or evaluation of work already published in the field.

Methodology A fundamental systematic approach or procedure that guides how the research or therapeutic practice should be conducted.

Ontology The study of being and existence, and an individual's beliefs about the nature of reality and what exists.

Paradigm A fundamental set of assumptions, beliefs and values that determine a therapist's or researcher's views and interpretations of the world. It provides a framework for understanding and investigating phenomena.

Philosophy The study of the fundamental nature of knowledge, reality and existence.

Pluralistic approach A way of practising, researching and thinking about therapy that is embedded in humanistic, person-centred and postmodern values, but also fully embraces a whole range of effective therapeutic methods and concepts. A pluralistic practitioner believes that there is a multiplicity of ways in which clients become distressed and, correspondingly, that there are different ways of helping them.

Projection The act of locating one's own thoughts and feelings on to another person.

Psychiatry The medical speciality dedicated to the study, diagnosis, prevention and treatment of mental disorders.

Psychoanalysis The first 'force' of psychology, a psychological theory and therapeutic practice that aims to understand and treat psychological problems by examining the interaction of conscious and unconscious elements in the psyche and bringing repressed fears and conflicts into conscious awareness.

Psychodynamic The interaction of conscious and unconscious processes and emotions that determine motivation and personality, and a form of therapy using psychoanalytic theory relationally to delve into the unconscious mind to uncover and address the root causes of emotional and psychological distress.

Psychological therapies Evidence-informed psychological treatments for mental and emotional problems. They are used by those in the counselling and psychotherapy professions, whose work is explicitly informed by psychological theories.

Psychology The scientific study of the human mind and its functions, especially those affecting behaviour in a given context.

Reflective practice The process of learning through and from experience, which facilitates gaining new insights of self and one's practice.

Reflexivity The process of examining your own judgements, beliefs and best practices. It involves questioning our own assumptions, values and prejudices, attending to them, and noticing their impact on you and your practice.

Relational approach A paradigm which overarches psychotherapeutic modalities and schools. In this approach, our self is formed through relationship with others. Through relationship, we attain wellbeing, grow, develop and solve problems. A relational approach can also be a core model of therapy.

Relational ethics A system of moral principles that guides working in ways that acknowledge the complex, diverse and challenging contemporary society in which we live and work.

Rupture A breakdown or disruption in the therapeutic relationship, often marked by difficulties that have an impact on engagement between the therapist and client.

Self-care The actions taken by an individual who understands their own needs and takes steps that promote their own physical and mental wellbeing.

Self-concept The way in which an individual perceives, experiences and understands themselves. This perception can encompass their beliefs, ideas and attitudes about their own abilities, personality and characteristics.

Self-disclosure The sharing of personal rather than professional information about the therapist to the client.

Social justice An umbrella concept of affirmative action to create a society in which individuals have equal access to opportunities, resources and rights, regardless of their background or circumstances. This is achieved by actively challenging oppression, marginalisation, discrimination, and working with others to create change.

Supervisor A qualified and experienced practitioner who provides professional guidance, support and feedback to other therapists, ensuring ethical and effective practice as well as supporting their professional development and self-care.

Theory A set of interconnected concepts that can be used to make sense of a specific aspect of the world. A theory is a statement about what the world is like.

Therapeutic frame The container in which therapy takes place and is held. This includes the context, the contract and the therapeutic relationship.

Third wave CBT A range of therapies in which the focus is on accepting and understanding thought, feelings and inner psychic relations rather than changing or controlling them. Examples of these therapies include ACT, DBT, and mindfulness-based cognitive therapy (MBCT).

Transference A term used by therapists to describe feelings, thoughts or memories that a client has from their past that they project on to another person, including the therapist. This is done out of conscious awareness and can manifest in complex ways that could include positive, negative or erotic feelings towards the therapist.

Transpersonal The fourth 'force' of psychology, which focuses specifically on the development of *being*, spirituality, potential for personal growth, transformation and a holistic view of the individual. A transpersonal therapist undertakes a guiding role in the client's process and journey.

Unconditional positive regard (UPR) An accepting, valuing attitude to another person without condition or judgement.

Vicarious traumatisation (VT) The cumulative effect of the therapist working with clients who are traumatised or distressed. This results in the therapist experiencing psychological or embodied symptoms similar to those of the individuals they are working with who are or have been directly exposed to trauma.

WEIRD psychological therapies These are therapies that prioritise Western, Educated, Industrialised, Rich, Democratic (WEIRD) theories, concepts and worldviews.

Working alliance This is the (therapeutic) relationship between the therapist and the client based on agreed goals and ways of working together.

Appendix 1

Client log for supervision

In order to make the most of your supervision sessions, it can be useful to make a note of questions arising after each client session.

Use this log to keep a record of these questions, so that you have them ready for supervision. You can also use this log to keep track of the clients you bring to supervision so that no client is overlooked.

	Client initials	Supervision question	Date of supervision session	Information gathered from supervisor. Any action required?
1				
2				
3				
4				
5				
6				
7				
8				
9				
10				
11				
12				
13				
14				
15				
16				

Appendix 2

Support and funding

Training in psychotherapy is costly, but funding opportunities are available. Check out the following:

- If searching for funding opportunities you can start with those listed within your own training institution: you can inquire whether there are any bursaries or scholarships available.
- https://www.bacp.co.uk/about-us/bursaries/
- https://www.psychotherapy.org.uk/join-us/ukcp-bursary/
- https://www.bps.org.uk/blog/early-career-conference-bursary-scheme
- https://www.bps.org.uk/black-and-asian-psychologists-fund
- For training in cognitive behavioural therapy, there are some fully funded training programmes for the following roles:
  - » mental health wellbeing practitioner (MHWP)
  - » psychological wellbeing practitioner (PWP)
  - » high intensity posts in IAPT services (now called NHS Talking Therapies).

  Please note that there is a two-year rule for the above posts, whereby a trainee cannot apply for further funding for two years after the award of the first training (see the NHS England website for more details).
- The Guild of Psychotherapists offers a Minority Ethnic Training Scholarship for its own training programmes. For more information visit: https://guildofpsychotherapists.org.uk/psychoanalytic-training-courses/scholarship/

Mentoring

Some organisations, like BAATN and BACP, provide mentoring services to help guide your professional development:

- https://www.baatn.org.uk/mentoring-programme/

Name index

N

O

P

Q

W

Y

Z

Subject index

T